A TRAVELLER'S ALPHABET

STEVEN RUNCIMAN

A TRAVELLER'S ALPHABET

PARTIAL MEMOIRS

THAMES AND HUDSON

Printed and bound in Great Britain by Butler & Tanner

CONTENTS

To
my great-nephews and great-nieces

PROLOGUE

THIS BOOK is not a serious contribution to travel-literature. I have made no attempt to interpret the way of life in the lands that I have visited or even to describe the beauties of nature and the works of art to be found there. My intention is only to record my own experiences in a number of places to which curiosity or circumstances beyond my own control have taken me, in the hope that they may serve to encourage or to warn travellers of the future.

In order to give some form to these disconnected anecdotes I have arranged them alphabetically, place by place. This has raised difficulties, as many of the places of which I have wished to tell begin with the same initial letter. I have had now and then to resort to names that are unfamiliar or archaic. For my Chinese experiences I have followed Marco Polo and put them under the heading of Xanadu. As the book begins with the Holy Mountain, so I wanted it to end with the Holy City: which means abandoning Jerusalem, the most mellifluous of all place-names, for the harsher word, Zion. The entries are inevitably of differing lengths, especially as I could not resist the temptation of introducing stories where they seemed to be relevant; and a certain amount of serendipity has crept in.

Not all my experiences were enjoyable at the time. But in retrospect the discomforts and anxieties of the past seem trivial or absurd. Instead, I remember the friendliness and kindness of many people in many countries. Most of them are dead long since; but my gratitude to them lives on.

Athos

PROVIDENCE never wanted me to visit the Holy Mountain. Twice I had set aside time for the visit; and on each occasion I had been obliged to hurry home with the journey unfulfilled. It was only at the end of June 1937 that I arrived at Thessaloniki one morning, ready to take a boat that was due to sail to Athos at 7 p.m. that evening. I had all the necessary ecclesiastical documents, but I still needed a police permit from the Government of Northern Greece. I discovered that it was a public holiday, the Feast of St Peter and St Paul; and all the offices were closed. Clearly I would miss the steamer and would have to wait till the morrow to try to discover some other means of transport. I was resting disconsolately in the hotel when at 6.35 p.m. a message was sent up to me to say that the Governor of Northern Greece was downstairs and was ready to sign the necessary papers. Hastily I gathered my belongings together and hurried to meet him. He kindly gave me my permit and, kinder still, sent me in his car to the quay. I caught the boat with five minutes to spare.

It was a sad error. She was called the *Maria L.* – what the 'L' signified I never discovered – and years ago had sailed on the Clyde before she retired to the waters of the Aegean, where she was now the oldest ship in the Greek mercantile marine. We were due to arrive at Daphne, the port of Athos, at 5.30 the next morning. At about 5 strange noises woke me; and then there was an ominous silence. *Maria L.*'s engines had broken down for good, and she was drifting on the current towards the rocks of Cape Drepanon, with Athos in sight some twelve miles away. All morning we drifted, occasionally bumping gently on a submerged rock. The captain was worried about the technicalities of insurance so would not send a wireless message for help. An American yacht appeared; but the owner refused to do whatever it was that our captain asked of him. In the afternoon there was a slight breeze; with the aid of a makeshift sail we moved into safer water. Next came a police-boat, which offered to take some of us to Daphne; but our captain refused to let anyone leave his ship. Then a tug appeared; but our captain decided that it was going to charge too much for its assistance. At last, towards dusk, a steamer of the same line came up and after some inelegant manoeuvring towed us into a natural harbour close by. We were then told that we must all tranship to this other boat, which was bound for Alexandroupolis in Eastern Thrace and would drop us at Daphne two days later. Some of us then asked if we

9

could remain overnight on the *Maria L.*, a message having arrived by boat from the Mountain promising to send boats over to pick us up. The captain said no; he was sick of us all, and if we did not leave his ship at once he would set sail for Piraeus with us all. As we knew now that the tug for which he was waiting would not arrive till next morning, that seemed an idle threat. It is wonderful how rage rids one of inhibitions. I found myself shouting in Greek with a fluency that I never knew that I possessed about his incompetence and general nastiness; and I turned angrily on an amiable Greek colonel, berating him for belonging to a country that allowed its ships to be captained by such idiots. He merely smiled sadly and congratulated me on my eloquence.

Two days later we arrived in the afternoon off Daphne. It was cold and it was raining; we might have been in the Hebrides. On arrival one had to make one's way some eight miles inland to Karyes, the capital of the Mountain, to obtain a further permit from the Greek governor and a document from the Holy Synod of the Mountain that told the various monasteries to offer one hospitality. For the transport of one's baggage and oneself one hoped to find a mule. But no muleteer had ventured to come to Daphne in the pouring rain; and the prospect of a wet tramp to Karyes was not alluring. On the boat I had made friends with an elderly ex-member of Parliament, who, as the dictator Metaxas had recently closed the Parliament, was occupying himself, as he told me not once but many times, in writing the history of Macedonia from the fourth millennium BC till modern times. He had come to inspect Athos accompanied by the son of an old friend, who was to look after him and take photographs for him. This youth, by name Iordani, was actually a Christian Turk, a descendant of one of the Turkic mercenaries whom the Byzantine emperors had settled in Anatolia long before the Moslem Turks had ever come there. They employed a liturgy in Turkish, written in Greek letters. At the exchange of populations in 1923, being Christians, they ranked as Greeks and were forced to leave their homes for Greece. He spoke good French, which he was glad to practise on me; and he decided that I was less boring than his patron and transferred his attentions to me. He found out that the monastery of Xeropotamou, some two miles along the road, was empowered to take in pilgrims on their way to obtain their permits at Karyes. So he and I started briskly up the hill, carrying our bags, while his friend, Mr Melfos, and three other elderly gentlemen followed more slowly.

The monks at Xeropotamou were not very welcoming. They were fasting, in preparation for a feast two days later in honour of all the saints who had been monks on the Mountain. But they provided us with some bean soup, helped out with mulberries from a prolific tree in the courtyard; and they put all six of us in a room with firmly closed windows, where we shared our beds with hungry bed-bugs. Next morning it was still raining; but the monks, having learnt that I had written a book about the Emperor Romanus Lecapenus, whom they claimed to be their founder, graciously showed me all their relics. When the rain stopped Iordani and I set out to walk to Karyes, while Mr Melfos and his friends waited for mules. It was a Saturday and every office in Karyes was closed. The Governor was away, but his deputy, when at last I found him, was helpful. It was only in the late afternoon that we could get our permits from the secretary of the Synod. So the deputy-Governor hospitably invited me to spend the night at Government House, a cottage with just one bed in it, which he kindly put at my disposal, and he invited the local bank-manager to dinner to meet me. They only spoke Greek; and my Greek was barely adequate for bright conversation. But we had a cheerful evening, after which I went to the midnight service in the old church of Karyes.

Next morning, being Sunday, it was hard at first to find mules. But eventually Iordani and I made our way with a mule along the path to the monastery of Vatopedi, the elderly gentlemen following sedately behind with two muleteers. The weather was now lovely, and the beauty of the journey through the chestnut woods was unparalleled. Vatopedi was a comfortable monastery. It had electric light, turned off soon after dark for the sake of economy. It had two W.C.s. Its clocks kept European time, instead of making twelve o'clock be at sunset, however long the day, as did the rest of Mt Athos. In consequence all the other monasteries considered it to be heretical. The monks were very friendly and eager to show their treasures. There was also a nearby cove where one could indulge discreetly in sea-bathing.

We spent two days there, then planned to go on to the monastery of Stavronikita, down the coast, and to spend the night at the great monastery of Iviron. Once again Iordani and I set off ahead with our mule, and Mr Melfos and one elderly companion followed with a muleteer. As we went down a narrow path we heard a commotion behind us and found that Mr Melfos had fallen from his mule and hurt himself rather badly. We conveyed him as tenderly as we could to the nearest monastery, a picturesque and impoverished establishment on a rock overhanging the sea. A doctor was summoned from some richer neighbouring monastery; and Iordani realized that he would probably have to escort the invalid back to Thessaloniki. In the meantime he helpfully arranged for a monk to row me along the coast to Iviron.

While we sat outside the monastery awaiting the doctor's arrival an aged monk came to talk to us. As he chatted away I noticed to my horror a cat with kittens lurking in the nearby bushes. It is well known that no female creature is allowed on the Holy Mountain, except for birds of the air, mice, reptiles and insects, whose presence cannot be controlled. The Mountain is dedicated to the Holy Mother of God; and in her honour there must be no other female presence there. The monk saw my look of surprise and hastened to give me an explanation. His Greek was not very easy for me to follow, but Iordani was able to provide a translation into French.

About a hundred years ago, said the monk – but like all good Athonites time meant little to him – the Mountain suffered from a constant plague of snakes. Cats were needed to deal with them. But they had to be tom-cats; and the supply was always having to be renewed, and the cat-merchants of the mainland kept raising the price higher and higher till the monasteries could no longer afford to buy any more. The Holy Synod met and decided to dedicate an evening of prayer to the Mother of God to ask for her assistance. This was done; and a few mornings later it was found that all the tom-cats on the Mountain had given birth to kittens. Great was the rejoicing until it was revealed that half of these kittens were female. What was to be done about them? The Holy Synod met hastily again. Some monks maintained that the females must be drowned at once. Others suggested that they might be sold; as miraculously born kittens they would fetch a high price. But the oldest and the wisest of the monks pointed out that it was the Mother of God herself who had provided them. She therefore could have no objection to them. Besides, if the monasteries got rid of them the same crisis would arise again in a few years' time; and the Mother of God might not be willing to perform the miracle twice. So we permit she-cats, said the monk.

I may say that I never saw any other kittens on the Mountain. Which was the sex of the cats that I subsequently saw, I had no means of telling.

A stalwart monk, standing facing the bow, rowed me rapidly to Iviron. There I ran into a youth whom I had met on the steamer, who was visiting an old friend who had become the monastery doctor. He took charge of me, talking in rapid Greek; when I did not understand he pinched me hard for emphasis, which made conversation rather painful. I found the monks of Iviron rather unfriendly and unwilling to show me their splendid library. The evening meal was barely edible. But the doctor and his friend provided lavish drink till it was time to attend the midnight service. After that I retired to bed, unwisely, as Iviron had the justified reputation of housing the worst bed-bugs on the Mountain.

Next morning I was able to hire a mule to take me up to the monastery of Karakallou, which I thought the most charming of all the small monasteries on the Mountain. It was beautifully kept, with a pretty garden. The monks were civilized and friendly; and there was a scholarly old abbot who radiated benevolence. They begged me to stay longer, but my days were running out and I had to press onward. After giving me the best cooked meal that I enjoyed on Athos they provided me with a mule to take me on the five hours' journey to the great monastery of Lavra, near the tip of the peninsula.

Lavra was clean, well cared for and orderly. Several of the monks spoke French and were ready to talk about their treasures and their history; and all were courteous. The food, it must be admitted, was unattractive, and I was running out of my own supply. I need not have worried. Next morning there arrived at the monastery an Englishman with a manservant and two mules, one to carry himself and the other laden with tins of provender, pots and pans and a rubber bath. He only spoke English and he liked to talk unceasingly. So he was delighted to find a compatriot and kindly allowed me to share in his amenities.

After two nights at Lavra I had to make my way back to Thessaloniki, to catch a boat that would take me to Constantinople. The guest-master promised to arrange for me to have a motor-boat that would take me from the little harbour of Lavra round the south-west coast of the peninsula to the port of Ierissos on the mainland. I had hoped to start early in order to have time to call in at the Russian monastery, on the western coast. I waited vainly all morning for news of the boat. In the afternoon the monk confessed that he had forgotten all about it; but he said that if I went down myself to the harbour I would probably find a boatman ready to convey me. And so I did; but it was too late now for me to visit the Russiko. I only had time to look in at Daphne to complete the police formalities necessary before my departure. It was a beautiful journey. But when we reached the harbour dusk was falling. The harbour consisted of a quay and a hut, the town of Ierissos being four miles away. I had to walk through the encircling gloom along a sketchy track, and soon I lost my way. Then through the darkness I heard goat-bells and was able to find the goat-herd. He answered my halting Greek enquiry in broad Lancashire English. After the 1922 war he had gone as a refugee from Anatolia to England and had worked in a mill there. But he had not much liked it, so had retired to become a goat-herd in Macedonia. When I reached Ierissos the inn was full but I was given a bed in a widow's tiny cottage, and arose early next morning to take the bus to Thessaloniki.

The bus was full of monks from the Mountain who had found some excuse for going to the great city. There were also a few laymen, and one woman who was all too clearly on her way to the city for the birth of her baby. As we chugged over the pine-clad mountains on the way, a fierce thunderstorm broke out, and a tree came crashing down not far from the road. The driver let go of the wheel to cross himself, then declared that he was too badly scared to drive any more. I was sitting next to him; and the conductor pushed past me and slapped him hard on the face, telling him to pull himself together. At that moment the woman began to cry out that her baby was coming. The conductor took charge. First he asked if there was a doctor among the passengers. The doctor from the monastery of Vatopedi replied. He had often, he said, dealt with childbirth in his secular days. He could manage. Then the conductor said that there was a hut by a spring a little further along the road. He would deposit the woman and the doctor there and take the bus on to the next village and return with a qualified midwife. We stopped at the hut. The woman was carried into it and laid on a large table. As the doctor descended from the bus he looked round all the passengers and pointed at me, telling me to come and help him as I seemed to be the cleanest of those present. We were joined by a youth who was the proud possessor of a spirit-lamp. While the doctor set about his business the boy brought water from the spring and I boiled it in a cup, so that any instrument that was needed could be sterilized. It was difficult to find a basin in which the doctor could wash his hands; but we discovered a crock that just held water. I averted my eyes as much as possible from the table, but even so, I saw sights that no innocent bachelor should have been permitted to see. However, all apparently went well; and I suppose that in fact we did not have to wait long before the bus returned, followed by a midwife in a rickety taxi; and we were rescued and were able to continue without further incident on our way to Thessaloniki. I was happy to arrive there.

B Bulgaria

It was through the groves of academe that I came to Bulgaria. When I graduated at Cambridge, aged not quite twenty-one, I wanted to do research in Byzantine history and was sent therefore to see J. B. Bury, the Regius Professor of History and the leading British Byzantinist. He was a frail shy man who many years ago when he had taught Classical history in Dublin may have had a few pupils; but after he had moved into Byzantine studies he neither had nor wished to have any more. It was an uneasy interview, as I too was shy. He told me firmly that Byzantine studies were far too difficult for any innocent youth to try to undertake. When he failed to damp my enthusiasm he declared that it was ridiculous for anyone to approach the subject unless he could read the Slavonic languages. I was able to answer that I had learnt to read Russian during the holidays when I was a school-boy. At once his attitude changed. He took me seriously and suggested that I might take as my subject the reign of a tenth-century Byzantine emperor, Romanus Lecapenus, during whose time Bulgaria had played a vital part in Byzantine history. If you can read Russian, he said, you will have no difficulty in reading Bulgarian. He took down from his shelves two heavy volumes of the *Proceedings* of the Bulgarian Academy, each containing an article by an eminent Bulgarian historian called Zlatarski, and told me to come back in ten days' time and report to him on what I thought of them.

It was not an easy task. I could not find a single Bulgarian dictionary in the whole of Cambridge to cover the gaps where the language diverged from Russian. But I struggled through and was able to satisfy him. So my commitment to Bulgaria was begun.

My dissertation on Romanus Lecapenus won me a Fellowship at Trinity; but I had by then accumulated more Bulgarian material than I needed for it. So I decided to write a history of early medieval Bulgaria. It is never wise to write about a country that one has not seen. I had passed through Bulgaria in 1924 in the Orient Express on my way back from Istanbul; but it was not till 1928 that I stopped in Sofia. It was in early April. I had been for ten days with one of my sisters in Istanbul, where it had been cold, foggy and damp. When we arrived in Bulgaria the sun was shining, on snow-topped mountains and valleys full of fruit-trees in blossom. Sofia was then a charming place, a market town with a few of the trappings of a capital added. I was able to meet the historians at its University. They were all German-trained, though most of them understood French. As my spoken German has never been good and my spoken Bulgarian was at that time minimal, I talked to them in French and they would reply in German. Professor Zlatarski was particularly kind, giving me copies of articles of his and showing me the way to sources that I had not been able to find in London or Paris. But one of his colleagues, Professor Mutafčieff, told me that it was absurd for a young man from Western Europe to think that he could understand Balkan history. When eventually my book appeared he repeated this view, though graciously saying that I had done better than might have been expected. As I knew that he did not read English, I was not greatly worried.

The great benefit that arose from this visit to Bulgaria was that I came to know the most interesting family in the country. When Ferdinand of Saxe-Coburg went there to be its Prince, he had some difficulty in finding young men well enough educated and intelligent enough to be of use to him. But he was greatly impressed by one called Dmitri Stancioff, whom he took into his service. Stancioff was to have a long career in public life, with periods of disgrace when he showed dislike of Ferdinand's policies or methods; but he survived to serve Ferdinand's son and heir, King Boris, ending his official life as Bulgarian Minister to London. His wife was a Savoyard countess who had come to Bulgaria as lady-in-waiting to Ferdinand's formidable mother, Princess Clémentine of Orleans. They had a son and three daughters, the eldest of whom, Nadejda, was the first woman diplomat, serving for a time as First Secretary at the Bulgarian Legation in London. She left it to marry a Scottish baronet with a large baronial castle near Stirling. I used subsequently to go and stay there, usually to meet an assortment of distinguished Continentals who liked to deck themselves in kilts in order to savour what they thought was Highland life.

On this first occasion it was the son, Ivan, who was in the Bulgarian Foreign Ministry, and his American wife, Marion, to whom I had an introduction. They were very kind to us, taking us to see all the local monuments and one day driving us right out into the country. At a small town called Radomir my sister lost her hand-bag. We had to summon the assistance of the town-crier to recover it.

My next visit to Bulgaria was in 1930, when I paid a short visit to the Ivan Stancioffs on my way back from Greece. I dined one night at the British legation. There had been a row between Greece and Bulgaria, the Greeks having accused the Bulgarians of opening their diplomatic bag. In the hope of being, socially at least, a mediator, our Minister invited amongst his guests the Greek Minister and the Bulgarian Foreign Minister. When we were comfortably seated at the table our hostess turned to the former and said loudly: 'Tell me, is it your people who have been prying into Bulgarian secrets, or is it the other way round?'

There was a pause; then, fortunately someone burst into laughter, into which soon even the protagonists joined, but not the British Minister, who looked as though he could have killed his wife.

Next afternoon I was summond to the Palace, not a very impressive building, to be received by King Boris. He kindly told me that I could dedicate my *History of the First Bulgarian Empire*, due to appear later that year, to him: a wrong-headed thing for me to have requested in the eyes of the Bulgarians of today. But they have forgiven me, it seems. That evening I took a night train to the village of Preslav, to see the widespread but scanty ruins of the early medieval capital of Bulgaria. The local Prefect and the local schoolmaster, Mr Gospodinov, who was in charge of the ruins and the little museum attached to them, were on the station platform to receive me but took no notice of me till there was no one else left in sight. They had expected, they then explained to me, to see a bearded professor, not a clean-shaven young man; and I had shamelessly to talk of my audience with His Majesty before they were fully convinced that I was really the person whom they had been told to meet. The Prefect soon disappeared, but Mr Gospodinov looked after me splendidly. We ended up the best of friends; and before I left to return to Sofia he took me again to the little museum and opened its cases, begging me to take a souvenir. I resisted the temptation to acquire one of its major treasures and selected a little piece of painted ceramic, which I thought it well could spare. I returned to Sofia overnight, and caught the Orient Express for home next day.

My next visit to Bulgaria was in July 1933, when I spent nearly three weeks staying with the old Stancioffs in a charming house on the Black Sea coast between Varna and the royal palace of Evksinograd. Ivan and Marion had, with their ever increasing family, a smaller house in the garden; it was they who took me round the churches and ruins of the province. One day Marion and I took a boat from Varna to the enchanting town of Mesemvria, now called Nisebar by the Bulgarians, on a peninsula jutting out into the sea and filled with late Byzantine churches. There the British Consul from Burgas, further down the coast, came to meet us. He gave us dinner at the Consulate; but his wife had just deserted him, and he thought that it would be improper to house a lady without having a chaperone. So Marion was sent off to a rather primitive hotel, while I was put in a bedroom only to be reached through the Consul's. He must have regretted his hospitality. I had eaten something that poisoned me; and all through the night he was kept awake by my frequent journeys past his bed. I recovered in time to travel back without discomfort to Varna.

I decided that on my homeward journey I would visit the old town of Trnovo, the capital of Bulgaria in the later Middle Ages, and then go on to Rustchuk on Danube, where I could catch a river steamer that would take me up through the Iron Gates to Belgrade. The day before I was due to leave the Bulgarian Prime Minister, M. Moushanoff, and his wife came to call on the Stancioffs. Hearing of my plans he pronounced that there was no decent inn in Trnovo; so he and the Stancioffs began to discuss where I should stay. At that moment King Boris, who used now and then to walk over from Evksinograd, slipped into the room. When the discussion was resumed the Prime Minister declared: 'He shall stay at the Arbanassi monastery'. 'But that,' said Mme. Moushanoff in horrified tones, 'is a lady's monastery.' 'I know,' said her husband, 'but he shall stay there.' I noticed then that the King was trying to suppress his giggles. When the Moushanoffs took their leave a little later, he explained to me that the Abbess of Arbanassi had been not so very long ago a lady of rather a loose reputation, and Moushanoff had been one of her gentlemen friends, as his wife well knew.

So to the nunnery I went. A night train from Varna deposited me at 3.40 a.m. at the nearest main-line station at Trnovo. There a young man called Karl, the Prefect of Trnovo's brother-in-law – but I never discovered his surname – met me and drove me over the hills while the moon was setting and the sun was rising down into the valley below Trnovo to Arbanassi, where a kindly nun showed me a room in which I could spend the rest of the night. I might have been more comfortable in one of the maligned inns. A stream ran through a corner of the room and seemed to serve as the establishment's main drain, as I found when I explored the toilet facilities. I slept a bit, then was summoned to have breakfast with the Abbess, who was still a handsome lady and spoke excellent French. After breakfast she showed me the beautiful little monastery church. Then Karl came with his car to take me round the churches of Trnovo, which is the most splendidly situated town in all the Balkan peninsula, and on to Nicopolis on the Danube, to put me on a train that brought me to Rustchuk and the steamer to Belgrade.

In September 1934 the International Byzantine Congress was held in Sofia. Before going there I spent a few days with the Stancioffs in Varna. The King and his brother, Prince Cyril, were in residence at Evksinograd and came over twice to see the Stancioffs while I was there. The Congress was a friendly affair and competently run: though, as with all international congresses, too many people were allowed to talk for too long. Perhaps the most memorable moment was when a young man looking like a grubby Lord Byron appeared, with a letter to the American archaeologist Thomas Whittemore. It was Patrick Leigh Fermor, on his way from England to Istanbul. Roger Hinks, then of the British Museum, and I were the only British delegates. The Bulgarians proposed giving us some decoration; but the British Legation pointed out that we were not official delegates and that we were anyhow too junior. So we each had to make do with a photograph of His Majesty.

When Britain declared war on Germany in September 1939, I was beginning to recover from a very severe attack of amoebic dysentery, acquired, it seems, in India. The treatment then in use to deal with the disease had no effect on me; and I was eventually saved by a drug that had been developed in Germany and had fortunately become available in Britain, just in time before war broke out. Early in 1940 my doctor told me that I could take on a civilian job, so long as I did not overdo things. So I went to the War Office to ask if it had anything suitable for me. The authorities there did not like my health record, but eventually offered me, if I was pronounced fit enough, the job of censoring the letters written by the Cypriot muleteers serving with the British army in France. Rather to my relief my doctor told me to refuse the offer. When I reported this, a kindly officer in the War Office told me to keep in touch and let him know when I was fit for service. They might, he thought, be glad to make use of my knowledge of the Balkans and of Greece. Meanwhile the Ministry of Information Foreign Service was looking for someone to take over its Bulgarian desk. The notorious Guy Burgess was then working in the Ministry. He had been one of my first pupils at Cambridge and was aware that I knew Bulgarian. He suggested me for the post; and I was appointed to it, thus owing my war career to a traitor.

I telephoned to my friend in the War Office to tell him my news. He seemed to be disappointed and asked me if the Ministry would retain me even when I was pronounced medically fit to serve abroad. I replied that that seemed to be its intention but that naturally I did not know what it would do with me should Bulgaria enter the war. 'Oh,' he said, 'should that happen, would you let the War Office know?'

In June 1940 the Ministry decided to send me out to Bulgaria to be Press Attaché at our Legation there. Italy had by now declared war on us; it was impossible to travel across Europe to the Balkans. So, early that July, I was put on a Union Castle liner that took me to Cape Town, and I went on by train to Durban. From there a civilian flying-boat carried me on to Cairo, stopping for the nights at Mozambique, at Kampala and at Wady Halfa. It was a delightful journey, the only disadvantage being that we had to arise at 5 o'clock every morning, as the heavy machine could only lift itself out of the water in the thin air of dawn. We flew low, with wonderful views of the scenery; and when the pilot spotted a herd of elephants or of giraffes he flew lower still so that we could see them clearly. In Cairo I was delayed for a week by illness, then flew on to Istanbul and there took a train to Sofia.

Life in Bulgaria was not so pleasant for me now. The Bulgarian government had decided that Germany was going to win the war; and it soon became clear that if Hitler wished to move troops into the country, they would be welcomed. As a British official I felt embarrassed to see much of my Bulgarian friends lest they should get into trouble later on.

Many of them, such as the Stancioff family, still greeted me cordially; and I made a few new friends. But there was always a strained atmosphere. The Prime Minister, Bogdan Filov, had been a professor of Bulgarian art, and I had known him quite well. But he was, not unnaturally, unwilling to talk to me. The King, though always courteous on the very few occasions when I saw him, could not now show that he had ever been familiar with a junior member of an unpopular Legation. The staff of the American Legation, headed by a colourfully eccentric Minister, were all friendly; and with Greece as our only ally at the time, fighting against the Italians, I became good friends with all the members of its Legation. It was a very interesting time for me, but uncomfortable and menacing so that it was almost a relief when the Germany army arrived. I stood in the street to watch the troops march in, magnificent specimens, obviously hand-picked to make a formidable impression, and all with the faces and expressions of robots.

With the German entry we broke off diplomatic relations with Bulgaria. After a week, spent largely in packing up or destroying documents and saying goodbye to such friends as would still know us, we left one morning in a special diplomatic train for Istanbul. We had been told to leave all our luggage, except for overnight cases, at the station the previous evening. During the night someone removed two of the suitcases, replacing them with two, each with a bomb inside, one timed to go off when the train was expected to be going through the outskirts of Istanbul, the other a little later, to complete the wreckage. When the luggage was distributed to its owners on the train, no one claimed them. But, as the Military Attaché and the Air Attaché had both left the country earlier, it was assumed that the cases were theirs, and the clerk of each Attaché took charge of one. One clerk opened his, and found inside some dirty clothes and what he took to be a wireless battery, an object that was much cheaper in Bulgaria than in Turkey. Unexpectedly the Turks provided two engines for the train when we crossed the frontier; and we arrived at Istanbul nearly an hour early. The British Embassy officials were late in discovering this; so the cars and taxis sent to escort us to our hotels did not arrive at the station for some twenty minutes. Some American journalists were better informed; and one of them with whom I had dealt professionally in Sofia, whisked me up at once to the Pera Palace Hotel. I had booked myself in and was in my bedroom when suddenly there was an appalling blast, and plaster from the ceiling fell in vast quantities upon the bed, into which, having a slight fever, I was longing to subside. After trying to comfort two children who were screaming next door I went down to the hall and saw a ghastly shambles. The suitcase had just been brought in to the hotel when the bomb exploded. Two of our girl secretaries had lost limbs and were bleeding to death. Three hotel clerks were already dead, along with two plain-clothes Turkish policemen and a taxi-driver who had been carrying in his passenger's luggage and whose remains blocked the doorway. There were others in the hall who were less seriously wounded. There was nothing to be done except to try to improvise bandages till ambulances arrived. Meanwhile the Military Attaché's clerk, who had brought in the suitcase, rushed out, bleeding and with his trousers in tatters, up the hill to the hotel to which his Air colleague had been taken with the other suspect suitcase. His colleague, hearing the blast and realizing what must have happened, had already run with the suitcase to an open space between the hotels and had found two Turkish policemen, to whom, having a smattering of Turkish, he explained what he had done. They made him come with them to the suitcase and opened it. The bomb was due to go off a few minutes later; but they had time to see that it was of German manufacture before they threw it into a convenient pit nearby.

After that grim experience thirty-four years passed before I came again to Bulgaria. I had kept in touch with two scholars there whom I had known when we were young together and who now were distinguished professors, Christo Danov, the archaeologist, and Ivan Dujčev, the historian. The latter had had his ups and downs with the ruling régime, as he refused ever to join the Party, but his international eminence was such that he had to be treated with respect. It was perhaps due to them that early in 1975 I received an invitation from the Bulgarian Academy to come to Bulgaria for ten days as its guest that March. This invitation was almost at once superseded by an invitation from the Committee of Culture, the equivalent of the Ministry of Culture, to be its guest. I learnt later that the Academy was not at all pleased at being thus brushed aside. The Chairman of the Committee of Culture was a formidable young lady, Liudmilla Zhivkova, the President's daughter and his First Lady, her mother having died. She had been educated at various institutions abroad, including St Antony's at Oxford, and spoke good English. She liked London and used to pay incognito visits there, to buy clothes at Harrods. She was on friendly terms with the British Ambassador, Mr Bollard, with whom she had arranged that I should stay at the Embassy when in Sofia. I had to give a lecture to the Academy. Then Professor Danov took me on a tour to Plovdiv and the enchanting monastery of Batchkovo, and to Kazanlik, where there was a tomb of a third-century BC Thracian monarch with unspoilt Greek frescoes of first-class quality. Only the most privileged of visitors were allowed into the tomb. For the ordinary public a replica had been made in a neighbouring cave, where the frescoes were already beginning to fade. We went on to Trnovo, which now had two hotels but very little water; and each hotel was only allowed a supply every other day. We arrived on the wrong day for our hotel. So an adjustment was made; in my honour the other hotel was deprived of its supply till the following afternoon.

The whole visit was very enjoyable. But Bulgaria had lost much of its simple charm. Sofia was now ringed with factories, and the town was full of ministries and offices built in a clumsy Soviet style and featureless high-rise apartment blocks. There were collective farms in the countryside, but not very many. The Bulgarian peasant had always had his own smallholding and was not willing to abandon it. So the authorities, more usefully, organized co-operatives. But it is still a beautiful country, with its mountains and its great forests, which owe their splendour to King foxy Ferdinand, who ordered that every goat should be shot on sight. When in the 1930s the Greek dictator Metaxas visited Bulgaria he was much impressed to learn of this. On his return to Greece he did not venture to be quite so drastic, so he offered a sum for every dead goat brought to him: with the result that the Greeks bred goats as never before.

Every three years the Committee of Culture summoned a congress at which its recent achievements were described. The Ministers from all the Communist countries and some of the Third World countries were invited to it, as well as individuals from Western Europe whom Mme Zhivkova personally liked. I was summoned to the Congress in 1977; and for a week I found myself treated as an honorary Minister of Culture. The Ministers, when they addressed the gathering, all spoke of the benefits of Marxism; but when I was called upon to say something, I was able genuinely to praise the work that was being done in Bulgaria to preserve its ancient and historic monuments. Well-trained fresco-restorers were to be found in the old churches, most of which, to the annoyance of visitors, were therefore closed to the general public. Archaeological excavations were encouraged. When an underground railway was planned for Sofia – for every up-to-date capital must nowadays have one – it was routed so as not to disturb the remains of the Roman city of Sardica, which were discovered beneath the modern town. Very few countries have done so much to look after the relics of the past.

My next visit to Bulgaria, in 1979, began badly. Mme Zhivkova had decided to celebrate in 1980 the thirteen-hundredth anniversary of the foundation of the Bulgarian state, when the Bulgars, a Turkic people, crossed the Danube and organized the Slavs of the Eastern Balkans into a formidable kingdom. She invited me to go round some of the historic towns in Bulgaria and encourage the local authorities to do something appropriate in honour of the occasion. Shortly before I set out she sent me an apologetic message to say that she would not be there to welcome me, as she had to go to represent her country at the United Nations. The Bulgarian Cultural Attaché in London provided me with a ticket to take me to Sofia on a Monday. But when I arrived there at 6.30 on the

Monday evening there was no one at the airport to meet me. I did not know what to do. I had no idea where I was to stay. I had no Bulgarian money. All the offices in the town were shut. I knew that my hostess was in New York, and I did not know the name of any of the members of the Committee of Culture; I only knew that most of its previous members had been replaced. I knew that the British Ambassador was away, as I had recently seen him in London; and the Embassy was closed for the night, and nobody answered the telephone there. Had there been an aeroplane going back to London, I would have taken it, as I did have a return ticket; but there would be none till the next morning. I settled myself in the V.I.P. lounge, where the young lady in charge of it was friendly but equally at a loss to know what to do with me. At 9.30 an official from the Foreign Ministry appeared, come to meet a diplomat from, I think, Czechoslovakia. He had been *en poste* in London, and he recognized me. When he heard my story he promised that when he had dealt with his visitor he would go to his office and find out who was the acting Chairman of the Committee of Culture and would telephone to him. He did so; but M. Lenchev, the gentleman in question, was away at the cinema, and it was some time before he could make contact with him. At last, at 11.15, I received a call from M. Lenchev, who told me to take a taxi and come to his flat. But by then no more passenger aeroplanes were to arrive at Sofia. There were no taxis at the airport, which was only open because the head of the Secret Police had come out to meet his Russian counterpart, who was coming in a special plane from Moscow. The young lady in charge of the lounge, desperate by now to get rid of me, appealed to him for help. Fortunately the Russian plane was slightly delayed; so he sent me in his car to M. Lenchev's address. M. Lenchev received me kindly; and while his wife, rightly suspecting that I was hungry, produced a supper for me and his son practised his English on me, he found me a hotel bedroom, to which he eventually conveyed me. It appeared that the Cultural Attaché in London, after giving me a ticket for the Monday, had telexed to Sofia to say that I would arrive on the Wednesday.

I spent twelve days in the country, mostly travelling round it. I visited places that I had not seen before, and everyone welcomed me. But the young man sent by the Committee to look after me was arrogant, self-important and not very competent. Fortunately he deserted me before my tour was over and I finished it happily on my own.

I did not expect ever to go to Bulgaria again, especially when a few months later Liudmilla Zhivkova died of a mysterious illness. Rumour said that she had been murdered by the Russians, who disliked her for having Western tastes and disapproved of the projected ceremonies, as they showed not only that the Bulgars were not a purely Slav people but also that their civilization was far older than the Russian. The ceremonies were held all the same, but muted by the absence of the remarkable lady who had inspired them. However, in 1988 I was invited to come to the opening of an Institute founded in memory of my old friend Ivan Dujčev, who had bequeathed his vast library to the University of Sofia, and then to the centenary celebrations of the University. I could not attend the former ceremony as I had promised to go that week to the island of Patmos, for the nine-hundredth birthday of the Monastery of St John the Divine. But I spent five happy days at the University for its centenary functions, where I received a high honour, the Blue Ribbon. Along with a few other honorands I had a large and heavy bronze medallion, hung on a broad royal-blue ribbon, placed round my neck by the Rector, who gave me as well a miniature to be worn on less formal occasions. In my young days in Britain the Blue Ribbon had been a symbol of teetotalism. It was very different in Bulgaria, where the wine flowed freely. I have learnt, too, that my *History of the First Bulgarian Empire*, half a century after its publication, is to appear soon in a Bulgarian translation, though shorn of its dedication to King Boris. So my long association with that beautiful and interesting country has reached a happy climax. I hope that with reforms in the offing it will itself be a happier place.

Cambodia and Cochin-China

I KNOW that both these names are out of date. But Cambodia is much more mellifluous than Kampuchea, and Cochin-China has a magic quality quite lacking in the grim word Vietnam. When I was there, in what is still called altogether Indo-China, the whole area was under French suzerainty. Only the district round Saigon, the old Cochin-China, was under direct French rule. It was, indeed, a Département of France. Elsewhere the native ruling dynasties lasted on, the Kings of Cambodia and of Laos and the Emperors of Annam. There were French Residents at each court, to control foreign policy and the military and the police. Otherwise there was little interference, except for a concentrated effort to promote French culture, in which Jesuit and Dominican missionaries played an active part, to the annoyance of the Buddhist authorities, who saw many of the leading citizens go over to the Church of Rome.

On 15 December 1938 I left Bangkok with a Cambridge friend, Eddie Bates, to go to Angkor, to visit the ruins of the great capital of the Khmer Empire. A clean, unhurrying train took us through rice-fields and savannah country to Aranya, on the frontier between Thailand and Cambodia, where a car was waiting to take us on. It was a pleasant journey. The savannah soon gave way to jungle, peopled by monkeys, parakeets and peacocks; Malay peacocks who are much more splendid than their Indian cousins and whose wives, too, are dressed in blue and green. The French Embassy in London had kindly told the authorities in Indo-China to look out for me; and when we arrived at Siemreap, the French Resident was there to greet us and to escort us to a hotel, explaining that the picturesque hotel close to the ruins of Angkor was closed for redecoration. The Grand Hotel at Siemreap, at which we stayed, was stark and bare, but adequate.

We were there till 20 December, going daily to the ruins. We had to have a car, to take us first some four miles through the jungle and then round the temples and palaces, which were spread over so wide an area that one could never have seen them all by foot. The buildings of Angkor have been so often described that there is no need for me to make the attempt. I can only record how awed one is to see these grand edifices with their towers and statues and the huge stone-carved faces of the gods twisted and toppled by the relentless force of the jungle, trees now centuries old, growing in their midst. Only the great temple of Angkor

Wat, inhabited by a few Buddhist monks, remained and, I hope, still remains almost intact. It is a building of almost Classical proportions, giving an impression, rarely to be found in the Orient, that here is a piece of truly three-dimensional architecture.

One morning the *Conservateur* of the site, M. Glaize, took us in his car some twelve miles into the jungle to see the temple of Bantei Seray. It is a small, delicately ornate building of great elegance, which seems almost decadent in its sophistication in comparison with the monuments of Angkor itself but is in fact some two centuries older than them. We drove on jungle tracks till we came to a ravine across which we could see the temple. We scrambled down the cliff and over stepping-stones across a stream and up the other side. Further up the ravine I saw the remains of a ruined bridge, and I asked M. Glaize why it was not repaired. He explained that a few months previously, soon after the bridge had been built, there had come by night a car driven by a Communist writer called Malraux who earned his living by collecting antiques for an unscrupulous dealer. He had made off with a number of carved stones that he had torn off the building. He was caught and was in prison now for theft. But the authorities thought it would be prudent to destroy the bridge, as no one could carry off heavy loot if he had to cross the ravine on foot. M. Malraux was later to make his name, deservedly, as a novelist, and, when he had repented of his Communism, he was to become General de Gaulle's Minister of Culture and to write books telling us all how we should look upon art.

One evening we were treated to a performance of the Cambodian Royal Ballet, in the forecourt of Angkor Wat. It was charming, though a little rough in comparison with a performance of the Thai Royal Ballet, which I had seen a few weeks earlier. On another evening we went mounted on elephants to a nearby hill, from which we watched a glorious sunset illuminate the jungle and mountains far in the distance.

Before leaving Angkor I wrote a rough poem:

> *Where the superb Khmer Emperors*
> *Offered disdainful prayer*
> *To Siva the Destroyer*
> *Amid the vast destruction*
> *Of all the works of Khmer,*
> *The peacock of the jungle*
> *Struts and spreads out his train,*
> *Where the Imperial elephants*
> *And concubines in palanquins*
> *Will never pass again.*
> *O proud peacock,*
> *Will the day ever come*

When there will be no more peacocks
In the Cambodian jungle,
And your harsh voice be dumb?

I am told now that with the wars that have devastated Cambodia that prophecy may well come to pass.

On the afternoon of 20 December a car drove us out of the jungle to the Cambodian capital, Phnom Penh. It was then a pleasant town, clustering round the Royal Palace, with few modern Western-style buildings to mar its proportions. We arrived in the evening and spent the night in a hotel where the mosquito-nets badly needed repair. Next morning we visited the museum with its collection of Khmer statuary, works of a classical purity whose faces wore a faint smile, reminiscent of the smile on the faces of the *korai* of ancient Greece. We went on to the Palace, with which I would have been more deeply impressed had I not come recently from the palaces of Bangkok. In particular the furniture suggested the *grands magasins* of Paris rather than the traditions of the East. We drove that afternoon to Saigon, crossing the great Mekong river by ferry, where I was stung by a hornet.

Perhaps because the sting made me feel unwell for a day or two, I did not care for Saigon. It seemed to me to be like a less picturesque Marseilles, a city whose reputation for immorality it shared; but I cannot tell first-hand of its facilities for sin. However, we found several kind friends there; and I liked the Jardin Botanique, which was beautifully laid out.

On the evening of the 23rd we set out to go by train to Hué, the capital of the Empire of Annam. It was a comfortable journey. We each had our own wagon-lit compartment; and we spent Christmas Eve winding slowly northward along the coast, eventually arriving at Hué three hours late, at 1 a.m. on Christmas morning. We were met by a secretary of the Résident Supérieur, M. Grasseuil, who took us to a hotel and showed us the programme that had been arranged for our sight-seeing for the next two days.

It had been planned that we were to have our Christmas luncheon with the young Emperor Bao Dai. But he had broken his leg the previous day when playing football – not, I thought, a suitable pastime for an Emperor. So the Résident and Mme Grasseuil entertained us. It must have been tiresome for them to have to include two unknown Britishers on such an occasion. But they were wonderfully cordial; and the luncheon was memorably delicious. We lunched again with them on the following day.

I was enchanted by Hué. The European buildings, including our hotel and the Résidence, were on the south bank of the River of Perfumes, and the unspoilt native city and the Imperial Palace on the north bank. The view up the river reminded me of the view up the Thames from Richmond which late eighteenth-century artists loved to paint. The Palace was Chinese in inspiration but, I thought, simpler and somehow more substantial than the palaces at Peking. The other chief sights were the tombs of previous emperors, each set in its own garden. It poured with rain when we visited the Palace. Otherwise our enjoyment was unalloyed.

The train back to Saigon on the 27th left at 6 a.m. Soon after we had embarked on it everyone was handed a notice, in French and in Annamese, telling us that when we reached a certain ravine we must leave the train and walk across the bridge, as it was considered to be in a dangerous condition. The train, emptied of its passengers, would then follow us. I asked the little Annamite guard why, if the bridge was in such a perilous state, we had not been made to get out of the train on the northward journey. Oh, he explained, the notices had not been printed in time. Again it was a lovely journey. On the way up darkness had prevented us from seeing the Col des Nuages, the mountains looking as though they were part of a Chinese painting. It was after nightfall that we crossed the ravine, to the light of swinging lanterns, the train following safely behind us. We reached Saigon at noon next day, four and a half hours late. There we found a Messageries Maritimes liner, the *Maréchal Joffre*, which was to take us to Singapore.

28

Damascus

IT WAS only on my second visit that I approached Damascus as it should be approached, from across the desert. On my first visit, in 1931, when I was on my way to Jerusalem, I had come by train from London, by the Orient Express from Calais to Istanbul, and from Haydar Pasa, across the Bosphorus, by the Taurus Express, which in those days ran across Anatolia by Konia, not by Ankara as nowadays, through the splendid gorge of the Cilician Gates to Aleppo, and then on into the Bekaa valley, where it split, half going to Beirut on the coast and half to Damascus. I left the train just before it split, at Baalbek. That afternoon and the next morning I wandered round the ruins of the great temples there. Then I went on by car to Damascus.

The road wound through the desolate hills of the Anti-Lebanon. Then suddenly the city came in view, surrounded by gardens and orchards, with the desert stretching away into the distance. It was a splendid sight. But then one came down through rather ugly suburbs into a city which had not yet fully recovered from the disaster of 1925, when, in the course of a Druze revolt, it had been bombarded by the French, who held the Mandate for Syria under the League of Nations; fires, some started by the rebels, added to the devastation. The greater monuments had survived intact; but the Grand Bazaar had suffered and was still full of wooden shacks with corrugated iron roofs. I spent only two nights there, passing the intermediate day almost entirely in the courtyard of the great Ommayad Mosque. The early eighth-century mosaics that had been uncovered there are a few years previously are of an extraordinary beauty. Obedient to Moslem rules they contain no human figures, but show houses and trees and gardens through which rivulets are flowing. They are the work of artists sent from Constantinople at the Caliph's request and are of special interest to Byzantinists as at that time Iconoclastic emperors were ruling in Byzantium, men who were almost as hostile to the depiction of the human figure as were the Caliphs. Pious Byzantines accused them of turning churches into parks. So similar mosaics, long since destroyed, may have at that time shimmered in the churches of Byzantium.

Seven years later I came back to Damascus, arriving this time, as one should arrive, from across the desert. I had been in Baghdad; and there was an excellent bus service, run by the Nairn Brothers, which went twice a week from Baghdad to Damascus. We left Baghdad on an afternoon in late March. Before dusk we had crossed the great River Euphrates and were well into the desert. At dawn there was nothing but desolation all around, not a bird, not a plant to be seen. Then suddenly there was a bright green line on the horizon; and soon, abruptly, we left the desert and were winding through lush greenery, with fruit trees in blossom, water everywhere, and the city walls rising ahead, and a background of mountains. It was easy to understand why to the Arabs of the desert Damascus was the pearl of cities and why the Prophet himself was said to have refused to visit it because no one had the right to go to Paradise till he was dead.

On this occasion I stayed with the French Résident, Count Stanislas Ostrorog. The Ostrorogs were a Polish family who had left their native land in the 1840s to escape from Russian domination and who, after prudently acquiring French nationality, had settled in Turkey, in a handsome *yali*, or wooden palace, on the Asiatic shore of the Bosphorus. It belonged now to Stas's elder brother Jean. He had married a Bourbon princess who was well-known to be the daughter of the armaments king Sir Basil Zaharoff and had inherited a large slice of his ill-gotten fortune. It was a happy marriage so long as they seldom saw each other. The Countess stayed in Paris, where Jean would occasionally visit her; and she was very generous in subsidizing the upkeep of the *yali* in Turkey.

Stas Ostrorog, who had been told by his brother to look after me, was a splendid host. He was highly intelligent, very well-read and witty, with a gift for making friends wherever he was posted. After the War he was to be French Ambassador first in Dublin, then in Delhi – I stayed with him in both cities. But his health had never been good and he died while serving in India. My days in Damascus were filled with sight-seeing and social occasions. We went to Bosra and to Hama, where we were entertained by a local magnate in a palace that was externally undistinguished but furnished within in luxury befitting an oriental fairy story. One evening we dined at the British Consulate, where I met General Wavell. When he learnt that I was hoping to write a book on the Crusades, he told me to come and see him some day, as he had studied their history when he was helping Allenby plan his invasion of Palestine in 1917. Some eleven years later I met him again and reminded him of his invitation, which he had naturally quite forgotten. But he kindly had me to lunch and gave me a fascinating account of Allenby's campaign. It was not wholly relevant to my work, as Allenby invaded Palestine from Egypt, while the Crusaders came down from the north. But it gave me a good lesson in military strategy.

When I arrived Stas Ostrorog had been having a difficult time with the Moslem authorities in Syria. The railway from Aleppo to Damascus ran for a stretch close to the River Orontes, and as the river was eating into its foundations it had to be moved further away from the bank. But at the crucial spot there was a tomb of a Moslem saint. Using all his persuasive powers Stas at last secured permission to have the little building moved a few yards further from the river, provided that the work was entirely done by Moslem workmen. They came and carefully dismantled it stone by stone; there was nothing inside. Then the engineers came to dig new foundations for the rail-track; and deep down below where the tomb had stood, they came upon the mummified body of a bull. It must have been a sacred bull, buried by the Egyptians when they controlled the country in the thirteenth century BC. Ever since the site had been holy, each religion that controlled the area paying it reverence. It was a wonderful example of the continuity of tradition in the East.

From Damascus I went on to Beirut, and from there to the north of Syria, first to Lattakieh and thence to spend a day at the great Crusader castle of Sayun, or Saone. The French archaeologist in control of the ruin met me there. He was greatly distressed because he had admired T. E. Lawrence's *Crusader Castles* till he came to Sayun and compared the measurements given in that book with the measurements that he himself had made; and it became clear to him that Lawrence had never in fact taken any measurements himself but had relied happily on guesswork. Many years later I was to share my French friend's disillusion when I was invited to meet Lawrence, only a few months before his death, at a small party given by his admirer, Sir Ronald Storrs. He gave me a feeling of mistrust and almost physical repulsion. I left the gathering as soon as I decently could.

From Lattakieh I went on to Antioch, which had not yet been ceded to Turkey. It was a small town, largely occupied by Armenians, looking rather lost within the great encircling Byzantine walls, which climbed up and down the mountains in the background and leapt across a great chasm. I spent six days there, well looked after by the director of the local museum, M. Merlat, and his wife. We were joined there by Henri Seyrig, the Director then, and for many years to come, of the antiquities of Lebanon and Syria: though in his later days he was to find himself notable not as a distinguished archaeologist but as the father of one of the most glamorous of French actresses. He and Mme Seyrig took me on to Aleppo, making a detour to see the monastery church of St Simeon Stylites, in its ruined grandeur on a bare hillside. I was not allowed to contemplate it for very long as Mme Seyrig was an ardent botanist and had been told that there was a patch of wild black irises near the monastery and we had to find it. Dark had almost fallen before we saw the flowers, looking magnificently black in the fading light. From Aleppo I travelled back by train to London.

During the War, I spent one night in Damascus, on my way from Jerusalem to Iran. In 1951 I was there again, anxious to complete my knowledge of the Crusader castles by visiting the great fortress that crowned a mountain-top above the town of Banyas, the Caesarea Philippi of the ancients. I also wanted to see the old Moslem city of Shaizar, near Hama, the capital in the Middle Ages of the highly civilized emirate of the Munqidite dynasty, one of whose members wrote the most entertaining book of memoirs to be produced in the Crusading era. It was not difficult to go to Shaizar, now a small village called Seidjar. I hired a car in Damascus and at Shaizar sought the local school-teacher, who seemed glad to take me round and show me what sights were still worth seeing. It was less easy to visit Banyas, as it lay in a military zone close to the Israeli border. Syria was at that time dominated by a man who contented himself with the modest title of Assistant Chief of Staff but was in fact a dictator. Thanks to the kindness of the British Ambassador it was arranged for me to see him, accompanied by an Arabic-speaking Secretary. He was gracious, but suggested that I might prefer to visit the other town of Banyas, which lay far from any frontier. It had a castle too, he thought. I told him that I had been there; it was the Banyas close to the frontier that it was important for me to see. He gave consent, and summoned a police-officer, whom he ordered in Arabic to accompany me, letting me see anything that I wished but keeping close to me wherever I went.

Two days later Major Mahmoud Abeid, of the Syrian Police, set out with me by car to the Israeli frontier. He spoke good French and had been much looking forward to this outing, at my expense. But when we arrived at Banyas and he realized that I intended to climb up a steep mountainside to see some ruins at the top, his face fell. He was a portly man, tightly packed into a uniform of rather heavy cloth; and the midday sun was strong. But he did his duty bravely and cheerfully, struggling up the slope behind me. First his belt was unbuckled and discarded, then his tunic was unbuttoned, and it soon came off. Fortunately we reached the summit before he had done more than unbutton his shirt. The peasant guardian of the ruins was surprised to have visitors and deeply shocked when I produced binoculars and a map – I wanted to check what other Crusader castles were in sight for signalling purposes. Major Abeid, so he told me as we descended, was sternly reproved for bringing a *farangi* spy to such a spot. By the time that I had seen all that I needed to see and we had gone down the mountain to have a picnic lunch at its foot, the Major was feeling pleased with himself. Never for fifteen years had he gone on such a walk, he declared, but he still could do it. Our camaraderie was enhanced on the drive back. The road ran for a bit close to the frontier; and a trigger-happy Israeli soldier, glimpsing, perhaps, a uniform in the car, started taking pot-shots at us. He was, happily, a poor shot; no harm was done to the car or to us. But to have been together under fire gave us a new bond of friendship.

As we drove back we stopped at every police post on the route, so that the Major could tell of his experiences and we could be given refreshments which did not all conform with the Moslem ban on alcohol.

My last visit to Damascus was in the spring of 1953. I was staying in Beirut, where my good friend the poet George Seferis (legally Seferiades) was Greek Ambassador. We had tried one day to reach the gorge of the river Adonis, which in early April runs red, with minerals dislodged by floodwaters from the melting snows of Lebanon. Unfortunately, that year the snows had not yet melted and the ambassadorial limousine stuck in a snow-drift on a mountain pass. So we never saw the blood of the slaughtered god. To console me George suggested taking me with him to Damascus two days later. He was accredited to Syria as well as to Lebanon; and his government had told him to see the Orthodox Patriarch of Antioch, who resides in Damascus, and ask him why he was accepting money from Soviet Russia. Greece, as the one officially Orthodox country, considers herself to have a special responsibility towards all the Orthodox Churches. We had a pleasant drive up to Damascus; and I sat in the car while George conducted his interview. He soon came out laughing. When he put his question the Patriarch simply answered: 'No one else has ever offered me any money.' I was then taken in to pay my respects to his All-Holiness, who was a kindly and unimpressive old gentleman.

I do not expect ever to visit that ancient city again. But to me, as to the Syrian leper Naaman, Abana and Pharpar, rivers of Damascus, are better than all the waters of Israel.

 *Egypt*

MY FIRST experience of Egypt was in the autumn of 1925, when I went through the Suez Canal on my way to China. I spent a few hours in Port Said, visiting the famous emporium of Simon Artz, where one was supposed to be able to buy anything that one wanted cheaper than anywhere else in all the world; but there was nothing that I wanted to buy. I also had my fortune told by an aged man who drew patterns in the sand. He told me, encouragingly, that I would have a long and happy life but warned me against having disreputable friends. It is true that most of the Bright Young People whose parties I attended in the late 1920s came to a bad end; and it is true that as a young don I knew all the Cambridge traitors – but as they regarded me as a hopelessly out of date old-fashioned Liberal I was in no danger of contamination. The following spring I returned through the Canal and went out again through it in 1938 and back in 1939, when I had time to make a brief excursion to Cairo, and to the Pyramids and the Sphinx.

In 1940 I spent a week in Cairo on my way via Cape Town to Bulgaria; but I spent it in hospital so have little to say about it, except that it rained one day, which, I was told, had never happened before in July. In the spring of 1941, after the German army had been admitted into Bulgaria and we had to leave, I was sent back to Cairo with orders to set up news bulletins on the Cairo radio, which was under British control, in the four chief Balkan languages. It was not a very happy time for me. The weather was unusually hot; and from the nature of my work I had to keep at it through the heat of the day, when luckier folk could enjoy a siesta. I was under the authority of the British Embassy, which was not always helpful. The Greek broadcasts were not troublesome, as there were many able and reliable Greek refugees in Cairo at the time. Once the broadcasts were set up I could leave things in their hands. It was not so easy to find Bulgarians, Serbs and Roumanians who were able to compose and to announce the bulletins. Members of the British Embassy regarded it all as an opportunity for finding jobs for the boys or, rather, for the girls, some of whom were far from suitable. Eventually we managed to set up a satisfactory organization. But by that time my health had given out. In July, after I had spent a week in hospital, the authorities decided to move me to the more salubrious climate of Jerusalem. I was greatly relieved.

Several novelists, notably Olivia Manning, whom I saw now and then, have described life in Cairo during those war years. It had an unreal glitter about it. We lived in comfort; we entertained each other. But the atmosphere was tense and uncertain. The war in the Western Desert was not far away. Soldier friends whom one met on their leave might go back there and never return. All the time we were wondering what was going on in Britain and feeling almost ashamed that we were not there to share in its dangers and its hardships. I have never found it easy to be unhappy for long. But this was, I think, the least happy period of my life.

I was back in Cairo in July 1944 on leave from Turkey. I had been away from Britain for four years and, for family reasons, I was anxious to go home for a while. The British Council, under whose aegis I was then working, told me that if I went to Cairo they might be able to arrange my journey. They did their best; and I discovered that they could send me home, but that they could not guarantee to send me out again; and I had to be back in Turkey by the autumn. I stayed nearly a month in Egypt. A kind friend who was on leave lent me his flat in Cairo. The tenseness had gone. The war had moved far away, though Egypt was now the base for commando raids on German-occupied Greece and, one hoped, for an ultimate invasion of the Balkans. I met Paddy Leigh Fermor again, whose exploits in Crete were already the stuff of legend. I spent a few days in Alexandria, where the old Greek and Jewish families still had their palaces. Coptic friends took me to see the monasteries in the Wady Natrun; and I made a brief expedition to Mount Sinai. I was planning to write a book on the Crusades and was able to talk about them to Egyptian scholars. It was a pleasant month even though I came to realize that I would not be able to make the journey to Britain. So, instead, I moved on to Jerusalem, and from there to stay with my brother, who was Air Attaché at our Embassy in Teheran.

When I was next in Cairo, for ten days in 1951, the atmosphere had changed again. The British presence was no longer to be seen, and King Farouk was ruling in his own extravagant way. The contrast between rich and poor was frightening. I wondered whether visitors to Paris in the years before the French Revolution had felt a similar sense of disquiet and doom. Nevertheless I enjoyed my glimpse of the glamorous life. I made friends with one of King Farouk's beautiful sisters, Princess Faiza, whose palace was full of carelessly collected treasures. At one of her smaller parties I offered to tell fortunes if she had any pack of tarot cards. It is usually said that no complete pack of old tarot cards survives. But her husband took me to a chest in which there were six or seven splendid examples dating, as far as I could judge, from the eighteenth century. One evening I went with her to a reception given by a cousin of hers, a princess; she had decided that her house was not big enough for the party so had annexed the whole street and had erected a large tent there, oblivious of the inconvenience that it caused to her neighbours. On the way there I asked Princess Faiza who would be present. 'Oh, all the family', she said. 'All?' I queried. 'If you mean my brother', she answered, 'we never invite him to our parties.'

My days were not, however, entirely taken up with party-going. I had come out to meet scholars at the University of Cairo and to lecture there. My theme was Christian–Moslem relations in the Middle Ages. The British Embassy vainly begged me to choose some less sensitive subject; but I have always found that, unless one is faced by fundamentalists – and Christian fundamentalists are almost as savage as are Moslems – it is easy to discuss religion with Moslems, so long as one is obviously sincere. Anyhow, that lecture seemed to be well received. I also spent two days in the Delta, seeing Damietta and Mansoura and other sites connected with the Crusades. My guide there was a large and genial schoolmaster, whose son's doctoral thesis I had examined in England. He was a kindly and assiduous guide; but his English, though fluent, was eccentric. Guesswork was needed to interpret what he said.

It was a depressing experience to go back to Egypt in 1964. I had never been to Luxor; and I wanted to see the temple at Abu Simbel before it was to be moved, stone by stone, up the cliff to escape inundation in the great lake to be created by the new high Aswan Dam. Cairo had lost its glamour. As usually happens after a social revolution, the rich were gone but the poor were as poor as ever. The streets were drab. The new ruling class of bureaucrats had no use for elegant shops and restaurants. The splendid monuments of the city were ill-kept, and the museums in a mess. The hotels, once excellently run by Swiss managers, were now in the hands of friendly but inexperienced Egyptians; and everything was becoming shabby.

I was glad to fly on to Aswan. I spent a pleasant day going up the Nile in a hydrofoil to see Abu Simbel, which I thought impressive in its situation but rather coarse in its architecture. But life in the Cataract Hotel was made perilous by hordes of unmannerly schoolboys, it being President Nasser's policy to encourage the Egyptian youth to see the country's antiquities. They would rush through the hotel, knocking over tables and chairs and an occasional American dowager. When I left to fly to Luxor I was nearly torn to pieces at the airport by a gaggle of schoolgirls, fighting to be the first on the plane. Fortunately, the Dowager Begum Aga Khan, who was also travelling on it, spotted me and beckoned me to join her, so that I could use the V.I.P. entrance.

At Luxor, thanks to Thomas Cook & Sons, I was put into an unfinished hotel. It was of the motel style; but few of the rooms yet had hot water laid on, and the electric bells were not yet working. If one wanted hot water it was necessary to stand at one's door in the hope that some attendant would soon pass by. The dining-room was staffed by untrained waiters who, in their eagerness to be obliging, would rush in and out of the tables spilling food, which they then scraped up from the floor and replaced on the dishes. When I asked for a clean fork a kindly youth picked one from a dirty plate and wiped it on his shirt. I went round next morning to complain at Cook's office; but no one took much interest. So I haughtily announced that I was far too grand to be treated in such a way and was so insistent on my grandeur that the Cook's representative at last discovered that there would be a room vacant at the old but still comfortable Luxor Palace Hotel. After two nights of squalor he came to escort me thither. There in the entrance hall were two British dukes, being 'Your Graced' by deferential clerks; and both of them greeted me. The Cook's representative was reassured that he had done the right thing, and my self-importance was justified.

One of the dukes told me that I had better have my meals with him and his duchess. She, being French, had been horrified by the food that the hotel provided and had herself cleared a corner of the kitchen, where she prepared the ducal meals. Unfortunately they went away next day and I was left to face the hotel's provender.

The quality of service is, I am told, higher now. When next I visited Egypt I went with an organized tour. The individual traveller not only pays more but is worse treated. The hotels prefer to deal with tour-managers. I was then able to see the Coptic monasteries by the Red Sea, which I had not known before, in comparative comfort, and to revisit the splendid monastery of St Catherine by Mt Sinai, now admirably restored and a holy place, but overrun by hordes of ignorant and unappreciative tourists.

France

In my young days, when air-travel was as yet unknown, journeying abroad nearly always meant passing through France. You could not fly direct to such unheard-of places as the Costa Brava. To reach Europe you had to cross the North Sea or the Channel. Hardy folk bent on visiting Scandinavia would brave the waters of the North Sea. Travellers to Central Europe might cross to Flushing or to Ostend; but for most Britons a journey to the Continent began with France. Even when aeroplanes came into use, few of us did more than venture to fly to Paris.

Most of my early journeys overseas involved a visit to France. I was, I think, aged four when I went there first, on my grandfather's yacht. We put in to Cherbourg; and I think that I still remember the look of the port, though my image of it by now is wholly fanciful. I am more certain about my next French journey, in May 1910. My father was then in the Cabinet, as President of the Board of Education – a far more sonorous and historic title than the modern 'Minister'. I suppose that it was the House of Commons's Whitsun recess that enabled him to escape for a few days. My mother had heard of a quiet inn in the woods near Dieppe and they took me there with them. I loved it. There was a large friendly patronne who let me watch her at work in the kitchen. Luckily we all had been taught to speak French when we were very young, and I was ready to be eloquent if none of the family was present. The idyll did not last for long. On the second morning, when we were at breakfast, the patronne burst in with tears streaming down her face. 'Le bon Roi Edouard est mort', she cried. About an hour later a special messenger arrived with a large envelope with the thickest black border that I have ever seen, containing a summons to my father to come home at once for the meeting of the Privy Council, to proclaim the new King. He left at once, but was too late for the ceremony. My mother and I followed next day. I was sad to go, but was somewhat consoled when we arrived back in London, and my father took me to see the King lying in state in Westminster Hall. I enjoyed still more the Royal Funeral procession, which I watched from a window in Whitehall. It stirred my romantic imagination to see all the kings and princes gathered together, in what was to be the last great royal occasion in Europe. I was enchanted by the sight of the widowed Queen Alexandra, sitting in her carriage and alternately mopping her eyes with a black hankerchief and smiling happily to the crowd.

In the spring of 1912 my mother, with great enterprise, took my brother, my eldest sister and me, then aged 11, 10 and 8, round by sea to the south of France. She brought a nursemaid to help cope with us, a Plymouth Brother – they do not seem to have Sisters – called Susie, who used to warn us of the dangers of Hell-fire, but quite gently, as she was a kindly creature. We spent several days in Saint-Rémy-de-Provence, then journeyed through Avignon, Arles and Nimes, to Carcassonne, where they were still building the medieval walls. It was a happy time for us all.

My next journey through France was fraught with anxiety. In March 1921 my parents, my brother and my eldest sister had travelled out in the family Rolls, with a very superior chauffeur, to Rome. There I joined them, having come by train, when the school holidays began. We had a pleasant time in Rome, Siena and Florence. Then my brother had to hurry back for the beginning of the term at Cambridge; and my parents decided that they would prefer to return by sea from Naples. So my sister and I were left to convey the Rolls and the chauffeur through France. Unfortunately, my parents did not provide us with much money for the journey; but they arranged for a further supply to await us at a bank in Tours, telling us to avoid the expensive glamour of Paris. It was an agreeable drive, but more expensive than we had expected; and by the time that we reached Moulins, hoping to go on to Tours next morning, we had little more left than enough for one night.

Moulins seemed to be full of witches. Never, before or since, have I seen so many sinister old crones gathered together in one town. When we arrived at the modest hotel that we had chosen, one of them came up and begged for alms. We were in no position to be generous and ignored her. She then turned and cursed the car. A few minutes later the chauffeur came to us in a state of alarm, to tell us that the back axle had been snapped neatly in half. So there we were, stuck in Moulins with our money running out, having to summon a technician from the Rolls representatives in Paris, who needed payment and who advised us that we would have to go to Paris to get the job completed. He was a kind man and lent us enough cash for us to take a sequence of cross-country trains from Moulins to Tours to collect the sums awaiting us there. That was a relief; but what had seemed once to be a lavish amount was barely going to suffice for our new expenses. We could not economize over the chauffeur, as he expected to be treated properly. So we starved ourselves and found a very cheap hotel in Paris for the two nights that we had to spend there. Providently we booked and paid for berths for ourselves and the car on the night ferry from Le Havre to Southampton; and on our last night in Paris we had enough left to enjoy a delicious dinner.

But our troubles were not over. When we reached Le Havre the next afternoon we were told that there had been a muddle and that there was no place for us on the boat. We were now penniless again; and I had to be back at school the next day. They refused to give us back the money that we had paid for the tickets. That could only be done through the head office in Paris or in London. In despair we drove to Dieppe, to see if we could do better there. As we approached the town we passed the Golf Club; my sister, who was nineteen and rather good-looking, decided to beg for money from one of its members. We drove in, and she approached the first respectably dressed Englishman that she saw and told him our sad story. Whether it was because of her good looks or, more probably, the sight of a Rolls-Royce in the background, he loaned us enough to get us onto the night boat to Newhaven and so to London. Ever since then I have advised travellers to France to avoid Moulins.

I often went back to France between the Wars, driving round the country, usually with Cambridge friends, or going to stay with that great lady, the writer Edith Wharton, who had an enchanting house on the castle rock behind Hyères and an exquisite *pavillon* in the Forest of Montmorency, near Chantilly. I usually spent the New Year with French friends in Paris and sometimes in the summer visited them in Normandy. I had known the son of the house, Louis, when he had come as an undergraduate to Cambridge. He was a promising artist, a pupil of Jacques-Emile Blanche, whose salon we would often visit. The family usually took a house in the country for the summer months. One August I visited them in a château overhanging the River Sarthe, near Le Mans. While I was with them there was a terrible disaster off Nantes, when a pleasure-boat sank with the loss of over a hundred lives. Next day we were calling on a neighbouring comte, a kindly old man, I had thought. He told us sternly that the accident was God's doing; for he had heard on reliable authority that most of the drowned trippers had been Socialists and some of them actually freemasons. I was glad to escape before he discovered that I came of Protestant stock.

After the end of the War I went less often to France. Edith Wharton was dead; and my travels were taking me further afield. I still visited my friends in Paris, and went with them to Normandy, where Louis had inherited a château. But he had had a bad war, spent almost entirely as a prisoner of the Germans, and his health had been ruined. He was working now as an Assyriologist, but struggling against tuberculosis. After his death I went on seeing his mother so long as she lived. She was a remarkable woman, a Norman brought up in an Anglophile family, and had been twice married, her husbands having been first cousins. When she was on her second honeymoon, in Palermo, a gypsy came up to her and said: 'I do not understand you. You are a respectable woman, but you are going to have children by two different men and you will give the children the same surname.' The gypsy went on to beg her so earnestly not to leave Palermo that afternoon that she was frightened and persuaded her husband to postpone their intended journey to Messina. It was as well. That night there was the great earthquake at Messina. The friends with whom they had planned to travel were among the thousands that perished.

I had always thought that Paris would retain its beauty for ever. But when last I was there, in 1977, though the centre was as handsome as ever, one could see in the offing high-rise monstrosities that made one long for a misty day. The Centre Pompidou is mercifully not too easily seen from outside. I went on that occasion to its opening, in our Ambassador's party. With us was Mr Edward Heath, who had come to attend the ceremony on the special invitation of Mme Pompidou. When we arrived and clambered up what should have been a moving staircase with some four thousand other guests to the large open space on the first floor – one could not in such a building call it the *piano nobile* – Mr Heath was brusquely informed that the platform was reserved for heads of state and Mme Pompidou and that he would have to stand along with the rest of us. Indeed, only President Giscard and his wife, the Belgiums, the Luxemburgs, Princess Grace of Monaco and three Presidents from Africa, as well as an embarrassed Mme Pompidou were seated in front of us. I managed to find enough space to sit on the floor; then, bored by the speeches, I went exploring. I found another staircase leading to ground level; but when I set foot on it I discovered that it was not attached to the platform, and I shot across the floor. When at last I was able to descend, the only exhibition that I could see was of shoes of the 1920s. It did not detain me for long. I was relieved when, on Mr Heath's insistence, we all returned to the Embassy.

The Centre Pompidou seemed to be graceless and unwelcoming, with all its entrails showing. I was saddened to learn that it was the creation of an English architect. I can only regard it as England's revenge for Joan of Arc. There are many among the French who admire it, I am told. But then, most Englishmen are in love with Joan of Arc.

Nevertheless, in spite of such an example of modern horror, and in spite of the glass pyramid that trivializes the dignity of the Louvre, France remains the most civilized of nations; and, living as I do in a house to which a sixteenth-century builder added pepper-pot turrets in the belief that they would make the house look French, I must record my loyalty to the Auld Alliance.

The Gulf

IN THE OLD DAYS we used to call it the Persian Gulf; and the name was justified in Classical and early medieval times, when the great kingdom of Persia dominated Mesopotamia and all the lands around, and even in later centuries when Persian shahs held a fitful suzerainty over all its shores. But now Persia insists upon the less mellifluous name of Iran, and Iran goes its own individual and unfriendly way in the progress of the nations: while the peoples that live on the western and southern shores of the great inlet are consciously and proudly Arab. It is more proper to call it the Arabian Gulf. But most of us when we speak of the Gulf mean that sickle-shaped, oil-rich sea that separates the huge bulk of Arabia from the rest of the Asian continent. It is true that the title has to some extent been usurped by the Gulf of Mexico. The Gulf Stream that comes from the west to lap our British shores has nothing to do with the Middle East; and when people talk of the Gulf States they are usually referring to those areas of the United States that border the Mexique Bay. But the ancient Greeks, who gave us the word from which 'gulf' is derived, knew of which gulf they were speaking; and we can follow their example.

I wish that I had known the emirates of the Gulf in older times when life there still followed its traditional lines, when, in spite of their barren shores, they enjoyed some prosperity from their pearl-fisheries and from their sturdy dhows that sailed across the Indian Ocean to bring back luxuries from far away to the markets of the Nearer East. By 1956, when I first reached its waters, the coming of oil had begun to alter everything. Oil-wells were burgeoning on land and in the sea; and wealth was pouring in. With wealth came many of the less attractive features of Western life. I was spending the early months of that year lecturing at the University College of Baghdad, and I escaped for two days to visit an old Cambridge friend who was working for the British Government in Kuwait. It was depressing. I had one glimpse of the old world. When I was walking along the quay the captain of a dhow beckoned me on to his ship and showed me round. She was a handsome boat, beautifully kept. Conversation was not easy. He had a few words of English, which did not always correspond to my few words of Arabic. But, over a cup of bitter coffee, I was able to understand something of his gloom. The sea-captains had been the aristocrats of Kuwait, with traditions of enterprise and of honesty and courtesy that stretched far back into the past. Now, with oil bubbling up all over the territory, anyone who owned a tiny piece of land might find himself suddenly a millionaire, quite untrained to cope with his sudden riches. The streets were lined with abandoned cars; for, if your limousine broke down, why go to the bother of having it repaired when you could easily afford to buy a new one? Older buildings were left to decay, to be replaced by ugly new villas. The dhows were the only things of beauty that remained; and their day was over.

There were compensations. Certainly new up-to-date hospitals were of benefit to the community, as were the works for the desalination of sea-water. But around them were arising monuments of extravagance. I was taken to see a school under construction, whose English architect had been ordered to spend far more money than the building required. So he was lining the class-room walls with mosaic; and in the boys' lavatory there was a charming row of thrones of all sizes, so that even the tiniest brat could be comfortably accommodated. Such elegance was not fully appreciated. Many of the smarter Kuwaitis still tried to send their sons to the tin sheds where the British community ran their school.

I have never been back to Kuwait. I suppose that by now it has adjusted itself to its opulence. Its main problem seems to be that, with the Kuwaitis themselves all too wealthy to deign to work, foreign labourers have had to be imported in quantities that threaten the stability of the state.

Over twenty years passed before I went to the Gulf again. Now it is Bahrain to which I like to go. Of all the states along the Gulf Bahrain has the longest history. With the presence, rare in those parts, of fresh-water springs, it was from earliest times a port on the age-old sea-route from Mesopotamia to the Further East. To the Babylonians it was known as Dilmun; and its lush fertility was such that they thought it to be the site of the Garden of Eden. From those distant ages to modern times its pearl-fisheries were famous. The centuries of desiccation that have afflicted all Arabia have left their mark on the island. It could hardly now qualify to be the Earthly Paradise. But its palm-groves and its gardens, encouraged by a ruler who loves flowers, give it a grace that sets it apart from its neighbours.

Man has been even unkinder than the climate. There is not much left of old Bahrain. Excavations have revealed what there is: the foundations of ancient Dilmun; temples and tombs with their seals and jars and goblets of good craftsmanship, dating from about 2500 BC down to Hellenistic times; and there are still burial tumuli to the number, it is said, of 172,000, which have been left in peace. There are one or two buildings dating from medieval times, notably the mosque al-Khamis. In the former capital Muharraq there are still a few houses built mostly in the nineteenth century in old traditional style, to suit the patterns of social life and to meet the demands of the climate. But today Bahrain gives an impression of frantic modernity. High-rise apartment blocks and hotels vie with grandiose office-buildings, all designed, as is usual with the work of modish architects, with no consideration for the buildings on either side. Smart residences and villas, some of them handsome and elegant, pullulate all round, with little regard for consistent town-planning. New mosques are continually built, for a population that is still dutifully pious, which necessarily follow traditional lines but too often lack the traditional sense of proportion. Not all the buildings are ugly. There is, for instance, a noble and well-designed National Museum, where one can see the best artefacts that the archaeologists have unearthed, as well as imaginative tableaux depicting the old way of life. There are well-kept avenues and gardens, and in the streets examples of modern sculpture which may seem admirable to those who like such objects. But the whole effect of the city of Manama, the modern capital, is not beautiful. However, that is the price paid for prosperity today. It is over half a century since the first oil-well in Bahrain came into action; and, though now the great days of Bahraini oil are probably over, kindred industries have been developed there. Meanwhile the off-shore banking world, which had made Beirut the centre of its operations in the Levant, when that once pleasant city collapsed into chaos, moved its centre to Bahrain, bringing fresh activity to its financial life. Bahrain moreover had become the main stopping-place for aeroplanes on their way to the Further East, while in 1986 a causeway, some sixteen miles in length, crossing the shallow sea that separates Bahrain from the Arabian mainland, was opened, to make the island serve, to its benefit, as a port on the Gulf for the Saudi kingdom.

It was, however, from no desire to profit out of Bahrain's prosperity nor even from a wish to gape at some of the enormities of modern architecture that induced me to pay three visits to the island during the last decade. It was to indulge in the pleasure of seeing an old friend and of visiting a land in the Levant that was welcoming and happy. Immediately after the last World War I was in Athens, in charge of the British Council. There were still British troops in Greece, under the command of General Scobie, who, more than anyone else, had saved Greece from falling into the hands of the Communists; for which he received little recognition in Britain, where left-wing opinion refused to believe in the atrocities committed by the rebels, but was regarded with grateful devotion by the Greeks. When the civil war was at its height round Athens, Scobie gave his A.D.C., Gerald Green, the task of seeing to the safety of two widowed Greek princesses, whom the Communists would have loved to capture and hold as hostages. Princess Nicholas, the mother of Princess Marina, Duchess of Kent, and Princess Andrew, the mother of the future Duke of Edinburgh, both of whom had endured life in Athens under German occupation during the War, were not fond of each other. Princess Nicholas, a Russian Grand-duchess by birth and insistent always that she was an Imperial and Royal Highness (in that order), was contemptuous of Princess Andrew, who was a mere Battenberg by birth; but Princess Andrew, as Queen Victoria's favourite great-granddaughter, had little use for haughty Russians. It was a tribute to Gerald's tact and charm that he not only persuaded them to live together in a secure place while the crisis lasted but also won and retained the deep affection of them both.

By the time that I came to Athens the civil war and the World War were over, and the princesses were back in their homes. I used to see both of them. Princess Andrew came several times to lunch with me in my little flat, to my great delight, as her conversation was wonderfully eccentric but often witty and always shrewd. I was more in awe of Her Imperial and Royal Highness, whom I never ventured to invite to my simple residence. But she sometimes invited me to her house and it was there that I first met Gerald; we have remained good friends ever since.

After he was demobilized and life in England had been soured for him by domestic difficulties, Gerald went out to Bahrain to be an officer in the Police Corps, then still under British control. There his courage, his good sense and his integrity impressed the Ruling Family; and after Bahrain obtained complete independence in 1971 he stayed on as English secretary and personal adviser to the Ruler. There he has remained. It is a life that is full of interest and responsibility, but a lonely one. A man who is intimate with the Ruler cannot wisely become a close friend of any of his subjects. The diplomatic world can provide pleasant company; but diplomats soon move on to other posts. The business world is seldom interesting except to its own members; and it, too, is transient. It was only when old friends came out to visit him that he could enjoy the ease and comfort of friendship. But Bahrain is not a place that many folk consider to be an alluring holiday resort; and few of us in this hurried world have time to stay there for long.

It was only in 1980 that I paid my first visit to Bahrain. At that time Concorde used to fly to Singapore, calling at Bahrain on the way. I decided that I must sample this new and well publicized method of travel. Once was enough. The machine may be a triumph of human ingenuity but it is designed for dwarfs. Never, before or since, have I travelled in such cramped discomfort. Moreover, the aeroplane that was to carry me back to London ten days later broke down in Singapore; so I had to wait on and on for hours while some vital part was flown out to Singapore to repair the stricken machine. I would have arrived home half a day sooner, and at infinitely less cost, had I not fallen victim to a form of travellers' snobbery. For my next visits to Bahrain, in 1985 and 1989, I chose less pretentious aircraft.

Bahrain may not seem to be an ideal island. But it has its assets. Those to whom the perfect holiday means lying in the sun, wooing skin-cancer, will find the sandy beaches that slope into the waters of the Gulf attractive and uncrowded during the early months of the year, before the damp heat of summer arrives. Night life is limited and expensive. There are not many sites or monuments of historic or aesthetic interest to lure the highbrow traveller. But Bahrain provides a spectacle, rare in the world of the Levant, where traditional values have come to terms with modern life. The infidel visitor is welcome. He suffers none of the restrictions imposed on him across the narrow waters in the Saudi kingdom. He can drink all the alcohol that he pleases. His womenfolk, so long as they are decently dressed, are free to wander through the streets by themselves. Local people all are welcoming. Even the Shia Moslems, who form a large part of the Arab population, show none of the xenophobic intolerance of their Iranian co-religionists on the other side of the Gulf.

For this most credit must go to the Ruler, Shaikh Isa bin Salman Al-Khalifa, the tenth of a dynasty that liberated the island from Persian rule two centuries ago. He is physically a small man. Seen standing next to our Queen he makes her appear like a giantess. But such is the dignity that he radiates that he dominates any gathering he attends. Bahrain is not a democracy in the Western pattern. The Ruler still rules. But, in the age-long Islamic tradition, every one of his subjects, however humble, can have direct access to him. On each of my visits I have been present at his *majlis*, where once a week he sits at the head of a palace hall, with his family and ministers, together with citizens and visitors who wish to pay him respect seated along the side-walls, and a sequence of Bahrainis, most of them simple and poor, comes up to him with a petition stating his aspiration or his grievance, knowing that the petition will be carefully read and adjudicated and that he will be given any help that he may need. Foreigners too may bring petitions; but those are rightly treated with caution. At one *majlis* which I attended I noted a gentleman, probably of Lebanese origin, and I whispered to Gerald who had brought me there that never had I seen a more obvious crook. He was the first that morning to come up with a petition; and I gathered later that my suspicions were not unjustified and that the Ruler, when my comment was repeated to him, heard it with delight.

One afternoon, when driving round the outskirts of the town, we tried to take a short cut across a sandy waste; and the car stuck in the sand. Our efforts to move it were in vain. But almost at once two men appeared and hurried to help us. They too were unsuccessful in their efforts; so they took Gerald off with them on foot to the nearest police station, to try to secure a van to tow the car out of its predicament, leaving me sitting in it. They had not been gone for long before two other men appeared and without a word to me tried their hands at moving the vehicle, and somehow succeeded. They then got into the car and began to drive me off. I thought for a moment that I was to be snatched away to be held as a hostage in some secret cell. They noticed my puzzlement and patted me reassuringly. In fact they had seen from a distance all that had been going on and knew the other men, one of whom was actually a policeman on holiday. So they drove me triumphantly to the police station just as the police were setting out in search of help. The episode ended in an atmosphere of congratulation and bonhomie. To suggest any remuneration would have been insulting. The policeman in plain clothes, not knowing who Gerald was, told him that they were all so happy under the Ruler that it was a pleasant duty to help anyone who visited his land. That trivial story explains why Bahrain is a pleasant place for travellers.

But I think that what pleased me most in the island was the park at al-Areen. I have always had a weakness for animals. When I was a small child and tiresome adults would ask me what I intended to be when I grew up, I used at first to say that I would be a thief and go to prison, an ambition that was checked only when my grandmother told me that in prison I would have to eat porridge, which I loathed. So then it was my ambition to become a zoo-keeper. It was an aspiration that never could have been fulfilled as I later found myself to be allergic to many forms of animal fur; so my affections had to be transferred to birds. I have always kept poultry and am on cordial terms with my hens, though ducks were my favourite creatures. I also learnt to be an efficient milker, a talent that is useless nowadays, when every dairy farm employs mechanical milking machines, which the cows are said to prefer. The Ruling Family of Bahrain shares this interest in animals. The Ruler's daughter, belying the notion that Arab women are obliged to lead repressed and narrow lives, runs in the island one of the largest and best-kept dairy farms in the world, supplying it with healthy milk. This is no mean achievement considering the climate and the need to import nearly all the food-stuffs. It is an impressive place to visit, particularly under the guidance of the Princess, who seems to know personally every one of her vast and happy herd. She also has a farm in Devonshire, which continually wins prizes at agricultural shows in Britain. The Ruler and the Crown Prince are interested in saving endangered species; and the park at al-Areen is the scene of their successful efforts. There, in an area of some five square miles, full of trees and irrigated with water pumped up from below the rock surface, you can see pools full of bird-life, largely of migrants; you can see zebras and ostriches, imported, it is true, from Africa, but in the hope that they will breed sufficiently to allow for colonies to be sent across to the Arabian mainland, where in the past such creatures could be found. You can see antelopes of many sorts and, above all that rare and lovely animal, the Arabian oryx, barely surviving on the mainland but here breeding happily. All being well, the oryx too may before long be seen again in its native land. There are roads through the reservation; and the animals are quite untroubled by the cars and buses to which they are used, so that visitors, and especially schoolchildren, can see the animals as they should be seen, living their lives unafraid of human beings. Beyond this reservation there is a larger one, more like to Arabian terrain, to which access is allowed to only a few specialists. There the animals that no longer need careful observation can roam without interference, as if in the unpeopled wild.

It is comforting to find such altruistic enterprise in the modern world. Each time that I have been to Bahrain I have come back happy to have renewed an old friendship and to have seen a land where sense and sensibility still are in control.

But now who knows what the future holds for the Gulf?

H Hamburg, Hildesheim, Hesse

MY MOTHER'S FAMILY was rich in forceful women. There was Great-aunt Flora, who was the first woman, apart from a few Royals, to be given an honorary degree in Scotland, as well as the Freedom of Edinburgh. Great-aunt Louisa was the first woman to sit on a hospital board. Aunt Bet was the first woman professor of economics. Various cousins achieved similar successes; and in the background there was Cousin Elizabeth Garrett Anderson. My mother herself was the first woman to get a first in history at Cambridge and, many years later, to sit beside her husband in the House of Commons. My parents both were in favour of women's suffrage, though the extravagances of the militant Suffragettes diminished their enthusiasm for the cause. Who would want to give votes to women who slashed pictures at the National Gallery or flung themselves in front of horses at race-meetings? It was women's work in the First World War that won them the vote, not the maenad disciples of Mrs Pankhurst, to whom the silly world has now erected a statue.

I, on the other hand, enjoyed the Suffragette movement. As my father was in the Cabinet at the time and our house in Westminster was therefore liable to be attacked, a policeman used to parade up and down outside it. To tease him my sister and I would go round to the Suffragette shop in Tothill Street to buy flags in their colours of purple, green and white, and drape our teddy-bears in them, placing them in the windows. But disillusion came with the opening of Parliament in 1911. The Suffragettes announced that if women's suffrage was not mentioned in the King's Speech every Cabinet Minister's house would have its windows broken. At noon two ladies appeared in the street, with huge handbags, doubtless containing hammers and stones. One was tough, clad in grey tweed jacket and skirt and a manly tie. The other was fluffier. We waited eagerly. But it became clear that the contents of the Speech would not reach the public till the early afternoon, when we had to go for our afternoon walk. In despair we went into the street, and my sister asked the ladies when they were going to break our windows, as we did not want to miss it and our governess was telling us that it was time for us to go out. The fluffy lady giggled; but her companion snapped out angrily something about this being no laughing matter, and taking her friend by the arm she marched away down the street, to the great relief of the policeman hovering in the background but to our furious disappointment. Of all the Cabinet Ministers' windows ours alone survived undamaged.

49

The long prelude is necessary to explain why I have never learnt to speak German properly. When they started me at the age of seven to study German grammar I was shocked to discover that the word for 'girl' was in the neuter gender. Having a suitable respect for the female sex, I thought this not only illogical but shamefully ungallant. I showed an obstinate resistance against further German studies. So they let me go off on to Greek instead. In later life I have greatly regretted my intransigent gallantry. I can read German; anyone interested in European history must be ready to do so. I can understand nearly all of what is said to me. But I am not at ease when I try to talk it; and I have never been long enough on end in Germany to overcome my diffidence.

In spite of this handicap most of my visits to Germany have been enjoyable. In late July 1911 my mother, for some domestic reason that I have forgotten, decided to take my eldest sister and me abroad for a week. My brother was at school and my younger sisters parked somewhere safely with Nannie. She just had the two of us on her hands. She found out that the boats of the old Orient Line – a line run by cousins of hers – after depositing travellers from Australia at Tilbury, went on to unload cargo at Hamburg and at Antwerp, and passengers for the round trip were welcome. So off we went to Hamburg, in those delightful days when no passports were needed for travel in Europe, unless you went to Russia or to Turkey, and when, with the gold standard in the background, all European currencies had a fixed value with each other and the British sovereign was gladly accepted everywhere. I was a trifle nervous about the journey. I knew my mother to be fluent in French, so all would be well when we reached Belgium. But did she know enough German to see us safely through Germany? I had never heard her speak German. In fact she spoke it quite adequately, though she told me much later that my obvious lack of faith in her was rather inhibiting. The boat docked for three days at Hamburg. We spent a morning at Hagenbeck's zoo, which I longed to see as it was famous then for housing its creatures in ample enclosures. It was not a disappointment. Then, in the afternoon, we took a train to Hildesheim – I think on the advice of our governess, who knew Germany well. It was an admirable place for romantically minded children to visit. After all these decades I can still vividly recall the churches and the old houses and the great rose tree that was said to date from medieval times. I had just been given a camera; and my first successful photographs were of scenes in Hildesheim. On our way from the hotel to the station, to return to Hamburg, a car wantonly ran into our taxi. In those days, when cars were still comparatively rare, such an accident seemed wonderfully exciting, none of us having been hurt in the least. The police were efficient, and we had the thrill of being driven to the station in a police van, amid re-iterated apologies from them that such a mishap should occur to visitors to their great country.

Bruges, when we went on there from Antwerp, did not leave such an impact on my memory, though I thought it very beautiful. But that may be because I have been there twice again, and my first impressions have been blurred.

My next visit to Hamburg was in 1922. That summer my grandfather took my parents, my brother and sisters and me on his yacht to Norway and back by Copenhagen. It was my first visit to that pleasant city; but I remember little of it except for a visit to the Tivoli Gardens and a party to meet old Prince Valdemar, the brother of Queen Alexandra. One of my sisters, then aged fifteen, was not used to curtseying while shaking hands and lost her balance, nearly pulling His Royal Highness down on top of her. The incident fortunately appealed to the royal sense of humour. From Copenhagen we sailed southward to the Kiel Canal and then up the Elbe to Hamburg, where my grandfather wanted to see again the shipowners whom he had known before the War. It was a moment when the German mark was falling rapidly, beyond all control. The shipowners, secure with foreign assets, entertained us lavishly; but in the shops there was panic. You could buy anything with a little foreign currency. I bought a number of German books and I found a bookseller where Russian books too were available. It was thus that I made my first acquaintance with the works of Aleksander Blok and of Anna Akhmatova, the latter then barely known as a poet. I was enchanted by her poems and can still recite one, a very short one, by heart, though I gave away the book long since.

It was not till February 1966 that I came back to Hamburg. I had been giving a lecture at the pleasant University of Göttingen and went on to give the annual lecture in English at Hamburg University, endowed by British American Tobacco. I spent a sunny day visiting Lübeck; but the next day was grey and cold. When in the early evening I gave my lecture I was gratified to see that the hall was packed to overflowing. I felt, however, that many in the audience had no idea of what I was talking. When the lecture was over I understood the reason. While I had been comfortably sitting in the Rector's room a wild snowstorm had started. Many of the students could not face walking or bicycling to their lodgings; but the University buildings were closing down for the night, and the only room to which they could go that was heated was the lecture-hall. So, though they may not have received much enlightenment from my talk, at least I had provided them with an hour of bodily warmth. Next morning the snow lay thick on the ground all over northern Germany. My train journey on to Bonn was slow and chilly. I arrived there many hours late, only just in time for a lecture that I was due to give at its university. In spite of the weather I remember with gratitude the friendliness of the people of Hamburg.

My first visit to Heidelberg was in July 1929. A French friend of mine, Robert Francillon, whom I had known when he was French lector at Cambridge, had been given a professorship at Heidelberg, and he invited me to stay with him there. On the way I visited Aachen and Cologne and went up the Rhine to Mainz. He met me there looking gloomy. We had planned to travel round several towns in the neighbourhood; but all that, he said, had to be cancelled as André Gide had invited himself to stay and had made it clear that he had no wish to go on excursions.

M. Gide arrived next day; I took against him at once. He was an unattractive man with a pale green complexion, and he never stopped talking. Robert had just become engaged to a pleasant girl, the daughter of the novelist Jean Schlumberger. (He had wanted to marry Martin du Gard's daughter Christiane, but she had preferred the Governor of Lake Tchad. She invited me to visit her there; but, to my regret, I never was able to take that opportunity to see Central Africa in the old colonial days.) Gide's own marriage had, as we all knew, not been happy, at least for his wife. He had himself made that clear in his autobiographical novel, *La Porte Etroite*, which I had read. It was particularly irritating to have to listen to him lecturing Robert on the duties of a husband, giving him advice that seemed to me to show little consideration for the feelings of a bride. He was, I suppose, conscious that I did not appreciate him properly; so he ignored me. The atmosphere was not improved by a series of wild thunderstorms, which left us all with our nerves on edge. After two days I could stand it no longer. I cut short my visit and went home. Robert said that he wished that he could escape with me. I have seen Heidelberg again under easier circumstances; but the memory of that first visit has always kept me from enjoying its beauty.

I was twice in Bavaria in the 1950s, and was charmed by it. My only visit to Berlin was short and strange. In 1936 my parents had taken us all on a yacht through the Baltic. Most of the family had gone home from Copenhagen; but I had fallen mysteriously ill after lunching at the British Legation in Stockholm and had spent the rest of the voyage lying in my cabin, fevered and unable to eat though not in pain. It later transpired that I had appendicitis; but my appendix was in the wrong place, so I did not feel the customary pain which would have been unpleasant but revealing. I had gone on with my parents to Oslo; but they then decided that I was too ill to face the journey across the stormy North Sea and that they must take me home by an easier route. So we went by train from Oslo through Sweden to Mälmö, and then a ferry across the Baltic to Stralsund in Germany and a train to Berlin, where we took the express train to the Hook of Holland. My father was again a member of the British Cabinet and when we arrived in Germany it was discovered who he was. At Berlin, to his embarrassed annoyance, there were officials to meet us at the station, who took us to the Adlon Hotel, where we reposed till it was time to go on to the Hook. The officials had discovered that he was taking a sick son home; so the unfortunate travellers who had planned to occupy sleeping-berths in the centre of the wagon-lit were pushed out to sleep over the wheels, so that the distinguished invalid could rest in comfort. I suppose that I ought to feel gratitude to Hitler's minions for this attention; but I still feel annoyed embarrassment when I think of it.

My happiest days in Germany for nearly forty years now have been spent in Hesse. A cousin of mine – distant, but a cousin twice, if not three times, over, as Scottish families in former days retained a clan spirit and only knew and intermarried with their relatives – married not long before the second War the younger son of the former Grand-Duke of Hesse and the Rhine. The marriage itself was marred by a nightmarish tragedy, when all the bridegroom's family were killed in an air-crash on their way to the wedding, leaving only one frail little girl who died soon afterwards. So, with her husband now thrust into the role of head of the house, my cousin had to go to live with him in Germany, under a régime that they detested, and which detested them, and soon to face a war in which their loyalties were cruelly divided. But courage and integrity saw them through it all; and after many difficulties, they were able at last to live in peace in the old grand-ducal hunting-box of Wolfsgarten. Peace is comparative, as it lies rather too close to Frankfurt airport, the biggest in Europe, and planes fly continually overhead. But the house itself, which consists actually of four buildings round a large courtyard garden, is beautiful and serene, set with a splendid park in the midst of a forest. Since my first visit there in 1953 I have been happily back there many times, usually sleeping in the old grand-ducal bedroom, in a bed almost equal in amplitude to the Great Bed of Ware, and with an old chest in the room which when opened reveals a bath.

To the sorrow of all his friends Prince Louis of Hesse died in 1968. He refused to take the title of Grand-Duke, saying that that denoted an office which he did not hold, but he was born a prince and remained a prince. He was, I think, the most civilized man that I have ever known, with a wide and sensitive knowledge of all the arts. He wrote beautifully, but far too little, in both German and English. His humour was delicious. He had always promised to provide me with a lexicon of what he called 'Victorian' English, the language talked by Queen Victoria's numerous German descendants, who used words such as 'also' in their German rather than their English sense and 'komisch' in its German sense of 'odd' rather than amusing, so that when they heard of an unusual but dreadful tragedy they would say 'How comical'. Sadly for me, he never had time to compile the work. He was immensely loved and respected throughout the former Grand-Duchy for his active patronage of the arts and all good causes. His funeral at Darmstadt might have been that of a reigning monarch, with the whole town in mourning and officials from what was a rather left-wing German state coming too to pay their respects.

Music was always the main delight of the Prince and Princess. Benjamin Britten was a close friend; and they made many journeys to far-off places with him and Peter Pears. It was at Wolfsgarten that I first met him, in 1953; and, several years later, when he was there recovering from a bad illness, I spent some mornings at his bedside, listening to him talk of his life, his hopes and his fears. The Aldeburgh Festival, of which the Princess is still President, owes a vast debt to the Hesses.

When I am in need of serenity it is to Wolfsgarten that I like best to go. After having lived through two world wars in which the Germans were our savage enemies, I felt for a time a little uneasy in Germany. But it is better to discard bitter memories. We suffered greatly from German bombers; but the Germans suffered too from ours. I never knew Dresden; but why did we destroy so much of Hamburg and of Darmstadt, and of the lovely old town of Hildesheim?

Istanbul

THERE IS a curious irony about the name of the great city that was once the capital of the Christian East. The Turks, to whom it has belonged now for more than half a millennium, insist that we call it Istanbul, which is in fact a corruption of the medieval Greek words, ''s tin polin', 'to the city', a usage similar to the English habit of saying 'going to town' to describe a visit to London. The Greeks insist that we call it Constantinople, a word never used by their Byzantine ancestors, but used by their Arab enemies and by the Prophet himself, in the form Konstantiniye, and used by the hated Westerners. It does, it is true, appear in the official title of the Oecumenical Patriarch, 'Patriarch and Bishop of New Rome which is Constantinople', and occasionally in writers with a fanciful turn of mind, though they inclined to prefer the term 'Basileousa', the Empress–city. Perhaps we should be neutral and talk along with the Slavs of 'Tsarigrad', the Emperors' city, or along with the Norsemen of 'Micklegarth'. But, with apologies to my Greek friends, I shall keep to Istanbul.

I came there first in 1924, yachting with my parents. Ataturk had taken over the city only the previous year, after the signing of the Treaty of Lausanne. He had abolished the Ottoman Sultanate. The Sultan's heir had been allowed to remain on as Caliph; but his office had been similarly abolished only about a month before our visit. The city, however, still retained much of its old Ottoman appearance. Respectable men still wore a tarboush on their heads. Moslem women were still veiled. Camels still carried their loads over the long bridge across the Golden Horn. The great Levantine families of British, French and Italian origin still maintained their compounds, though they no longer enjoyed the Concessions that had enabled them to follow the laws of their ancestral countries and they knew that their days of prosperity and influence were over. I was glad to have a glimpse of the past. There were no buildings then outside the great line of the old Byzantine land-walls, only gypsy encampments where you could have your fortune told. (Mine was satisfactory. I would have illnesses but would survive to a ripe old age.)

I was only there for less than a week, as I had to go back to my studies at Cambridge, travelling for the first time on the old Orient Express. When next I came there, in the spring of 1928, everything was changed. There were no more camels in the streets. The men all wore cloth caps and the women had been ordered to remove their veils. This was not altogether popular. Many years later I made friends with a Turkish lady who had been a great beauty in her time. She told me that the enforced removal of the veil had spoiled her life. When you were veiled, she said, you could deceive your husband under his eyes. Ladies would go, properly veiled, to the hairdressers at the Grande Rue de Pera, now renamed Istaklal Caddesi, and their lovers would be let in by a back door. A husband might suspect the worst; but it was impossible to identify any of those heavily covered women. The absence of the veil destroyed that useful anonymity.

One of my sisters was with me on that journey. We came by boat from Venice, calling at Corfu and Athens on the way. A fellow-passenger on the boat as far as Athens was the great Greek statesman Eleftherios Venizelos. He had known my father; so I ventured to accost him and was very kindly received, especially when I told him that I was engaged on Byzantine studies. I thought him witty and genial and highly intelligent, but was somehow left with an impression of deviousness. But I am very glad to have met him.

It was March when we came to Istanbul, and the weather was cold and grey. That and the drabness of the people depressed us. We went conscientiously round all the Byzantine and old Ottoman sights that were open to visitors; and we had one sunny day on the Princes' Islands, ruined for me by an attack of hay-fever due to riding in a horse-drawn victoria. I am sadly allergic to horses. On the whole we were glad to move on to Bulgaria, a journey which I have described earlier in this book.

It was not till the summer of 1937, after my visit to Mount Athos, that I next came to Turkey. On this visit I travelled a bit round the country, going to Bursa, which is one of the loveliest of towns, redolent of its Ottoman past, and to Yalova, which, like Bursa, was famed for its medicinal waters, popular even in Byzantine days. With a young Cambridge friend, Michael Grant, I took a steamer along the Black Sea coast to Trebizond, from where we drove through lush forests up to the top of the Zigana Pass and on into the bleak valleys of Eastern Anatolia. As we ate our lunch by the roadside near the summit of the pass a detachment of the Turkish army went by, on its way, as it was politely expressed, to 'assimilate' the Kurds. The men in their thick uniforms had been marching for hours uphill in the summer heat. The aroma that they left behind somewhat ruined our picnic.

I spent most of that visit to Turkey in Istanbul. At that time a remarkable American, Thomas Whittemore, was engaged in uncovering mosaics in the great cathedral of Saint Sophia. He was a man whom professional archaeologists and scholars dismissed as a pretentious amateur; and, indeed, he had a gift for making himself appear to be a charlatan. But we should all be very grateful to him. He was wonderfully persuasive and had induced Ataturk to secularize the building from being a mosque and to declare it to be a museum, so that the Christian decorations could be brought back to light; and he had secured permission to take charge of the operation. His persuasive powers enabled him also to raise funds for the work from rich American ladies, whom he handled with superb artifice. Amateurish he may have been, but he saw to it that he had first-class craftsmen to assist him, the chief of whom, Ernest Hawkins, was to become the world's finest authority on the uncovering of mosaics and frescoes. It is due to Hawkins's later work that we can now see the incomparable decorations of the Kahriye Cami, the Church of Saint Saviour in Chora, which is, I think, the loveliest thing to see in all Istanbul. I had known Whittemore for many years, having first met him in Istanbul in 1928, and I always enjoyed his rather eccentric company. He would let me come whenever I liked to watch him and his craftsmen at work in the great building.

At the same time excavations were going on to uncover the floor mosaics in the Great Palace of the Byzantine Emperors. These were being done under the direction of a professor from St Andrew's University, J. H. Baxter, who, like Whittemore, had the air of being a charlatan. Perhaps for that reason, the two were not on speaking terms. I had to hide from Whittemore that I used to go to watch Baxter's team at work, while in Baxter's presence I could never mention Whittemore's name. It all added to the amusement of life. At the same time Turkish friends saw to it that I learnt to appreciate the Ottoman mosques and palaces in the city. The various embassies had all moved down from the bleakness of Ankara to enjoy the pleasures of the Bosphorus; and I was asked to a number of informal parties. The British Ambassador, Sir Percy Lorraine, used to invite me on his yacht, to sail up the Bosphorus or across to the Princes' Islands. It was a pleasant time; and it made me reflect how enjoyable life must have been for visitors to Ottoman Constantinople who had the right contacts in the easy-going days of the nineteenth century, before the austere reign of Abdul Hamid.

When I came back from Trebizond there was an International History Congress in full swing in the city. I avoided its meetings. But Ataturk himself decided to give a party to the delegates in the Palace of Dolma Bahçe, to which ambassadors were also invited. Percy Lorraine asked permission to take me with him. There, amid the sugar-cake fantasy of that nineteenth-century baroque palace, I was privileged to meet the great man. He was stocky and upright but obviously sick, with a complexion that was pale olive-green. His eyes, however, were unforgettable. They were steely blue in colour, and they seemed to pierce right through you. He was very gracious. My father, on behalf of the British government, had recently arranged a trade treaty with Turkey; and Ataturk spoke of it with appreciation. When I told him that

I was a Byzantinist he expressed his approval of the work being done in Saint Sophia. Indeed, though he liked to promote historical theories intended to bolster Turkish self-esteem, his favourite being that the Turks were the descendants of the Hittites and thus had an ancestral right to Anatolia, he did not himself take them very seriously. Some years later the young lady who was my assistant at the University of Istanbul told me that when she was studying archaeology at the University she used to lodge with an uncle who was an old friend of Ataturk's. One day Ataturk came to the house and, seeing her in a corner, asked her what she was doing. Trying to read Hittite, she replied. 'It is like old Turkish', he said. 'No', she answered. 'It is more like old Armenian.' Her uncle was aghast; but Ataturk laughed. 'I sometimes think that I shall have to prove that the Armenians are really Turks', he said. Yet his theories did have their effect. The same young lady told me that her husband was of the purest Turkish stock; he was descended from Abraham and the Prophet.

Five years later, in the early spring of 1942, when I was living in Jerusalem, working for the Government Information Service there, I suddenly received word from our Foreign Office telling me that I was to go to Istanbul. It seemed that Ataturk's successor, President Ismet Inönü, had been driving round Istanbul and had noticed a building that he did not recognize. He made enquiries; and at last someone said that it was probably Byzantine, but no one could tell him anything more. He was angry to find that none of his officials knew a thing about Byzantium. It was, he said, all part of the history of the city and the country. It was disgraceful that Byzantine studies were not taught at the University. He sent for his Minister of Education and told him to find a professor at once who could teach the subject. The Minister appealed for help to the head of the British Council in Turkey, who happened to be my friend Michael Grant, with whom I had journeyed to Trebizond in 1937. Michael at once suggested that I would be suitable. The British government at the time was anxious to do what it could to please the Turks. So, when a formal request for my services arrived in London it was granted at once.

I was not at first pleased. I was enjoying my life in Palestine. Now, at rather short notice, I had to dispose of a very pleasant house and the furniture that I had collected. I had to remember and try to increase my slight knowledge of Turkish. I had to take leave of all my friends in all the various communities in Jerusalem. The Orthodox Patriarch, I remember, was eager that I should go to see his brother-Patriarch in Istanbul, but the Armenian Patriarch said that his brother-Patriarch there should be avoided – I never found out why. On 24 February I left Jerusalem before dawn, to drive to Beirut and on to Tripoli, where I took a train that left in the evening to go northward through Aleppo. The British Ambassador to Ankara, Sir Hugh Knatchbull-Hugessen, was on the train with his wife, whom I had to protect from the lecherous advances of a drunken wagon-lit attendant. After several hours at Aleppo the train went on to Ankara where we arrived the following evening. I spent two nights there, arrived in Istanbul on 1 March and was plunged at once into Turkish academic life.

I spent three and a half years as a professor in Turkey. From a purely academic aspect it was not very rewarding. I had to give an outline course of lectures on Byzantine history, in English, which was translated sentence by sentence into Turkish by my excellent young lady assistant, who had learnt English at the American College for Girls up the Bosphorus. But to facilitate her task I had to write out a text and to remember to keep to it. My audience consisted of all the first-year students of history, Turks all of them, for members of the minority races – Greeks, Armenians and Jews – were discouraged by the authorities from studying history. They liked this method of lecturing as it gave them time to take down every word of translation. Then, when the time for examinations approached, you would see them with their notes memorizing the texts by heart. The examinations were all oral; and you had to face having your lectures repeated back at you, word for word. It made marking rather difficult, as you could not mark down anyone who remembered exactly what you had told him, even though it was clear that he did not understand a word of what it meant. It was very noticeable that the girls, though far fewer, were of a higher standard than the boys. This was, I suppose, because a Turkish girl needed to be keen and enterprising and to come from an enlightened family to get to the University, whereas a boy would go there as a matter of course. In addition to my history lectures I had a small class studying Byzantine art and archaeology. This was much more enjoyable. I could run it more as a seminar; the authorities, I do not know why, did not object to Christians and Jews studying art and archaeology; and the Turks in the class were all intelligent, though here again the girls were abler than the boys. Nearly all the class was at home in English or French so there was not the need for verbatim translation.

Istanbul at that time possessed the only university in Turkey. The professors were of mixed origin. There were a few Britishers besides myself, some already there when I arrived, some coming later. Among them was the eminent Classical historian Ronald Syme. The senior archaeological professor was a German citizen with Nazi sympathies, a good scholar but not a lovable man. I had to deal with him over the arrangement of the art and archaeology classes. We spoke to each other in French. A large number of the professors were Jews. The University had been wise enough to offer Chairs to refugees from Hitler's government, especially from Vienna after the Anschluss. They made a valuable contribution to Turkish academic life, especially in the sciences.

When I arrived I found them all rather chilly and hostile, which puzzled and distressed me till I discovered the cause. I had been appointed, on the orders of the President, in the middle of the academic year, and there was no provision for me in the University budget. So the refugee professors, having no embassy to look after their interests, all had their salaries docked to pay for mine. They were repaid in the next budget; but they had for a time been rather short of cash. I was horrified when I found out their plight; but by then they realized that I was innocent and ignorant of it, and I became good friends with many of them. Salaries were indeed a little uncertain. One year, when money was short, we were subsidized by gifts of cloth, enough to make each of us a suit. The British professors were given a useful subsidy by the British Council, so were never in difficulties. Some of our colleagues were not so fortunate.

On the whole, however, life was easy in comparison with what was happening elsewhere in Europe. There were occasional shortages. Coffee, that mainstay of Levantine life, was occasionally unavailable; and one had to make do with rather nasty tea, grown near Rize, on the Black Sea coast. There was a period when the whole of Turkey ran out of toilet-paper. But there was always enough to eat and drink.

I lived for my first two months in Istanbul in the Pera Palace Hotel, which had recovered from the effects of the bomb that had exploded when the British Legation had arrived there from Sofia. It was not very comfortable; but there was an old-fashioned splendour about its high later nineteenth-century rooms. Then I found a small flat at the top of a block in Beyoglu. It had a lovely view across the Bosphorus. But it was so cramped that I could not entertain friends in it; and when, as was usually the case, the lift was not working, it was an arduous climb to reach it. So, a few months later, I moved up the Bosphorus to the village of Bebek. Nowadays there is a suburban sprawl all along the European coast of the Bosphorus. The newer village of Bebek lay by the water, clustering round the landing stage and the terminus of the tramway into the city, with an older village climbing up a small valley behind. It was in Old Bebek that I found a wooden house standing by itself. It was larger than I needed; so I closed some of the rooms, putting in them my landlord's not very handsome furniture and filling the rooms that I used with furniture that I acquired. It involved a steep climb from the village to reach it, up a lane which, I was warned, was haunted by the ghost of a huge black dog; but I never saw him. There was a garden which, given time and energy, could have been made charming, and a pleasant view over the old village and over the water to Asia. I was very happy there, with the village postman's wife coming in to look after me every day. My one anxiety was that the house might catch fire. By Turkish law at that time a tenant was not allowed to summon the fire brigade without permission from the landlord; and, as my landlord was a Turkish army officer stationed near the Russian frontier, the house would have burnt down long before the necessary permission arrived.

There had been a bad fire some two years previously at the University buildings, up near the great Suleimaniye Mosque, in the centre of old Istanbul, and the humanities departments were temporarily housed in a pleasant palace on the Bosphorus, the former home of an Ottoman princess. There was a tram-stop opposite its entrance; so I used to go in from Bebek by tram. Having joined the tram at the terminus, I could always have a seat; but as it approached the city the tramcar became crowded. At first, being well brought up, I would offer my seat to some heavily laden woman. This produced surprised looks from the men in the car and embarrassed reactions from the women. I stopped the practice after an occasion when I rose to give my seat to a woman who was carrying several packages and a puling baby. She motioned me to sit down again, but she handed me the baby, which dribbled on to me for the rest of my journey. I usually returned in the evenings in the little steamer which went every few hours up the Bosphorus, calling at the village landing-stages.

I spent two years in the house in Old Bebek. Then the colonel who owned it returned from the army and wanted it for himself. I moved into the lower half of a house in the newer part of Bebek. It was more comfortable and more compact, and very convenient for the tramway; and I still could see the Bosphorus from my windows. I missed the quiet of the old house, though in spring that quiet was broken by a plethora of nightingales. But it was all more convenient, especially when I had a long bout of illness. The upper half of the house was occupied by an amiable Jewish professor and his wife, with a son who was an able young doctor, who attended to me with kindly competence.

One advantage of living in Bebek was that I was not far from Robert College, the American institution that had provided a higher education in English to Turks and members of the minorities alike, for years before the University of Istanbul was founded and was still patronized by the more progressive Turkish families. It is now incorporated into the state university system but in those days it was run by Americans, though the chairman of the governors was always a Turk. There were almost as many British as American professors there. Indeed, the students' parents insisted that English should be taught by an Englishman, not an American. I made friends with many of them. Robert College also possessed a good academic library, for which I was very grateful, as the only good library in Istanbul itself was that in the German Institute, which naturally I could not use. It is true that the chairman of the governors had removed some important volumes, intending some day to translate them into Turkish and determined that meanwhile no one else would be able to forestall him.

From the point of view of academic research my years in Istanbul were wasted. On the other hand I came to know every inch of the city and its environs; and the Turkish authorities encouraged me to travel round the country, so long as I kept away from military zones. Nor did they object to me going off in the long summer vacation to Syria and the rest of the Arab world. I was already contemplating a book on the Crusades and was thus able to trace the Crusader routes across Anatolia and to visit all the Crusader sites further to the south. Thomas Whittemore was still working fitfully in Saint Sophia, and I was able to increase my knowledge of the great church. It was now fully functioning as a museum, under an amiable and rather pathetic director. His appearance gave rise to the story that his family had been eager for influence at the Sultan's court and so when he was a small boy had had him castrated. It was too late. By the time that he was ready to enter the Sultan's service Abdul Hamid had fallen and the new regime dispensed with the services of eunuchs. His marriage in later life to a plain, though agreeable, spinster long past her youth, did nothing to dispel the story.

The Turkish professors at the University were all very kind to me. I was particularly fond of the Dean of Humanities. He was of Cretan origin, the descendant of Greeks who had adopted Islam; and he had therefore ranked as a Turk in the exchange of populations in 1923. I once came unannounced into his office on some urgent matter and found him making notes in Greek. He confessed to me that he still found it easier to think in Greek than in Turkish, but he begged me not to reveal his secret to his colleagues. His bright and elegant daughter was one of the best pupils in my art and archaeology class. I was lucky in the young woman who was appointed to be my assistant, whom I have already mentioned. She belonged to the old Turkish family of the Karacalarli, who had owned tobacco fields in Macedonia, with a grand house in Kavalla. They had had to move from there in 1923, and were compensated with fields of far less value near Samsun, on the Anatolian coast. They had rich relatives. In the 1760s a daughter of the house had been married to the son of a neighbouring land-owner. But when he unveiled her after the marriage ceremony, her looks were such that he at once repudiated her. She lived on, divorced and disgraced, at her parents' house, till one day an Albanian adventurer appeared in Kavalla and, hearing of her story, went to her father and offered to take her on. They were given a small house in the grounds of the family mansion, and there their son was born, called Mehemet Ali. Backed by the influence of his mother's family, he entered the Sultan's service and eventually became the Khedive of Egypt, the ancestor of the Egyptian royal house. In gratitude he offered his mother's family some estates in Egypt. But they were rather ashamed of him, especially when he rebelled against the Sultan, and ignored the offer. They remembered it again in 1923, when they found themselves much poorer; but the King of Egypt told them then that they were a hundred years too late.

My assistant married into an even grander family. Her husband was the Çelebi Effendi, the hereditary head of the Mevlevi, the Whirling Dervishes, descended in the direct line from their founder, the great mystic Jelal ad-Din ar-Rumi. The Sunni Moslem establishment in the Ottoman Empire had never quite approved of the Mevlevi, being suspicious of their mystic practices, their rhythmic dances that brought them into a state of ecstasy, in communion with God. They were also too ecumenical in outlook. But the Çelebi Effendi had commanded great prestige. It was he who at a sultan's inauguration had the right to gird him with the sword of Islam, the ceremony that had made him Caliph of the Faithful. All that had disappeared. My friend had had a difficult life. The Mevlevi headquarters had been at Konya, but the Order had possessed *tekkes*, or meeting-places all over Turkey, with properties to support them. Ataturk had abolished the Order in Turkey and had annexed all its property, though he left the Çelebi's family with its estates. The young Çelebi Effendi had therefore moved to Aleppo in Syria, his establishments in Syria, Lebanon and Cyprus being left in operation. But when in 1938 Syria was obliged by international pressure to cede the Hatay, the district round Antioch, to Turkey, the angry Syrians, backed by the French who still controlled them, banished every Turkish national from Syria. The Çelebi Effendi, who had kept his Turkish citizenship, was then forced to leave the country where the Mevlevis still flourished to move back to Turkey where they were forbidden. It was impossible for him to get a visa to revisit Syria, particularly after the outbreak of the Second World War. His first wife had refused to leave Aleppo and had been allowed to stay there. So he divorced her; and when he settled in Istanbul he met and married my future assistant.

I went many times to their house. It was there that I first smoked a hookah. He sat me down with a very splendid specimen, which he offered to give me if I could smoke it all evening without being sick. I succeeded in so doing; and I have the hookah still, though I have given up such smoking and use the bowl as a handsome flower-vase. He also gave me a small seal, which, he said, would admit me into any *tekke* of his dervishes. Then suddenly, in the spring of 1944, he died of a heart-attack. He had living with him in Istanbul his son by his first marriage, a boy of sixteen, who now became hereditary head of the Mevlevi Order. To be accepted as such it was his duty to go round all the *tekkes* and have his knee ceremoniously kissed by the members. But they were all in Syria and Lebanon, countries for which no Turk could obtain a visa. By then Syria was under the control of the Free French, and high up in the administration was my friend, Count Stanislas Ostrorog, with whom I had stayed in Damascus before the War. He had been brought up on the Bosphorus, and I knew him to be fascinated by old traditions. So I wrote to him to explain the situation. He answered at once, enclosing a large envelope addressed to 'His Highness the Çelebi Effendi', giving him permission to enter Syria and Lebanon with any of his entourage and to travel there wherever he wished. Armed with this, as soon as the school and university terms were ended, the boy set out with his step-mother and was formally received as head of the Order in every *tekke* that was still active. I followed them a few days later. When I arrived at Aleppo there was a delegation of dervishes waiting at the station to greet me; and they insisted on looking after me entirely for the day and a half that I was there. They honoured me with a special whirling ceremony, which I sat and watched along with the late Çelebi Effendi's first wife, who had come out of the seclusion in which she lived to thank me for my services to her son. As I went on my way there were delegations to meet me at Hama and at Homs, at Tripoli and at Beirut. At Homs they whirled for me; but elsewhere I managed to refuse their offers of a similar honour. Wherever I went I was told I was their brother now. So, though no whirler myself, I am an honorary Whirling Dervish.

Sad to say, things have not gone well for the Mevlevi since then. A few years later the Syrian government decided to abolish the Order and annex its property. By so doing it called down on itself the wrath of Allah. Two members of the Syrian cabinet suddenly died, as did the wives of two others. It also called down the wrath of the Turkish government, which sued it for taking away the property of a Turkish citizen, though that was just what the Turks had done some twenty years earlier. It seems that the Syrians, and the Lebanese who followed suit, paid up enough to pension off most of the dervishes. But their long tradition was brought to an end. Worse was to follow when a member of the Çelebi's family persuaded the Turks to revive the whirling ceremony as a tourist attraction. He collected a number of followers who were prepared to dance in the old manner before a paying public, at the old headquarters in Konya and elsewhere in the country, thus reducing a deeply felt religious ceremony to the status of a ballet performance. There could be no worse insult to the memory of one of the greatest of mystical teachers, Jelal ad-Din ar-Rumi.

Life for a Britisher working in a neutral country during the War was not always easy. As a professor at the University I was a Turkish official. It was essential that I should do nothing that might arouse the slightest suspicion that I was a secret agent. When the Italians caved in they handed to the British Embassy in Ankara their Embassy's list of suspected British spies. It seems that I headed it, with the flattering description 'molto intelligente e molto pericoloso'. It was unfortunately quite untrue. The Turks have always run their secret police efficiently. At this time there were three separate bodies of them, one dependent on the government, one on the President in person, and the third on the Governor of Istanbul. Each was said to despise the others. There was a handicap: as surnames were newly come to Turkey, foreigners seem to have appeared in their files sometimes under their surnames but more often than not under their first names. But that did not damage the thoroughness of their investigations. In 1943 I spent a week at the pleasant resort of Yalova, recuperating after an illness. One of the Government secret police was there, to keep an eye on foreigners visiting the resort. As I was the only one there at the time and as he wanted to improve his English, he spent much of his time with me, and told me details of the private lives of many of my British friends in Istanbul, of which I had had no idea. I asked him if his colleagues had a similar dossier on me. Yes, he said, but it was uninteresting.

In fact I never had any difficulty with the Turkish authorities. I was always perfectly open about my British contacts. When a former Cambridge pupil of mine came to Istanbul to work in the Embassy special service, I warned my friends at the University that I intended to see him; but, as I had no secrets to tell him, no one need worry. Indeed, the only occasion when I was accused by a Turk of being a spy was when I was visiting an old mosque across the Bosphorus with a Turkish friend and the guardian heard us talking in English.

The German Ambassador to Turkey was von Papen, the one eminent man to emerge legally unscathed from the Nuremberg trials. Most of the Germans in Turkey loathed him. Ribbentrop's sister, who was the wife of the German Military Counsellor, perpetually pleaded to Hitler through her brother to have him removed. Their loathing was not without cause. Von Papen and his family usually talked in English among themselves; and his favourite ploy, when a newcomer arrived at the Embassy, was to ask him what he planned to do when Germany was defeated. But the Turks loved him; and Hitler had no wish to upset the Turks. Before the War von Papen had come to London as Foreign Minister, and my father had taken me to a party where he was present. We were introduced to him; but my father, who had no wish to talk to him, quickly edged away, and I was left bravely trying to make conversation, while von Papen's eyes searched desperately for someone more important. But he had the gift of remembering faces. Soon after I arrived in Istanbul I went to an antiquary's shop in the Grand Bazaar, and there I saw von Papen with a Turkish detective in tow. I knew the detective. As he was word-perfect in English as well as German, he used also to be attached to the British Ambassador when he came to Istanbul, and I had met him more than once. He came over to greet me, while von Papen stared at me with a look of half-recognition. When he went back, von Papen obviously asked him who I was. When he was told he looked at me and gave me one slow wink. We met in the Bazaar on several other occasions, and I always received the same accolade.

Outside the University, Turkish officials and Turkish friends were very careful to ensure that we and the Germans never met each other. But I was to have one not unpleasant contact with the German Embassy. I was in Ankara for a few days in the spring of 1944 and went to dine with the First Secretary of the Swedish Embassy. He was not there when I arrived at his house but appeared some twenty minutes late laden with bottles of Mumm champagne. 'These,' he said to me, 'are a present to you from the German Embassy.' He had gone there to meet a new German First Secretary. When he rose to leave, saying that he had someone coming to dinner, the German had asked him whom he was entertaining, and on hearing my name, exclaimed that he had been to Cambridge and used to go to my lectures there. The occasion called for celebration, he said; and he sent a porter down to the Embassy cellars. So, thanks to the German Embassy, we had a festive evening. My Swedish friend retained most of the remaining loot, remarking that I might find it difficult to explain to my compatriots how I was in possession of drink that could only have come fron an enemy source. In fact I think that this had not been just a casual friendly gesture. By now German diplomats who disliked the Nazi régime were beginning to try to cross over to the Allied camp, and Turkey provided the easiest route, as von Papen turned a blind eye to such attempts. This young man probably had some such ambition and wanted to find a Britisher who would speak up for him if he succeeded. He did not succeed, as the German authorities, who may have been suspicious of him, did not allow his wife to join him in Ankara, and he could not well leave her behind in Germany. Indeed, he was disgraced soon afterwards for having friends in the group that so nearly succeeded in assassinating Hitler. He appeared some years later *en poste* in the German Embassy in London; but I had forgotten his name and only identified him after he had left. So I never thanked him as I ought to have done.

Even while we were still at war with Italy, the Turks never thought it necessary to keep us apart from the Italians, or from the nationals of other countries allied to the Axis; and after Italy changed sides we all made many Italian friends. In 1945, during my last months in Istanbul, I came to know the newly arrived Papal legate, Monsignor Roncalli. To look at, he was a short, rotund peasant, but with a quick mind, a wonderful sense of fun and a serene and tolerant benevolence. I have never known anyone else who gave one such a happy feeling of sheer goodness. He was loved in Istanbul, even by the Moslem Turks and by the Orthodox Greeks, whom history has made deeply suspicious of anything emanating from Rome. It is not often in a hierarchy that a good man reaches the summit. Roncalli's elevation as Pope John XXIII restored one's faith for a while in a divine ordering of things. But his reign was to be short. I wish that I had paid him a visit in Rome. A mutual friend from the Istanbul days went to see him there and reported that he had asked after me and would be glad to see me. But too often one puts off to tomorrow what one should do today. I planned to make the journey the following year; but by that time he had died.

Of the nationals of enemy states I saw two or three Bulgarians, refugees whom I had known in Sofia; and I saw some Roumanian friends. Elizabeth Asquith, daughter of the old Prime Minister, had married a Roumanian diplomat, Prince Antoine Bibesco. They had been living on his Roumanian estate, which was said to include 100,000 plum-trees, when the dictator Antonescu brought the country into the War on the German side; and their daughter had not been discreet in airing her anti-Fascist views. They obtained permission to go with her on a visit to Istanbul, and there they deliberately lost her; and she was able to make her way to Egypt and eventually to her relations in England. I had known Elizabeth since my childhood; her brother Puffin Asquith had been my closest friend at our preparatory school; and I saw no reason why I should not continue to know her. It was sad: her health was bad, and she hated life as it was in Roumania. She was rescuing her daughter from it, but at the cost of probably never seeing her again. Indeed, she died very soon after the Russians entered Roumania.

I saw rather more of Antoine's cousin, Princess Marthe Bibesco, whom also I had known before the War. I shall talk of her palace in Roumania when I write about that country. She was devoted to it but was essentially an international figure, who would have been better at home in the days before 1914, the days of the great royal and imperial courts, when the European aristocracy saw itself being above the bonds of nationalism. She had been a great beauty; and she had succeeded in meeting almost everyone of importance in her time, some of them, it was said, very intimately. She was also an accomplished writer, whose works, mostly novels, written in French, eventually won her member-ship of the Belgian Academy. She arrived in Istanbul in 1944, with some vague and unreal idea that through her international connections she might somehow inaugurate a peace-movement. But the British Embassy was not sympathetic when she tried to obtain papers that would let her go to London and see her old friend, Mr Churchill. We British in Istanbul were told that she was a dangerous woman whom we should not see. I paid no attention to that ban. Beneath her pretensions she was a highly civilized woman, interested in everything, widely read, and with a sharp wit. I found her a wonderful companion with whom to wander round the old churches and mosques of the city. I made no secret of my friendship with her; and, if the British authorities objected, they never did anything about it.

Indeed, I found the British Embassy always kind and helpful. Sir Hugh was a man of great charm whose air of easy-going nonchalance hid a wise and far-sighted brain. He received bad publicity owing to a notorious spy at the Embassy, known as Cicero, whose story was told, without over-much accuracy, in a book which was turned into a film. Long before the time when his activities according to the book were discovered, my former pupil in the Embassy at Istanbul, hearing that I was going to Ankara to dine at the Embassy told me to look out for this Albanian-born valet-footman who was known to be trying to sell information to the Germans. But that British Intelligence should have been intelligent for once rather spoiled the story. Sir Hugh's successor, Sir Maurice Peterson, won my admiration when my old friend Ivan Stancioff, whom he too knew well, escaped from the Communists, who had just taken over Bulgaria and were out to get him as a friend of the Royal Family. Sir Maurice insisted on welcoming him as a guest till he could find somewhere to live. This was reported to London; and the Foreign Secretary, Anthony Eden, sent orders that Ivan should be evicted. Sir Maurice took no notice and continued his hospitality. Lady Peterson was the daughter of a respectable clergyman, a friend of my father's. She was an unpretentious lady who liked to wander round the old quarters in Ankara and Istanbul, where the sight of a lone Western lady invariably produced a rabble of impertinent urchins. She would then turn on them and give voice to a string of Turkish curse-words. Where she acquired the vocabulary we never could find out. We hoped that she never knew what it all meant. The naughty boys used to flee in terror.

I spent much of my time with Turkish friends. One of the closest was Osman Okyar, the son of a distinguished statesman, an old friend of Ataturk's, who had been Ambassador in London. Osman had been to Cambridge, where he had won first-class honours in economics and was on the way to becoming Turkey's leading economist. I was fond of all his family. His uncle, Sedad Eldem, was an eminent architect, from whom I learnt much about Ottoman architecture. At that time the leading young lawyer in Istanbul was a lady, Süreyya Ağaoğlu, whom I used to see often. She was formidably bright, but also well connected, which helped. She said to me once: 'Don't you enjoy being clever?' To which I tactfully replied, 'I would enjoy it if I were as clever as you.' But Turkey was still a man's country. Her gardener refused to take orders from a woman, and she had to summon her much less successful brother in to tell him what to do. Prince Zeid, the youngest brother of King Abdulla of Jordan and King Feisal of Iraq, was living in Istanbul at that time with his Turkish wife, a handsome, ample lady who was a prominent artist. I used to meet a number of artists at their house on the Bosphorus. I was lunching with them there once, on a terrace by the water-side, when there was an earthquake, and we had to hurry up the steps into the house before a great wave swept in, upsetting the chairs and tables. I knew also a charming old Egyptian princess – like all the Egyptian royal family of mixed Turkish and Albanian stock – who had been a great beauty when young and then had had her face lifted; but unfortunately one side fell, and she never could be bothered to have it repaired. It took a little time to get used to her Janus-appearance. One lunched and dined at her house in the old Ottoman fashion, remaining seated in a comfortable chair while a retainer brought up a small table on which one's meal was laid out. To these and to many other hospitable Turkish friends I owe much gratitude.

No city is more splendidly situated than Istanbul; but its setting has one cruel disadvantage. I have often thought that the inherent melancholy and pessimism of the Byzantines was due to the climate of their imperial city, to the cold wind that blows in winter down the funnel of the Bosphorus from the Black Sea and the steppes of Russia beyond it, to the hot enervating wind, the *melteme*, blowing from the south in summer, and to the all-pervading damp. At the end of February 1945 I was stricken by a bad attack of sciatica. For a month I was in agony and practically immobile. Then, after treatment at the American Hospital and a few days taking the curative waters at Bursa, as many Byzantines had done before me, I returned to work in early April. But in less than a week the sciatica returned, seemingly worse than before. Eventually the University gave me leave to go away for a month, provided that I was back in time to deal with the end of term examinations; and meanwhile my excellent assistant, who had the text of my lectures, read them out in Turkish to my classes. I spent the month of May in the kinder climate of Cyprus, where I had several friends who looked after me. I was there, in Kyrenia, on VE Day. Life there restored me; and I was able to return to Istanbul for the examinations. By the terms of my contract with the University I was due to spend another year. But I could not face another winter in that climate, and both the University and the British Council, which was sponsoring me, agreed that it was better that I should resign.

It was indeed time for me to go. I rather enjoyed the examinations. For the History Department I had two co-examiners, both Turkish, one an ardent pan-Turanian, only interested in Turkic races, the other a pious Moslem, only interested in Islam. Each marked the students according to their views rather than to their historical knowledge, and were consequently apt to quarrel; and I could hold the balance between them. However, for this last examination, the pan-Turanian professor was absent, in disgrace for having been involved in a plot against the government, organized by other pan-Turanians who considered that the authorities were not taking sufficient interest in the plight of the Turks in

Soviet Turkestan. The conspirators were said to have planned to invade a meeting of the cabinet armed with flit-guns filled with noxious gases, and, with every minister thus rendered unconscious, they would take over the government. The professor was soon pardoned; but in the meantime his place as examiner was taken by a University hack who was anxious to please his superiors. One of our examinees was a youth who had clearly done no work at all, relying on the fact that his father was a highly respected member of the Establishment. When I failed him, my fellow-examiners asked me anxiously, did I not realize who the boy was? When I remained obdurate, they both of them raised their marks so that he should pass with distinction. I realized then that I was unsuited for oriental academic life. It was time for me to leave.

So, after five years in the Near East, I was at last able to go home, wondering what I should do next. The Arabian explorer Bertram Thomas had just been made Director of MECAS, the establishment set up in Lebanon by our Foreign Office to give concentrated training in Middle Eastern studies to would-be diplomats. He asked me to be his Assistant-Director. I protested that my Arabic was far too poor for me to be suitable. He replied that in that job I would be able quickly to learn Arabic properly. I was tempted; but I felt certain that the Foreign Office would prefer one of its own flock for the job; and meanwhile I had been invited by the British Council to take on the post of Representative in Greece. I spent the next two years in the dry and salubrious climate of Athens, in those days before pollution, and have never suffered from sciatica again.

I have been back many times to Istanbul since my academic days there. While I was writing about the Crusades I found that there were several sites in Anatolia that I needed to revisit. It is often impossible to understand the course of a battle if one has not examined the actual terrain. Sometimes one goes there too late. I once made a long journey through central Italy to look at the site of the battle of Tagliacozzo, where Charles of Anjou defeated the young Hohestaufen prince Conradin, only to find that the plain had long since been drained and the water-courses moved. But my most useful visit was to Eskisehir, to find out what had really happened at the great battle of Dorylaeum, where the soldiers of the First Crusade succeeded in routing the Seljuk Turks. It was only when I saw the lie of the land that I understood how the Crusaders managed to turn a near-disaster into victory.

It was always pleasant to see my Turkish friends again; and I made new friends, of which by far the most important was the Oecumenical Patriarch Athenogoras. Like Pope John he was a man who radiated goodness. Like the Pope he was a villager in origin and had the same simplicity of outlook, the same benevolence, the same ecumenical tolerance. Physically he was very different. He was very tall and erect, with a long white beard. When clad in his full Patriarchal robes he could have stepped down from a Byzantine mosaic. His splendid appearance, together with his courtesy and his unfailing correctitude towards the Turkish authorities – technically he was a Turkish citizen – won him the grudging respect of the Turks, especially as when he arrived in Istanbul from the United States, where he had been Archbishop of the Greek Church, to assume his position, it was in President Truman's own aeroplane, the President being one of his admirers. I saw him first in the autumn of 1947, soon after he had arrived in Istanbul; and thenceforward I went to the Patriarchate whenever I was there. One year I was there for the Orthodox Easter, when I thought he would be too busy to see me. But he spotted me when I went to the midnight service on Easter eve, and sent me a message to tell me to come round to the Patriarchate on the Monday morning. He would be receiving visits from the faithful, but we would chat in between the visits. I found him seated on the Patriarchal throne in the reception hall; and next it there was a lesser throne in which he placed me. So I too, like some lesser Patriarch, had respects paid to me. Some of the visitors seemed surprised to see a stranger seated there. But all went well until some Greeks whom I knew in Athens appeared. At the sight of me they could not restrain their giggles, in which His All-Holiness soon joined. Later, in 1963, he invited me to go in his party to the millennary celebrations on Mount Athos. I could not manage it: which was perhaps just as well, as the monks of the Holy Mountain, considering that they lived in eternity, thought it unnecessary to celebrate a mere millennium, and resented the Patriarchal intervention and did their best to sabotage the visit, making sure that it ran short of food.

The Patriarch liked the book that I wrote on the Patriarchate under the Turks, *The Great Church in Captivity*; and in 1969 he gave me the title of Grand Orator of the Great Church. In the good old Ottoman days that would have made me the senior lay member of the Holy Synod of the Patriarchate and would have allowed me to bear the hereditary title of Prince. But in these secular days it was an empty, though deeply appreciated, honour. I was lecturing in America at the time of his death and sadly could not go to pay my last respects to a man whom I loved and admired.

In May 1983 the Turkish government kindly invited me to come to the opening of a Council of Europe exhibition in Istanbul, devoted to Anatolian art down the ages. I had never thought that Anatolia, Asia Minor, was part of Europe; but I was glad that it had reached that honorary status, as the exhibition, though a little weak in the earlier periods, unless one had a taste for Hittite tablets, produced a splendid spectacle of the whole range of Ottoman art. The opening ceremony was especially effective, with carefully trained Janissaries marching in their special gait, to the whining but haunting sound of their authentic musical instruments. I had not been to Istanbul for over fifteen years; and I was glad to find it less badly damaged by modernity than most great cities, though its skyline has been ruined by high-rise hotels on the top of the hill in Pera. As you approach it now from the Sea of Marmara, you no longer find the domes and minarets of old Istanbul dominating the view. Still more kindly, the Turkish government arranged for me, with an assortment of other foreigners, to spend beforehand four days on the Aegean coast, to see as many sites as could be fitted in. We spent our days going to Ephesus and to other ancient cities, some now being carefully excavated, some romantically untouched. We were housed for the nights at Kuşadasi, the one resort that was well endowed with hotels. There was, however, a World Congress of Rotary Societies taking place there; and though we were given a hotel in which to sleep, we had to dine with the Rotarians at their main hotel. They did not provide very enlivening company. But on the third night we were told that there would be a cabaret show there, to which we went full of expectation. We were not disappointed. The show consisted of four young persons, two boys and two girls, completely naked and gilt all over, who pranced between the tables and leered at the guests. The expression on the faces of the worthy Rotarians and their still worthier wives will remain in my memory for ever.

The last time that I went to Istanbul was in the early spring of 1986, when some friends had bullied me into allowing a film for television to be made of my career, and they wanted some scenes to be shot in Byzantium. The weather was lovely, with a hazy sunshine giving a cloak of mystery to the whole city. I cannot in my heart approve of the great new bridge across the Bosphorus. No man, I think, should join continents that God has put asunder. But in the misty light it had great beauty. Why is it that bridges, alone of large modern constructions, usually manage to be beautiful? I suppose it is because they are not designed by architects. I was able to visit the Patriarchate once more, and to attend a special liturgy in the little church of St Mary of the Mongols, the one building to survive as a church from the days of Christian Constantinople. I was able to spend some time in my favourite Ottoman mosque, the Mosque of Söküllü Pasha, the loveliest, I think, of all the buildings of the great architect Sinan. Thanks to hospitable Turkish friends, I stayed in one of the very few wooden *yalis* left on the banks of the Bosphorus, on the Asiatic shore. So on my last nights in the shadow of the great imperial city, I went to sleep with the waters of the Bosphorus lapping beneath my window.

Japan

It is a grave mistake to revisit after an interval of years a country or a city that you have loved. You will find it changed, and never changed for the better; and your happy memories become sullied. On the other hand, if you revisit a country that you disliked, there is no risk of disappointment, and it is possible that you may discover beauties and charms that had evaded you when you were there before. So perhaps, after more than sixty years since I was there, I ought to go back to Japan. I am doubtful. Tokyo, when I saw it in 1926, was still half in ruins after the great earthquake of 1923. But, from all accounts, the city is now a vast accumulation of buildings devoid of charm. I suspect, too, that other, older cities have been invaded by triumphant industrialism, and the historic resorts have been ruined by misguided attempts to lure tourists, which, as in many other countries, spoil all that the civilized visitor wishes to see.

I might have liked Japan better had I not come there straight from China. I had loved Peking and the country around, the vast dusty plain and then the great mountains, with the Wall winding away into the distance. After such monumental splendour even the prettiest things in Japan seemed, to use a dreadful modern word, so twee. Only Fujiyama had some grandeur; but there was nothing surprising about it; one had seen it all before in numerous prints and pictures. I had liked the Chinese. They clearly had little respect for Western barbarians, but they were courteous and kindly – I am speaking of the old days before Mao's Cultural Revolution. In contrast the Japanese were self-conscious. They too did not have much respect for the barbarians, but they wanted to impress them. On the one hand they wanted to make us realize that theirs was an ancient civilization, older, they erroneously claimed, than the Chinese. On the other hand they were determined to show us their skill in adopting Western technologies; and, indeed, their successes were remarkable, but that did not make them more attractive. Arthur Waley had just published his translation of *The Tale of Genji*, written in the early eleventh century AD by the Lady Murasaki, which is, I think, one of the greatest novels in the world's history. I had read it avidly; but in the Japan that I saw there was little to remind me of it, except, perhaps, in the lay-out of the older palaces.

When I was in Tientsin I had met a Japanese dealer who made his living by importing antiques from Japan and selling them to tourists as being Chinese. Prompted by my hostess, the wife of the British Consul-General, he offered to take me round Japan when next he went there to collect his goods. I did not much like him; but she pointed out to me that this would be a wonderful opportunity for seeing Japan from a Japanese angle. She persuaded me to accept his offer. To my shame, I cannot remember his name and I seem never to have written it down in my diary. He had gone to Japan before I was ready to travel; so he arranged to meet me there on my arrival.

On 3 February 1926 I set sail from Tientsin in a small Japanese steamer, the *Nanrei Maru*. The passengers were all Japanese except for myself and two missionaries, one an American Methodist and the other a French Trappist, who was being moved from the large Trappist monastery near Peking to one near Nagasaki in Japan. He was released from his vows of silence for his journey and was determined to take full advantage of this opportunity to talk; but, owing to the long years of silence, he knew no language but his native French. He was delighted to find someone who could converse in his tongue. As the steamer wound its way down the Pei-ho river he never stopped chattering. He would ask me questions about the outside world and seldom waited for an answer but started up again. There was an endearing innocence about him; I was happy to listen to him. In the late afternoon the boat crossed the bar at the mouth of the river and went out into the Yellow Sea, where it was extremely rough. The two missionaries retired to the cabin which I had to share with them. When I joined them later the Methodist was being rather sick and the Trappist very sick. The former, conscious that he was bearing up a little better than the latter, would now and then lean from his bunk and say: 'Put your faith in God, and all will be well.' The Trappist asked me anxiously what he was saying, and, when I conscientiously translated the trite remark, he raised his eyebrows in surprise. After all, he had spent his life putting his faith in God. After a while the stench in the cabin was too much for me, and I spent the night on a sofa in the saloon. It was still rough next morning, when we sailed past the Shantung peninsula, its mountains covered with snow; but the wind abated, and by evening we were under the shelter of the Korean coast. The missionaries recovered; and I found myself having to act as interpreter while the Trappist tried to explain the nature of his Order to the Methodist, who found it all very odd. Next day we progressed in comfort through the islands off the south Korean coast; the sea remained moderate as we crossed the strait to Japan. The following morning we arrived at the Japanese port of Moji. There my Trappist friend was met by his new Abbot, who came aboard with several of his flock, all released for the moment from their customary silence and all chattering like starlings. I was introduced to the Abbot, who thanked me solemnly for having been kind to his brother. Without him the boat seemed very quiet as we sailed up the Inland Sea, to reach Kobe at 10 o'clock next morning.

There my bear-leader met me. (A faint memory now suggests to me that he was called Mr Nogawa.) We went by train to Kyoto and there he installed me in a little Japanese hotel. I had been very nervous about going to a Japanese hotel, being aware that if you wanted a bath in one you went to a bath-house, where, after carefully washing yourself you stepped into a tank full of naked Japanese of both sexes and all ages. In this hotel, however, there was no bath-house, only a cauldron which could not take more than one body. The proprietress, a kindly, motherly woman, used to come with her girls to watch me bathe and to giggle at the whiteness of my body; but I soon grew used to that. I was embarrassed on the first night, when one of the girls came into my room to undress me. I kept saying one of the few Japanese words that I knew, *sayonara*, which means good-bye. She went on with her task; but, to my relief, I found that one was expected to sleep in one's underclothes. I found it hard to like Japanese food. I soon became adept with my chop-sticks, but I never could manage to eat raw fish.

I spent six nights in Kyoto. My bear-leader was conscientious in looking after me. He took me to see all the sights of the city, and we would go by tram or bus or train to see the shrines and temples in the neighbourhood. He was a competent guide, who organized the journeys efficiently and could give sound basic information about the sights. But I soon began to suspect that he was making money out of me. I naturally paid for our journeys and our meals, and depended upon him to tell me how much I ought to pay. Nothing was cheap, in what was then considered a country of low prices. I did once manage to decipher a restaurant bill without him noticing me. It was for rather less than the sum that he asked me to give him. Maybe he was justified; he was certainly using up his time in looking after me. But he was always stopping to see what was for sale in junk-shops and would be triumphant when he discovered a bargain.

All the same, thanks to him, I saw many places of interest and of beauty. I was particularly impressed by the temples at Nara. We went there on a public holiday, the 2586th anniversary of the foundation of the Japanese Empire. The crowds were such that we could not find a place in any native restaurant and had to go to a Western-style hotel. The food was indifferent but at least I was not expected to eat raw fish.

We left Kyoto to go by train to Kozu, where my bear-leader put me into a car to take me to Miyanoshita. There, he said, the local antique-dealer, Mr Shibu, would look after me. Miyanoshita was a pleasant town with hot springs, high in a valley on the far side of Fujiyama. I spent three happy days there. I stayed at a largish Japanese hotel, with a kindly proprietor, whose personable young son prided himself on his English and was determined to see that I enjoyed myself. He insisted on accompanying me to the public bath in the hotel, to make sure that I learnt the proper technique for bathing. Mr Shibu turned out to be a charming old man. His old-fashioned English seemed to be derived from his reading of Shakespeare, from whose works he made frequent apt quotations. He took me, usually by bus, to see the neighbouring villages, through mountainous country, with the plum-trees in the valleys just coming into bloom. He insisted on paying for everything himself, though I did persuade him once to dine with me at the hotel. He hinted very delicately that he did not think highly of my bear-leader, whom he knew as a fellow dealer, and hoped I was not being exploited. He and the son of the hotelier were the two Japanese whom I really liked.

From Miyanoshita I travelled by bus and then train, with two changes, to Kamakura, where a great statue of the Buddha stands by the shore of the Pacific. There my bear-leader joined me; and in the afternoon we took a train to Yokohama, where he had some business to conduct. On the train I found myself next to an American, a very ordinary commercial traveller. But after ten days of seeing no one but Japanese, I fell on him as though on a long-lost friend. From Yokohama we went on to Tokyo. I disliked Tokyo; and my dislike was not lessened by being taken to see a No play. The No theatre is, I suppose, an acquired taste. For me to have to sit for hours on a very uncomfortable seat watching the slow progress of an uninteresting story was not an enlivening experience. The delicate gestures of the actors were fascinating to watch at first, but soon they became monotonous. I left long before the drama was over.

After two nights in Tokyo I went by myself by train to Nikko. Nikko impressed me. It seemed to be on a larger scale than the other old Japanese cities, with an unself-conscious serenity. It was the only place where I felt that I was in the world of the Lady Murasaki. The hotel was friendly; and there were very few tourists about, though I had some difficulty in escaping from a garrulous American couple. When I returned to Tokyo my bear-leader had left, but Mr Shibu had come down from Miyanoshita to see me again. Next day I returned to Kyoto. After two nights there I went down to Kobe, to embark on a French liner, which carried me over stormy seas to Shanghai.

I am glad that I went to Japan and that I saw it in Japanese style. I am glad that I met the kindly Mr Shibu, with whom I kept up a correspondence for a year or two, till I received a letter from the son of the Miyanoshita hotel telling me that he had died. To express my not very sincere gratitude to my bear-leader I sent him from London two pieces of old Worcester china. From his letter of thanks it was clear that he thought them of little interest; and I wished that I had not taken the trouble to make the gesture.

Perhaps I ought to return to Japan. The Japanese are said to love the very aged; so I would doubtless be well received there. Those whom I have since met have all been very amiable and polite. A few years ago the works of George Orwell were very popular in Japan. It being known that I had been at school with him, I received letters and even visits from eager young Japanese scholars asking me for my impressions of him. It was difficult to try to explain to them what life was like in College at Eton during the First World War. So I doubt if I was of much use to them. I wish them all well; but I cannot feel much affection for Japan.

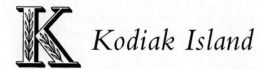

Kodiak Island

KODIAK ISLAND, off the coast of Alaska, is not a well-known resort. Its fame, to those who have heard of it, lies in being the home of the largest genus of grizzly bears. When I visited the island, early in November 1975, the bears had all gone to sleep for the winter. I had no hope of meeting any of them. My interest in going there came from another direction.

The State of Alaska has had an extraordinary history. It is the only territory in the world that has been voluntarily, indeed eagerly, disposed of by the Russians and taken over very grudgingly by the United States. Its existence was vaguely known to cartographers of the sixteenth century; but it was in 1741 that the navigator Vitus Bering, a Dane in Russian employ, crossed the sea now called after him and made a survey of its southern and western coasts. He was followed later in the eighteenth century by the British explorers James Cook, George Vancouver and Alexander Mackenzie. But its grandly inhospitable shores did not lure settlers to follow in their wake. However, by the end of the century Russian fur-traders had learnt that the waters were full of seals and sea-otters and the mainland of small fur-bearing mammals. The market for furs in Russia was insatiable; so small trading-stations began to appear, the first in 1783, situated on Kodiak Island. In 1799, owing to the exertions of a trader turned statesman, A. A. Baronov, the Russian American Company was founded and given by Imperial edict administrative control of the settlements and a monopoly to exploit the natural resources of the coastal lands, as far south as 55°. Its headquarters were established at New Archangel, the town now known as Sitka. In 1825 a treaty between Russia and Great Britain fixed the boundary between Russian America and British Columbia, giving the Russians the territory that is now the Alaskan panhandle, as well as the huge, as yet unmapped, peninsula to the north-west.

The Russian American Company governed the settlements for sixty-two years. Its officials showed little aptitude for administration, and they were ill-supported by the Imperial government. The charter was not renewed after 1861, when a governor from St Petersburg, Prince Maksutoff, was sent out to take charge of the territory. With the end of the American Civil War the United States began to take an interest in the Pacific coast, with its fisheries and its furs, and in the possibility of laying a telegraph line through Russian America to Asia.

The Russians were by now sick of trying to govern lands that were so far away, across a stormy ocean, and that seemed never to pay their way. At that time Britain was their bugbear. They suspected the British of planning to invade Russian America from British Columbia and thus to threaten the Russian establishments on the Pacific coast of Asia. When the United States began to show an interest in acquiring the territory they gladly responded. They could not know of the riches that lay beneath the soil, of the gold in the Yukon valley or of all the oil to be found in the Northern Slopes by the Arctic Ocean; they did not realize that the United States would be a far greater menace to their Empire than ever Britain could be. When the American Secretary of State, William Henry Seward, offered to buy all Russian America for the sum of $7,200,000, they gladly accepted the offer. The treaty arranging the sale was signed on 30 March 1867, and the United States formally took over Russian America at a ceremony at Sitka on 18 October that year. Many Americans regarded the deal as a ridiculous extravagance. It was suggested that the new territory be called 'Icebergia' or 'Seward's Folly'. But he meantime christened it 'Alaska', from an Aleut word that meant 'the great land'.

The Russians departed, but they left something behind them. The natives, the Tlingit Indians of the panhandle, the Eskimos of the mainland and the Aleuts of the southern coasts and islands, had been pagan animists. The Russian settlers had brought their priests with them and they set about the conversion of the natives. They acted with sympathy and tact. While I was in Alaska I had the opportunity of seeing copies of the instructions sent out by the Orthodox Metropolitan of Moscow, suggesting how they should proceed. They were remarkable for their tolerance and wisdom. The missionaries were told not to attempt brusquely to abolish established native customs, but merely to modify them if they seemed to be anti-Christian or if possible somehow to incorporate them into Christian practice. A polygamous chieftain should not be ordered at once to give up all his wives but one. That would risk upsetting the social pattern too drastically. It would be better gently to suggest that monogamy might be more suitable for the next generation. The churches built by the Russians, small though they were, appealed to the natives, with their candles and their icons and the simple dignity of their ceremonies. They suggested another world but one that was not out of reach. The Russian priests were nearly all of them simple men, often of peasant origin. They were impressive when in their robes they performed the Mysteries; but outside the church they fitted easily and unpretentiously into the community. The Tlingit Indians and many of the Eskimo and Aleut tribes gratefully accepted Russian Orthodoxy.

The coming of American rule meant the coming of missionaries of a different calibre, mainly Baptist. Protestant missionaries have almost always been harsh and impatient in denouncing sinful practices. My mother once found herself sitting next to Cosmo Gordon Lang, when he was Archbishop of York, and in the course of conversation asked him why missionaries in Africa insisted on converts promptly expelling all their superfluous wives. 'Dear lady,' answered the Archbishop, 'should we not rather call them concubines?' Such was the attitude of the Americans in Alaska. Concubinage, and many other customs, were sinful. They must be stopped at once. There were converts to this newer form of Christianity among natives who wished to ingratiate themselves with their present rulers. But many of the tribes remained faithful to the Church that they had learnt to love. In many towns and villages you still see little churches built in the Russian style, fitting far better into the northern landscape than the gothicized barns of the Protestants. Few of them are old. They were all built of wood; and sooner or later carelessness with the candles led to a conflagration. But the icons and the church plate were usually rescued and still receive due reverence. The liturgy is no longer in Slavonic; but the English into which it has been translated keeps a simple dignity and avoids the vulgarities that disfigure the American-English translation of the Catholic Mass.

It was a desire to see the survival of Orthodoxy that helped to make me eagerly accept an invitation in the autumn of 1975 to give some lectures at the University of Alaska. A doctor friend of mine from the Southern States, whom I had known in New Orleans, had moved to Alaska, to Anchorage, where he had many friends among the University professors; and it was he who persuaded them to invite me. Alaska, though by far the largest state in the American Republic, has the smallest population, with its towns scattered far from each other. The University therefore consists of distant units. I was based at the branch in Anchorage, the largest city in the State, which was the centre for the humanities. But I also visited Fairbanks, in the middle of the State, the original University, now given over mainly to engineering and the sciences, and Juneau, the State capital, in the panhandle, as well as outlying colleges at Sitka and at Kodiak Island. I also escaped for a few days to the gentler climate of Seattle, in the State of Washington.

Life at Anchorage was very agreeable. I stayed with Martin Palmer, my doctor friend, in a wooden house on a tree-covered hillside, some ten miles from the town. No other house was in sight, though some were near. One looked through the trees at snow-covered mountain peaks. At any moment one expected to see a moose or even a bear pass by the window, though I was not so honoured. Everyone was very hospitable; though I soon felt that I never wanted to eat salmon again. The University was lively and the students keen. I was a little put out at being addressed by some of the younger academics as 'Steve', not a name that appeals to me. The older professors preferred to call me 'Sir Runcimán', stressing the last syllable as Americans are wont to do when faced with an unfamiliar or alien word. Foolishly I tried to amend their ways by composing a limerick:

> *The bright young professors of Anchorage*
> *Pay little attention to rank or age.*
> *Quite right, you may say;*
> *But it wasn't the way*
> *To give poor old Sir Runcimán courage.*

But when I recited it no one thought it funny. I suspect that in America limericks have to be dirty to be acceptable.

One day, owing to the kindness of British Petroleum, I spent visiting its installations at Prudhoe Bay, on the shore of the Arctic Ocean. We flew for some $2\frac{1}{2}$ hours over snowy mountains and bleak prairies to land on a desolate plain. The ocean was already frozen; and a light covering of snow made it impossible to see where the land ended and the sea began. In the pale winter light of that empty landscape the strangely shaped erections that the oil industry requires had a fantastic beauty. I had seen similar constructions in the East and had thought them there to be eyesores. Here, amid the desolation, one seemed almost to be in a fairyland world. Encased in furs, to keep out the deathly cold, with our faces barely showing between the wrappings, we were taken round the field. Having no empathy with machinery I could only gape and wonder and make the tritest comments. Less beautiful but almost more impressive was the enormous building in which all the staff were housed. It contained not only sleeping quarters but offices and sitting rooms, a bathing-pool, a squash-court, a hospital ward and every other amenity considered necessary for modern life, as well as a vast cafeteria, where I enjoyed an excellent luncheon, not surprisingly, as it was run, so I was told, by the best-paid chef in all America. He was a charming man, well contented with his life, so long as he could escape for two or three days every fortnight to the comparative freedom of Anchorage. He was surrounded by cheerful minions who told me that in wintertime they never went outside the great building except when they left to go on leave. He showed me round room after room of stores of food, all necessary to guard against the times when for days on end blizzards made contact with the outside world quite impossible. We flew back to Anchorage after dark. The town seemed banal after that glimpse of a futuristic world.

Sitka, on an island in the archipelago off the Alaskan panhandle, seemed to me, in spite of its lovely situation, a rather melancholy place. It was a town that had seen better days. It had been the capital of Russian America and of Alaska till 1920. Now the government offices had moved to Juneau, on the mainland. Its finest monument, the Orthodox cathedral of St Michael, built in the early nineteenth century, had been burnt down in 1966. Only the crypt survived. It was snowing on and off throughout my visit, which added to the atmosphere of melancholy and nostalgia for a past that would never return. Juneau, perched on the edge of a splendid fiord, was a livelier and happier city. I saw it in sunshine.

But the place in Alaska that I shall remember with the deepest affection was Kodiak Island. The little town there had no architectural distinction; its Russian church was the only building of note. But, as the oldest settlement in Alaska, it had its quiet dignity, in spite of occasional disasters, caused by tidal waves or tempests. Alaska is disaster-prone. Apart from such man-made horrors as the recent leakage of oil from a wrecked tanker, the worst leakage in the world, which has defiled the sea and destroyed the creatures that live in it over a long stretch of the coast, and apart from the general harshness of the climate, it is right on the earthquake belt. The great earthquake of 1964 was the most severe ever recorded on the American continent. As well as the devastation round its epicentre, it set off great waves that swept the ocean over a number of coastal towns. On Kodiak Island the buildings by the sea had been overwhelmed, but the church, on higher ground, had survived. It was this church that gave a special quality to the island. Attached to it was a seminary. Here, under the authority of a Russian-American nun, Sister Victoria – helped by a simple, pious and cheerful Tlingit Indian deacon, and by a young man from New England, a convert to Orthodoxy, who seemed a little out of place – eight young Eskimos were learning to become Orthodox priests. I was accompanied on this journey by Dr Palmer who had met Sister Victoria on a previous visit and who introduced me to her as soon as we arrived; and I spent as much time as possible with her. Like all the best saints, she was clearly an excellent and much loved teacher, something of a disciplinarian, and with a lively sense of humour, radiating kindliness. It was moving to see the young acolytes sitting at her feet as she talked to them, and still more moving to see them taking part in a service in the church. In their simple robes, with their bright, fresh, slant-eyed faces, they seemed rather like animated dolls, yet with an air of simple devotion. It was cheering to see that the Orthodox Church was living on, to give to the natives of Alaska a religion that suited them so well. I believe that since I was there Sister Victoria has been summoned back to her convent in New England. But the seminary goes on and, with God's help, its work will be continued far into the future.

So, when I think of Alaska, I remember the splendour of the scenery, I remember the hospitality of my friends, I remember the fantasies of the oil-world. But it is Kodiak Island that remains foremost in my memory.

Los Angeles

IT WAS IN THE SPRING of 1955 that my friend George Hoyningen-Heune, the photographer, brought me a message from George Cukor, the film producer, to say that he was coming to London in May and wished to see me. Would I be interested, he wanted to know, in being Artistic Adviser for a film that MGM were planning, entitled *The Female*? I felt greatly flattered to be considered a specialist on such an important subject till I remembered that there had appeared recently a book under that name which concerned the life of the great Byzantine empress Theodora. All the same, I decided that it would be amusing to learn more about the proposal. So, when Mr Cukor came to London that May, I went to a dinner-party that he gave in his suite in the Savoy. He received us dressed in black silk pyjamas, which made me feel a trifle over-dressed. He explained to me then that the film was indeed about the Empress, that Miss Ava Gardner was to take the title-role, and that it would be shot in Rome. Would I be prepared to spend two or three months there next year, to give the film-company my advice? When I reported this to my academic friends, they were all horrified. That would be prostitution, they said. My name would be associated with a vulgar and unhistorical production, and what reputation I had as a serious historian would be ruined forever. But I rather liked the idea. To be paid — and, I gathered, well-paid — to spend some months in Rome would not be disagreeable. I knew that the last thing wanted from an Adviser was that he should be about the place all the time advising. He should merely look in from time to time to correct any really blatant anachronism or, perhaps, to insist on the leading lady having a hair-style proper to the period; for actresses, however much they may be ready to wear period costumes, cannot bear to have to alter their coiffure. So I said that I was not uninterested in the proposal.

Months, however, passed and I heard no more. Then I had a message to say that the project was postponed. Finally, next spring, when Mr Cukor was again in London, I was summoned once more to dine at the Savoy, and he told me that when Miss Gardner saw the script she pronounced it to be lousy. He had to admit that she was right; and when later I saw it myself, I agreed with them.

That August 1956 I was sitting one morning in my house in St John's Wood when the telephone rang. It was a call from Paris; a voice said: 'I am Dora Levine Hovey, and I am in charge of the scripts for Metro-

Goldwyn-Mayer. I want to fly over to London and have tea with you.'
When she arrived she explained to me over the tea-cups that MGM, and
various other film companies, were worried about the impact of television. They planned therefore to do a number of short films on historical subjects, which would go round the television circuit and then could
be shown in schools all over the United States. Would I be prepared to
write some suitable scripts? I asked what sort of subjects she had in mind.
She said that they would have to deal with historical characters that
people had heard of. 'And what historical characters have you heard of,
Mrs Hovey?' I inquired. 'Oh, you know,' she replied, 'Joan of Arc and
Queen Elizabeth.' I did not think that I could tell many stories just about
those two ladies. I also gathered that these films would be done on the
cheap. So I politely told Mrs Hovey that I would not be of any use to her.

I then wrote to Mr Cukor to explain my unwillingness to co-
operate. I was not prepared, I said, to have my lovely stories dressed in
butter-muslin. I received an indignant reply. Come to Hollywood, he
said, and he would show me the MGM costume museum, where every
costume that had ever been made for each of their films was stored, ready
to be used again if necessary. In any case he would be delighted if I would
come and stay with him in Los Angeles for a week or two; and we could
then perhaps plan some historical film in which I would be interested.

It was an invitation that I was happy to accept. I had to give lectures
in Toronto and in Chicago early the next year, and then find my way to
the Philippines and Borneo. It was an unexpected delight to be able to
break my journey for two weeks in California. George Cukor was the
kindest of hosts, and he felt that we had a special affinity as we shared the
same date for our birthdays. He lived in a handsome house with a fine
garden on Beverly Hills. He had a number of good Impressionist
pictures and a vast number of books, many of which he had actually
read, though I could never discover when he had the time for reading.
My bedroom opened on to the garden. It was oval-shaped and elegantly
furnished. The bathroom, however, presented a problem, as the bath-
tub was L-shaped, or, rather, it was a square with a corner filled in. To
judge from the salts and essences provided, it was meant for use; but I
never learnt how to fit into it.

George was a wonderful host. As he was busy all day directing a
film, a not very noteworthy production called *Les Girls*, he provided me
with a car and a young student to drive it. I was taken to Disneyland, to
the huge cemetery at Forest Lawn, to Malibu Beach, to the gardens
around Pasadena, and everything else that a good tourist should see.
Social life was a little restricted. Just as in England the best families came
over with the Conqueror, so in Hollywood the best people had come
over with the Goldwyns and the Mayers; and if, like George Cukor, you
belonged to that select group, you did not mix with the riff-raff of

the movie world but only with actors and actresses who came from respectable backgrounds. In consequence I spent much of my time, very happily, with Katherine Hepburn. She was staying nearby, in a house that had a private cinema; and she was shocked to find that there were a number of good films that I had never seen. So I went round three times to her house, once with George and twice by myself. We began the evening with champagne and caviare, then watched a film, after which there was supper, where we were joined by Spencer Tracey, who never seemed to be quite sober and was obviously annoyed to find another gentleman at the table. She handled him with gentle tact, and he would calm down. George's leading lady in *Les Girls* was an enchanting young actress, Kay Kendall, who came often to the house. She was engaged to be married to Rex Harrison, who was then rehearsing for *My Fair Lady* in New York and who would come to Los Angeles at week-ends. She twice brought him to dinner while I was there. Sad to say, she died very soon after her marriage. Her co-star in *Les Girls* was Gene Kelly who came to the house once or twice; but one felt that he was not considered to be quite of the same social background.

I was soon made aware of the social form. A prominent film-star and his wife used to give parties which were said to be somewhat louche; and a friend offered to get an invitation for me to one of them. But it was firmly told me that no guest of Mr Cukor's would be permitted to go to such a party. So my chance of attending a Hollywood orgy was lost. George could be stern on other matters as well. When I made fun of the Forest Lawn cemetery, which is, I still think, hilariously horrifying, I was sharply reminded that it had brought comfort to numbers of sorrowing relatives and it was not for me to mock at it. But, in spite of such reproofs, the visit, I think, went well. I was allowed to go down to the studio now and then, to see George in action. I was shown round the MGM costume museum, happily now with no feeling of obligation, as any idea of making short historical films had been abandoned. And, within the circle of George's friends, I was made welcome. Anyhow, he invited me to come again whenever I wished.

Two years later, in March 1959, I visited him again, for three days. I arrived in time to attend a star-spangled dinner party. Gladys Cooper was there. She had been the leading pin-up girl long ago, in the days of the First World War, and she had aged with elegance and grace, to become a beautiful old lady. Laurence Olivier was there, and Spencer Tracey, and Sophia Loren. In my younger days I used to practise fortune-telling, with some success. Indeed, for a time I was Court fortune-teller to King George II of the Hellenes. I was often quite uninspired; but in some inexplicable way I knew when I was foreseeing things correctly. Sophia Loren insisted on being told her future. I began by talking with some puzzlement about marriage. But one of my fellow-guests began kicking me under the table so I soon changed the subject. I ought to have known that her marriage, or marriages, were in a muddled state and that she was faced with a possible prosecution for bigamy in Italy. So I went on to tell her that she was going to be the victim of a burglary. I was right. She went soon afterwards to London, where all her jewels were stolen from her hotel bedroom. Many years later I met her at a party at the Italian Embassy in London. When I came up to her she looked at me strangely and then said: 'But I know you. You were the man who warned me about that burglary.' I was next asked to take on Laurence Olivier, but I refused. I was too tired, I said. A few months earlier, in London, I had told Vivien Leigh her fortune; I had foreseen misery. As she and Olivier were still married I thought it wiser to keep clear of it all.

I never stayed with George Cukor again, though I always went to see him when I was in Los Angeles. I found it easier to stay with a friend in whose house I did not always have to be on my best behaviour. Frank Lysinger has the distinction of being the great-grandson of Joseph Smith, the founder of the Mormon Church. He is, I fear, what is called a Jack Mormon, that is, a Mormon who does not conform to the strict discipline of the sect. He is ready to drink such stimulants as tea and coffee and even demon alcohol. Yet when he goes into a Mormon temple he is received as a Prince of the Blood. I knew him for some time before I learnt about his ancestry. We had gone together for a journey into the Mojave Desert, and I had been intrigued to find in my motel room not only the usual Gideon Bible but also the Book of Mormon. When I remarked on this, a little too flippantly, to Frank, he reproved me and pointed out how strange it was that an almost illiterate peasant boy should have been able to produce that lengthy and, I fear, to me unreadable, volume. He too was a friend of George Hoyningen-Heune and of George Cukor. So it was easy to maintain my old connection with them. Whenever I had occasion to pass through California again I would stay with him; and he would often take me for excursions into the interior. I remember very vividly a journey to Death Valley, a bleak arid area lying far below sea-level and surrounded by strangely coloured mountains. Its desolation, however, was broken by the arrival of three buses filled with ladies of uncertain age, all shaped like hippopotami, all wearing pastel-coloured pantie-suits, and all chattering like starlings.

Early in 1971 I was invited to spend a few weeks at UCLA, the University of California, Los Angeles. I had lectured there two or three times already; and the eminent professor of Byzantine Studies there, Milton Anastos, was a good friend of mine. He it was who had me appointed Regents' Lecturer for a term. It was not an arduous position. Indeed, I was only expected to give one lecture, though in fact I gave two. It was my duty simply to be about the place, so that students who were interested in my line of history could come and talk to me. I knew that there would not be very many of them. But UCLA has a magnificent library; and I thought that I could spend my days happily and profitably among its shelves.

I arrived on a Sunday evening, and was taken by Professor Anastos to a pleasant apartment that he had found for me, high up in a tall building, just below the apartment in which he and his wife lived, together with his huge collection of historical works. I spent the Monday settling in, meeting members of the Faculty and some of the students, being introduced to the librarians, and being shown the supermarkets where I would have to do my shopping. On the Tuesday morning at six o'clock I woke up with a jerk. A minute later the earthquake began. There were two shocks, neither lasting for more than two minutes, with a minute or so between them. The whole building swayed alarmingly. But I remembered being told that if a building swayed it probably would not fall. So I stayed patiently in bed. But I could not help wondering whether at any moment Professor Anastos's vast library would come tumbling down on to my head. To be battered to death by Byzantine texts might have been appropriate for me but I did not fancy the idea. It was the worst earthquake that Los Angeles had suffered in recorded history. The epicentre was a little to the north of the University, in an area where there were two hospitals, both appallingly damaged, and where there was a junction of motorways. I went out to see the site two days later. There was a viaduct which looked as though a giant had taken it in his hand and crumpled it like a piece of paper.

My office on the campus was in a building the architect of which had been responsible for one of the wrecked hospitals; and, as it was not an alluring office, I preferred to see students in my apartment, which was close to the campus. To my sorrow, as a result of the earthquake the University Library was closed for the rest of my visit. All the books on the east–west axis had been shaken from their shelves; and it was a lengthy task to put them back in their places and to repair the volumes that had been damaged by their fall. So I spent my spare time in seeing old friends like George Cukor and once again tasting the pleasures of the film world. My week-ends were free and I usually went away for them. I visited San Diego, with its splendid zoo, where the animals live in such large enclosures that you seldom can see them. Of other visits I shall tell later in this book. Apart from the earthquake and lesser tremors that continued for two or three weeks after it, I enjoyed my term at the University. The weather was pleasant; and even when most of Los Angeles is veiled in smog, the area round the University seems always to be free of it. There are many worse places in the world in which to spend the grim month of February.

Los Angeles usually receives a bad press in comparison with San

Francisco. It is a huge sprawling city without any centre. It has few good buildings and far too many districts filled with squalid slums. There are pleasant residential quarters; but the houses built along the shore are periodically wrecked by storms or tidal waves. Other houses are built on hillsides that soon start slipping into the sea. Others, built further back, are liable to perish in the fires that now and then sweep over the waterless hills. The distances are such that you cannot live there without a car. Indeed, if you walk anywhere, especially after dark, you are liable to be arrested as a suspicious vagrant. One moon-lit evening, when I had been dining at a house barely a quarter of a mile from my apartment, I decided to walk home. Almost at once a car drew up and an anxious couple asked if they could help me. Had my car, perhaps, broken down? When I explained that I was walking for pleasure they were aghast. Did I not realize how dangerous it was? They bundled me into their car and drove me to my apartment block waiting to see that I was safely inside the door before they left.

Yet, for all its faults, I prefer it to San Francisco. The site of San Francisco is magnificent, or was so till a barbarous horde of high-rise buildings sprang up to dwarf the hills. There are charming quarters and charming people in the city; but the smug, complacent air of moral laxity is, I find, unattractive. It takes away all pleasure from sin. I feel far more afraid of earthquakes there than in Los Angeles. One year I was returning home from New Zealand and paused for a week in Fiji. I found it quite impossible to realize that, because of the date line, on leaving Fiji I would arrive in San Francisco on the previous day, and so had misinformed my hosts there about the time of my arrival. There was no one to meet me at the airport. A telephone call revealed that my hosts were away till the morrow; but after further calls I found a kind friend who was willing to house me for the night. He took me to his apartment, high in a tower block, and showed me into a room furnished with a water-bed. As I lay there sleepless – for the waves would not allow me to lie on my side but kept pushing me on to my back – I kept wondering what would happen were there to be an earthquake. The heavy contraption would quite certainly bring the building down and would itself burst open. So, if I were not crushed to death I would undoubtedly be drowned.

Morea: Monemvasia and Mistra

GREECE is to me a second country. But were I to try to tell of all my experiences there, up and down the mainland and through the islands, there would be little room left in a book to cover my journeys to other lands. So I must restrict myself to places that begin with the letter M. Happily they include many that I love best. There is Macedonia, the grandest of Greek provinces, more Balkan, perhaps, than Mediterranean, with its plains and lakes and great rivers flowing through it. There are old towns there, such as Edessa or Florina or Kavalla that as yet have not been ruined by tourism. Its capital, Thessaloniki, is a noble city, containing within its walls some of the finest of Byzantine churches, and an excellent university. Then, in Thessaly, a little further to the south, there are the strange monasteries of Meteora, perched on isolated crags with precipitous sides. It is hard to conceive how the first monks ever managed to reach the sites of several of them; and to some, within living memory, the only means of access was to be hauled up in a basket. Queen Marie of Roumania claimed to be the last visitor to be welcomed in this manner. She had never, she told me later, been so terrified in all her colourful life. When I went there first, in 1928, steps had been cut in the rock, to replace the baskets; but the result was almost more perilous. It was a very steep climb, with nothing to support one; it was only suited to those who had a strong head for heights. There were still a few monks in each establishment, eager to welcome a visitor and to show off their icons and manuscripts. The monasteries fared badly during the last World War. They were thought to be centres of resistance. The monks were removed, the treasures vanished, either looted or rescued and lodged in museums. Now, though the Grand Meteora, the largest of the monasteries, still houses a few monks, in the others there are only custodian-monks, and the churches and cells are empty and bare – empty, that is to say, of treasures, but full of tourists. For, alas, a road now leads up to the top of the neighbouring mountain, and the visitor can reach each building by merely crossing a bridge over the intervening chasm. Cars and buses bring crowds of sight-seers, many of them angrily ignoring the notices that remind them that these are holy places and visitors are requested to be decently dressed. I do not wish to see the Meteora monasteries again.

It is further still to the south that I am happiest in Greece. The great peninsula known to the ancients and again today as the Peloponnese, but for which I prefer the more mellifluous medieval name of Morea – 'the mulberry tree', so called from the likeness of its shape to that of a mulberry leaf – though parts of its coast-line have been ruined by ugly tourist-hotels, and buses clog the roads that lead to such haunted sites as Mycenae, another M, but now only fit to be visited during the bleaker seasons of the year, still has many districts attracting only travellers who know what they are doing. It is the part of Greece where one is most conscious of the Middle Ages. There is no greater tragedy in history than the Fourth Crusade, when Frankish knights from the West sacked the holy city of Constantinople. But the Frankish conquest of the Morea, which followed soon afterwards, had its compensations. It brought new life to a province that had been somewhat neglected by the Byzantine government. The new-come princes and lords worked hard to enrich their estates. Trade was encouraged, and intercourse with the outer world. The castles that they built, though now romantic ruins, bear witness to their bellicosity, it is true, but also to their determination to run an orderly administration. They showed a certain contempt for their Greek subjects; but they were far too few to take the risk of alienating them entirely; and they were resented by the Greeks less for their secular government than for the attempt of the less prudent of them to force the authority of Rome on to the local Orthodox congregations. Slowly the Greeks recovered their land, in efforts lit with flashes of romance, only to fall, when at last they had won it all, under the harsher domination of the Turks.

The Frankish invasion of the Morea began in 1205. By 1213 Geoffrey of Villehardouin, who bore the title of Prince of Achaea, was in control of the whole peninsula, apart from a corner in the south-west, including the ports of Corone and Methone, prudently retained by the Venetians as part of their reward for having taken part in the Fourth Crusade, and apart, too, from the town of Monemvasia, on its rock that juts out into the sea near the south-eastern tip. This was a nest of Greek pirates, preying on the trade that the Princes of Achaea were now building up.

The Principality reached the summit of its prosperity under Prince William, the younger son of Geoffrey, who succeeded his brother, Geoffrey II, in 1246. He had been born in Greece and reared by Greek nurses. He spoke Greek as easily as French. His third wife was Greek, a princess from Epirus. He regarded the Morea as his native home. His administrative capital was at Andravida, or Andréville, in the north-west of the peninsula, a town of which none of the medieval buildings remain, except for the ruins of a small Gothic cathedral. But his favourite residence was the palace that his father had built near the town that the Franks called La Crémonie, the ancient Lacedaemon, or Sparta. It lay in the most turbulent corner of the Morea, with lawless tribes all around –

the Milengi in the Taygetus mountains, the Tzakones in the Parnon mountains on the other, eastern, side of the vale of Sparta, and the wild Maniots to the south, on the peninsula that ends at Cape Taenerum, or Matapan. Prince William's first task was to capture Monemvasia, which fell to him in 1250, starved into surrender after a three-years' blockade. Next, he built two great castles, one, Maina, or La Grande Maigne, close to Cape Matapan. Its site now is unknown. It is usually thought to have been on the coast to the east of the Cape; but I am inclined to place it on the western side of the peninsula leading to the Cape, on a hill jutting out into the Gulf of Messenia, where a few meaningless ruins are to be seen. The other was a few miles to the west of Sparta, on a cone-shaped hill called Myzithra, from its resemblance to a cheese of that name, which was made in the shape of a cone. The name was soon shortened to Mystras or Mistra. At the same time he strengthened the fortifications of Monemvasia. From these three castles he could control that truculent corner of his principality and live in security in his palace at La Crémonie.

That security was not to last for long. William had ambitions to be lord of the whole Greek peninsula. He realized that a threat to this ambition came from the revival of Byzantine power, under the energetic Emperors in exile at Nicaea. When by the middle of the century Macedonia was back in Byzantine hands, the independent Greek Despot of Epirus was alarmed. He had two lovely daughters, one of whom he gave in marriage to Manfred of Hohenstaufen, King of Naples and Sicily, and the other to Prince William. His two sons-in-law shared his dislike of Nicaean Emperors. When he decided to attack the Nicaean army in Macedonia, Manfred sent him a contingent of his finest knights and William came in person with his leading vassals. The Nicaean throne had just been taken over by an able usurper, Michael Palaeologus, whose army was commanded by his brother John, a competent and experienced general. The crucial battle took place in July 1259 at Pelagonia, near the modern Monastir. There were quarrels among the allies, and when the battle started the Epirots withdrew from the field, leaving William and the Italians outnumbered and outmanoeuvred. Within a few hours they were routed. William's chief vassals were slain or captured. William himself attempted to escape disguised as a peasant but was recognized by his remarkably prominent teeth. It is interesting to reflect that had the art of dentistry been further advanced the Greeks might not have recovered the Peloponnese.

William and his fellow-captives were taken to Nicaea. After two ·years the Emperor Michael, who had by now captured Constantinople from the crumbling Latin Empire, offered terms for their release. William was to give over to him his three great fortresses, Maina, Monemvasia and Mistra. The High Court of the Principality met, consisting mainly of the wives of the captive lords, and known in history as the Parliament of Ladies; and the terms were accepted. In the autumn of 1261 William and the other captive lords came home, followed by Byzantine officials, to whom the three fortresses were ceded. The Greek reconquest of the Morea had begun.

I cannot speak of the lost castle of Maina; but Monemvasia and Mistra remain my most loved places in Greece. It was at Monemvasia that I first set foot in Greece. My parents had borrowed my grandfather's yacht, a three-masted schooner called *Sunbeam*, famous in the 1870s as having been the first yacht to circumnavigate the world, under its first owner, Lord Brassey. We had set out from Naples in March 1924, on our way to Istanbul, and had spent two nights storm-bound at Catania in Sicily. I had not regretted that delay, as it enabled me to have my first experience of a provincial Italian opera-house – we saw a spirited performance of Puccini's *La Fanciulla del West*. Travelling with us was Sir Rennell Rodd, later Lord Rennell of Rodd, and his wife. He had recently retired from the post of British Ambassador in Rome. Many years previously he had been *en poste* in Greece and had fallen in love with the Peloponnese and its medieval monuments, and in 1907 he had published a book in two volumes called *The Princes of Achaea* and *The Chronicle of Morea*, the first work in English to be devoted to the story of the Frankish occupation. But, widely though he had travelled through the Morea, he had never been to Monemvasia; and now, to my delight, he prevailed upon my father that we should make a landing there.

On a perfect day in early April we sailed past Cape Matapan and round Cape Malea into the anchorage below the rock of Monemvasia. Its bulk, a thousand feet in height, rose out of the sea, joined only by a narrow causeway to the mainland. Its name in Greek means 'one entrance'. To the Franks, with their inability to twist their tongues round local wording, it became Malvoisie, which the English translated as Malmsey; and in the later Middle Ages it was above all known for the rich wines of the Morea which were exported from its harbour. Indeed, the barrel in which the Duke of Clarence met so sad an end must have passed through the bay in which we now were anchored. From the sea it was all beautiful; but when we landed we came into a melancholy town. It sprawled along the southern side of the rock, between a steep precipice and the sea. Walls still protected it at the eastern and western ends, and there was a long wall along the shore. To the north it backed on to the precipice. The entry was through a vaulted passage beneath a great bastion. But inside the walls, apart from a few churches in ill repair, the narrow streets were lined with deserted houses, some of which had been handsome in their day. More and more, we were told, the population was moving across to a new settlement on the mainland, where modern amenities such as drainage and electric light were promised. The churches were locked, and no one seemed to know who kept the keys. I was disappointed as I wished specially to see the icon of Our Lady Chrysaphiotissa, which had flown one day from a church in the village of Chrysapha, near Sparta, to take up residence in Monemvasia. The villagers of Chrysapha suspected theft, and some of them came by night to steal her back again. It was in vain. A few days later she took once more to the air and, it was reliably reported, was seen flying over the mountains to Monemvasia, where a church was built to house her.

It was sad to see decay in such a lovely setting; and it was a relief to climb the path that went zigzag up the side of the precipice to the ruins of the upper town on the summit. There, half-hidden in the scrub, you could see the foundations of churches and mosques, barracks and houses, Byzantine, Venetian and Turkish, carpeted round about by a profusion of spring flowers. One building stood intact, the church of St Sophia, built on the edge of the northern cliff at the end of the thirteenth century on the orders of the pious Emperor Andronicus II. It was in good repair, though the frescoes in the interior were fragmentary and fading. It stood solid and dignified among the desolation.

We sailed on that evening to Syra, then Myconos (one of my less favourite Ms, as already it had been discovered by tourists), and on to Mitylini, which was worthier of its initial letter. We had no time to explore the island, but I loved the town with its lively harbour and its grim Genoese castle. I still, however, feel indignant over an episode there. I was painting a water-colour sketch of the town and thought that it was, at least for me, who am a poor artist, a promising work. But Lady Rodd, who was painting in oils close by, snatched it from me and improved it with several strokes of her oily brush. It was a long time before I forgave her. It helped to remember that when she was an ambassadress she was universally known as Lady Rude. She was indeed given to curious habits. When some years later, in 1932, I stayed with the Rodds in their handsome house at Posilipo, on the Bay of Naples, I found that during the season when the house was full of guests, the domestic staff received no pay but lived on the tips that the visitors were expected to leave for them. The service was in consequence impeccable, indeed, too much so. If you left your shirt in your room to go for a swim, when you returned it had vanished, to be given back to you next morning, beautifully washed and with a laundry bill, which Lady Rodd vetted before she collected the cash from you. She mellowed in later years; and I ended up very fond of her.

Fifty-eight years passed before I came again to Monemvasia. I kept away from Greece from 1967 to 1974, during the rule of the Colonels, not wishing to see a country that I loved so cruelly misruled. Soon after they fell, I went to Athens. Mr Karamanlis, the provisional Prime Minister, kindly found time to see me. In the course of our talk he asked me when I had first come to Greece. I said that I had been to Monemvasia in 1924. He then told me that the town was being re-habilitated and that I ought to be given a house there. Indeed, a young architect, Alexander Kalligas, and his archaeologist wife, both trained in London, were determined to bring the town back to life. It had by now been almost entirely abandoned in favour of the growing, prosperous village on the mainland. They bought what houses they could afford and set about tactfully restoring them and providing them with basic modern comforts. The government of the province of Laconia soon began to take an interest in the work and to organize the restoration of more houses, all with unpretentious care; and Alexander Kalligas has been able to keep an eye over it all. The town has been given new life; and it is now a delight to visit it. It is true that most of the houses are now occupied as holiday homes, by owners coming from all parts of Europe, but all of them happy to lead quiet lives in a historic setting, and eager to attend the symposia organized every summer by the Kalligases. And enough of the native population are living there, running shops and tavernas, to keep the town from seeming to be an artificial creation.

The houses seem mostly to date from the Venetian occupation of the town, in the early sixteenth and late seventeenth centuries. Some date from Turkish times; and a few seem to be Byzantine. When I stayed there in 1982 I was housed in what remains of the building in which the Emperors lived on their visits to the town. I have twice been back there, always in summer. It must be windy and bleak in wintertime. Yet, were I prepared to lead an expatriate life, I would be happy to instal myself in a little old house in Monemvasia.

But I would perhaps be happier to make my home in the village that lies below the ruined city of Mistra, the Byzantine capital of the Morea. I was there first in 1928. In those days there was a remarkable travel-agent living in Athens called Mr Ghiolman. He had his tentacles all over Greece. You told him where you wished to go and everything was arranged for you. I had made use of his services for a visit to Delphi. I took a train from Athens to Livadia. At the station a muleteer awaited me with his beast; and we set out to walk over the gap between the mountains of Helicon and Parnassus to the splendid monastery of Holy Luke, on its lonely hillside. It has been too often described for me to need to do so here. To me its unique charm is that in the greater of its two churches you can join in the Orthodox liturgy in a setting of coloured marble and gleaming mosaics, unchanged since Byzantine days. So many of the churches where mosaics survive are now cold monuments, closed at nightfall. There is nowhere else, except in the church of St Sophia in Thessaloniki, where you can see mosaics at their best, in the light of lamps and candles; and the mosaics of Holy Luke are among the most majestic in the world. In those days visitors of both sexes were allowed to spend the night in the monastery. When I was there on this visit among my fellow-guests was an American lady who, when we sat down to a simple evening meal and were offered wine by the guest-master, sternly refused to let him fill her glass. She disapproved of alcohol, she said. He was puzzled and hurt. Was there something nasty about the wine, he asked? I begged her to take a little and then fill the glass with water, till the alcoholic content was minimal. But no alcohol would ever pass her lips, she said. It cast a gloom over the whole evening. Next day my muleteer and I tramped along a mountain path to Delphi, while on the other side of the valley engineers were building a road to link Delphi with Athens. Perhaps it was necessary. But nowadays when, even in the off-season, you see some thirty tourist-buses lining the narrow main street of the town, you wish that it had never been made. Delphi had few visitors then. You could sit in the ruins in unbroken quiet. From Delphi I took a bus down to the port of Itea, and so by boat back to Athens.

Mr Ghiolman organized my journey to Meteora a few days later, and after that my journey into the Morea. I took the train from Athens to Tripolis, in Arcadia. It was a leisurely journey through lovely country. Nowadays we travel swiftly by car. A well constructed road takes us over the great pass that leads from the Argolid to Arcadia. The railway climbs slowly up the hill, giving us time to see the views from a new angle at every bend. Many years have passed since I last went on the railway that crosses the Morea to Kalamata (and on that last journey I was suffering from food-poisoning) but some day I hope to wind slowly through those hills again. In 1928 after leaving the train at Tripolis I found a decrepit bus that carried me on to Sparta, happily stopping for a moment when we crossed over the last pass and saw the green vale of the Eurotas spread before us, backed by the snow-covered peaks of Taygetus. I stayed for three days in Sparta, walking each day the four miles to the modern village of Mistra and a mile on to the entrance-gate of the old city.

This is not a history-book or a guide-book. I have written elsewhere of the story of Mistra and its buildings. In 1928 very few tourists came there. I had the ruins almost to myself, except for an old goatherd who took his flock through the ruined streets each afternoon, and except, too, for the nuns in the monastery attached to the church of Our Lady Pantanassa. There were several of them then, kindly old ladies who welcomed me each morning with a glass of ouzo and a spoonful of jam. They asked me questions about England and about Queen Victoria, whom they seemed to think was still alive; and I answered them as best I could in my halting Greek. Very little had been done as yet to put the churches and their frescoes into good condition. I was torn between my pleasure in seeing ruins that had been left unspoilt and unimproved and my awareness that much needed to be done if the monuments were to survive.

After my three days in Sparta a muleteer, provided by Mr Ghiolman, appeared, to take me over the Taygetus range through the Langhada Pass to Kalamata. The road that now crosses the pass was not yet reconstructed; and we would now and then leave the existing road to take short cuts along the precipitous paths. It was a wild day, with clouds swirling round us and occasional showers. I remember it as an arduous experience. We spent the night in a village near the summit. I was given a bed in a peasant house. It was horribly cold, and I was footsore and weary. The journey next day was easier, though walking down a steep slope is almost as exhausting as climbing up it. The sun began to shine. The hills were bright with wild flowers. Suddenly, as we emerged from a narrow defile, the view opened out; and there was Kalamata in the plain far below. I was glad to reach the town and to take the train next morning back to Athens. That long walk now is rather like a dream to me. I did not cross the pass again till the autumn of 1977, when I took a bus from Kalamata to Sparta. Everything looks different when you travel in the opposite direction. I recognized very little of the scenery, and I entirely failed to identify the village in which I had spent the night. Foolishly I had neglected to note down its name at the time.

I was next in Mistra for the inside of a day in 1947. I was working in Athens at the time and with two colleagues spent the Orthodox Easter holiday in driving round the Morea. Civil war was breaking out at the time in northern Greece, where the Communists had Yugoslav backing, and there were rumours of Communist brigands in the Morea. We ignored them. But, after attending the midnight service in Tripolis we drove on hoping to have our Easter lunch in the small town of Dimitsana, but as we approached it, through a pine forest, we came upon a bus standing by the roadside, empty and with bloodstains on the seats. They told us in the town that it had been waylaid by brigands and the soldiers in it, on their way to spend Easter with their families, had been shot as they sat there. The town was in mourning, and we had to push on. We went to Andritsaena, and from there walked to Bassae, to which there was not yet any road, and to Karitsaena, the most romantic of all the towns of the Morea; and then we spent a day in Mistra. There was no one else there, except for a shepherd–boy who eagerly supplied us with a mass of misinformation about the ruins. During the War and the German occupation it had been impossible to do any restoration work. But since those dark days the buildings and frescoes in the old town have been given new life. We must all be grateful for the careful and sensitive treatment that they have received.

In September 1976 the Fifteenth International Congress of Byzantine Studies took place in Athens. Earlier in the year I received a message telling me to arrange to come to Greece a few days before the opening of the Congress in order to attend a ceremony at Mistra. Soon I heard a rumour that they were planning to call a street after me in the little modern town below the ruins. When I had been in Athens, in charge of the British Council organization in Greece for two years after the War, one of my happier duties had been to allot scholarships to Britain to young Greeks of promise. It was not difficult to find worthy candidates from amongst the generation that had grown up during the years when Greece had been isolated from the outside world. Most of them justified their scholarships and came to play a part in Greek public life. One of them was by now Deputy for Sparta. I was told that it was he who thought that it would be pleasant to show gratitude for those scholarships of long ago by giving my name to a street in some town of which I was fond. As Mistra lay in his constituency it seemed to him to be a suitable location. What the people of Mistra thought, I never discovered. It is to be doubted if any of them had ever heard of me. But they were amenable. The idea also won the more effective approval of my old friend Constantine Trypanis, the eminent authority on Greek literary history, who was then Minister of Culture in Athens. It was he who sent me an official invitation to come for the ceremony.

Early in the morning of 2 September 1976 we set out from Athens in a procession of three cars. I travelled in the Ministerial car with the Minister. In the second car were Madame Trypanis and Professor Dimitri Obolensky from Oxford, and in the third the Director of Antiquities with Stavros Papastavrou, the lecturer in Medieval and Modern Greek at Cambridge. We paused for an early lunch at Tripolis. When we reached the province of Laconia we found a police car, with flashing lights, which pushed the tourist buses to the side of the road to let us pass. I liked that. On the outskirts of Sparta the governor of the province was waiting, and I was transferred into his car. We were allowed a few moments at the hotel in Sparta to tidy ourselves before going on to Mistra.

There, in the main square, Palaeologos Square, the whole population of the little town seemed to be gathered. There was a small street that ran off it to the west, and on the wall of the building at the corner, facing the street, a Greek flag was draped over something, and on the wall facing the square there was a Union Jack. As I stepped from the car a buxom blonde lady came up and presented me with a bouquet of pink roses, in the name of the women of Sparta – an undeserved tribute, as I had never done anything for them. Remembering how royalty behave on such occasions, I handed it to Madame Trypanis to carry for me. Then the local schoolmaster, who was Mayor of the town, delivered a speech of welcome in such careful *katharevousa* Greek that I barely understood it. He was followed by the Minister who, at the end of his simpler speech, pulled a string, and the two flags came down, revealing a plaque giving the name of the street in Greek letters, where the Greek flag had been, and in English, where the Union Jack had been. I then gave a short address in Greek, which had been vetted for me, and almost entirely rewritten, by Stavros Papastavrou. Afterwards we walked with the local notables down to the local hotel – I marched between the General of the district and the Bishop – and were refreshed with sticky cakes and lemonade.

We went back to the hotel in Sparta to rest, but soon had to start out again for a banquet in the inn by the gate of the old city. I had been suffering from influenza just before setting out to Greece and had not wholly recovered. That evening my temperature rose again. By the time that we arrived at the banquet I was feeling barely conscious. But, just as slight intoxication or great rage releases inhibitions, so does a fever. I found myself chattering amd making jokes in Greek in a way I usually can only manage after spending a week or so in Greece. But I was glad to be able to retire to bed.

The Minister and his wife returned to Athens early next morning. My friends from Britain and I stayed on at Mistra till the afternoon. But, while they went round the old churches I sat fevered in the car. Back in Athens that evening I was due to dine and stay the night with Greek friends. But when I arrived at their house I retired at once to bed. Fortunately one of their dinner-guests was an eminent doctor. He gave me some drug. I do not know what it was, but it enabled me to attend without collapsing the long-drawn out opening of the Byzantine Congress next day.

The Mayor of Mistra had given me a document proclaiming me to be an honorary citizen of the town. I did not know how to show my grateful appreciation, except by writing a book about Mistra and dedicating it to him and his townspeople. I went back to Mistra the following year, to refresh my memory of the buildings. I had been with the then British Ambassador to Greece and Lady Richards to the ceremonies which every year celebrate the Battle of Navarino. They dropped me off at Kalamata on their way back to Athens, and then it was that I took a bus over the Langhada Pass. I did not want to bother my friends in Mistra; so I stayed in Sparta and took a taxi to the gate of the old city, in which I could wander unobserved. On my way back I walked back into the town square, timing it so that I could catch the bus without waiting. But the bus was late; and while I stood about an old man recognized me. He sat me down in a café and summoned a number of friends; and I was kept there while the bus went off to Sparta without me.

The last time that I came to Mistra was in the spring of 1986. I could not then try to be anonymous, as I was with a film-crew which was foolishly doing a documentary about me. We had already been to Istanbul and to Monemvasia. Mistra by then had been beautifully tidied up. Goatherds no longer wandered through the ruins, to the great advantage of the wild flowers on which the goats used to graze. That spring, after a wet winter, the profusion of flowers was almost unreal. The weather was flawless. Had it not been for the tedium of having to enter each church with a bright impromptu remark some six or seven times over till the camera men and the sound men were satisfied, I would have loved it all. The townsfolk welcomed me kindly. The Youth Club, all eight members of it, gave me a dinner for which their mothers cooked delicious dishes. The nuns in the Pantanassa Convent allowed a liturgy to be sung in their church in my honour. They would not be present themselves, as they followed the Old Calendar and regarded the actual hierarchy as being sadly heretical. They only attended services there when an aged priest of their persuasion tottered up the hill to minister to them. But they were tolerant of heretics and entertained us kindly after the liturgy.

I left Mistra impressed more than ever by its beauty and its atmosphere, and happy to see how well the work of conservation was maintained, though a little alarmed by grandiose plans to restore the Palace of the Despots.

On my way from Monemvasia to Mistra I had been able to visit Yeraki, the town whose name means 'falcon', with its great ruined Frankish castle and its many churches scattered in the neighbouring fields and up the citadel hill, none of them of any great aesthetic importance but all with a simple charm. The same applies to the churches at the village of Chrysapha, which I had seen on an earlier occasion, though one of them contains a fine seventeenth-century icon sent by the Monemvasiots in recompense for the icon that insisted on flying to Monemvasia.

There are other sites beginning with M in the Morea that are well worth a visit. There is Methone, the Venetian Modon, with its great fortress, the finest work of Venetian architecture in the peninsula. There is the monastery of Megaspilaeon, the 'Great Cave', built over the mouth of the cave under an over-hanging precipice, in the mountains inland from the Gulf of Corinth. I spent my birthday in 1934 in a little inn nearby. The other guest in the inn was an able young American scholar, Alison Frantz. She had obtained permission to catalogue the treasures of the monastery. The monastery building lacked distinction, apart from its sensational situation; but its treasures were many. The following day, having finished her task, she travelled back with me to Athens. A little train took us down from the mountains to the coast, where we caught the Athens train. As we left she remarked that she wondered if anyone else would ever see what she had seen. When we arrived in Athens the evening papers were full of the news that the great monastery of Megaspilaeon had been destroyed by fire. So I have always accused her of having set a match to it just before we left. In truth she may have been indirectly responsible, as her catalogue would have probably revealed that many treasures that had appeared in earlier catalogues had disappeared. To avoid the accusation of having illegally disposed of monastery possessions, it was better to burn the whole lot. One could then safely say that Miss Frantz had overlooked several items. Its greatest treasure, a wax icon attributed to St Luke, was saved, as well as relics connected with the monastery's foundress, St Euphrosyne. The monastery has now been rebuilt and is of remarkable ugliness. But the view from the windows of its great gallery is superb.

One of the most charming buildings in the Morea is the church of the Virgin at Merbaka, in the Argolid plain, twelfth-century in date, and remarkable for the decorative brickwork and faience of its exterior walls. Inside, its frescoes are all faded. Close by is a charming small church of the same date, dedicated to the Zoodochos Pigi, the Fountain of Life; and nearby is the spring, known to the ancients as Canathus, in which the goddess Hera used to bathe every year to recover her virginity. I have never been able to persuade any of my lady friends to see if the magic still works.

Then there is the Mani. Patrick Leigh Fermor has written so well about it that I need not attempt to describe it. The true Mani, the lower part of the promontory that ends at Cape Matapan, though it has a stark beauty, is too bleak and harsh to be lovable. I have driven through it twice, fascinated by its strange tower-houses, but glad always to escape to a less cruel countryside. Patrick, as an honorary Maniot, is right to admire it; but he lives himself on its very edge, in a lush and welcoming countryside; and in his house you receive a welcome that his Maniot chieftains would never have given you.

There are other Ms in Greece that I have forgotten to mention, Metsovo, for instance, at the top of the pass that leads from Epirus into Thessaly, a small town whose charm is unspoiled through the care of its great local family, the Averoffs. There is Marathon, which still has the power to move me, even though irritation at the uncritical enthusiasm of English public-school masters for Classical Greece sometimes makes me wish that the Persians had won the battle. There is Missolonghi, haunted still by Lord Byron, and by Dr van Millingen, the medical youth who did not know how to treat him, and whose son lived to be one of the most distinguished of Byzantine scholars. I should perhaps include Melos; but it has never seemed to me to be among the most endearing of the Greek islands – and I have never thought that the Venus de Milo added to the beauty of the Louvre. I cannot think why the French did not hand it back to Madame Mercouri when she was Greek

Minister of Culture – an M for whom, though a person and not a place, I have a true respect.

Despite all the competition it is the Morea that keeps my affection, and in the Morea Monemvasia and, still more, Mistra. I hope that I shall see them again.

N Nevada

I AM NOT BY NATURE a gambler. It is certainly pleasant to receive unexpected dollops of money; but a Calvinist family background leaves a recipient with a feeling of guilt. Riches should come as the reward for hard work, preferably one's forebears'. Some people seem to enjoy the thrill, or at least the risk, of losing everything. But that involves a streak of masochism which I do not possess. Yet when I have been in California the temptation to cross the border to visit the gambling hells of Nevada has always been hard to resist. My plans to go to Las Vegas were twice thwarted. Maybe my ever watchful guardian angel disapproved. On the first occasion when I was about to fix up the journey there, I was summoned home by a glamorous engagement in London. It was, I think, Princess Alexandra's wedding. On the second occasion it was a sudden engagement with a different sort of glamour that made me change my programme.

In the autumn of 1965 I was in Australia, lecturing for the British Council, and planned to come home through the United States. I had lectures to give there in Los Angeles and in Dallas; and I wanted to go to Philadelphia to attend the autumn meeting of the American Philosophical Society, the 'Society for the Promotion of Useful Knowledge', founded by Benjamin Franklin and now the oldest Learned Society in the world after the Royal Society; and I had arranged dates so as to have a Friday and Saturday free, on my way from Los Angeles to Dallas, intending to spend those days in Las Vegas. But when I was in Canberra I went to dinner with the British High Commissioner and there met the American Ambassador. He had been Mrs Ladybird Johnson's attorney in Texas and had earned a reward; but, as he was not highly polished in manner, it was thought that in Australia any uncouthness would be forgiven, in view of his unfailing bonhomie. It is true that he had somewhat startled Canberra society when, as he went to present his credentials to the Governor-General and was marching up between the Guard of Honour, temptation overtook him as he passed the drummer. He snatched the drum-sticks from the youth's hands and beat a tattoo himself before proceeding. Then, after the ceremony, his euphoria was such that he shouted to everyone in Government House, guards, typists and footmen and all, to come and join him at a party at the Embassy. The Governor-General and his wife found themselves left in solitude.

By the time that I met him he had quietened a little, and he was very popular. He was a conscientious ambassador who did his homework about anyone whom he was going to meet, even about me. He asked me about my movements; and I told him that I was going on to California and Texas. Where in Texas? he asked. I told him that I was to lecture at Southern Methodist University in Dallas. What! he exclaimed indignantly, was I going to Texas and not to Austin, to the University of Texas. It was his university, and it was Mrs Johnson's university; and, why, Miss Linda Bird Johnson was there at the moment. Now what was that subject in which I was interested which began with a B? Byzantium? I ventured. Yes, that was it. Miss Linda Bird was studying Byzantium. I must go to Austin and lecture to her.

Next morning the British High Commission telephoned me to say that the American Ambassador was demanding to know on what day I would go to Austin. The only day that I could manage was the Friday which I intended to reserve for Las Vegas. I offered that, hopefully remembering that American universities are apt to be deserted by Friday evenings, everyone having left for the week-end. What I did not know was that the University of Texas football team was due to play a major match at Austin that afternoon, and all the loyal University folk would therefore be staying there. A few hours later I had a call from the American Embassy, informing me that I would shortly be receiving a cable from the University of Texas, inviting me to give a lecture there on that Friday afternoon, and I must accept it, as the Ambassador had been in touch with the White House about it. So there was no escape.

However, on that Friday morning, when I left Frank Lysinger's house in Los Angeles to take the plane to Dallas, where I had to change into another for Austin, I did not allow enough time to reach the airport and we were held up by traffic on the freeway. So I missed the plane. But when I telephoned ashamedly to Austin they took my delinquency very lightly. People were always missing planes, they said, and anyhow the weather was so bad in Texas that it was doubtful if any planes would be able to land there. I should take the next plane; and they would put off the lecture till after the dinner. They were right about the weather. I learnt later that I was lucky to have missed the first plane, as it went flying on into Arkansas, and I would never have reached Austin that evening. The plane that I caught managed to land, rather late, at Dallas; but I had to wait there till a plane could be found brave enough to fly on to Austin. Eventually, after having telephoned to say that I would have to miss the dinner, I arrived at Austin airport at 8.10 p.m. and was rushed, unwashed and unkempt, to the lecture-hall.

Sitting modestly in the third row was a good-looking young lady and behind her two huge thugs. I noticed, to my gratification, that as I was ending my lecture on the Fall of Constantinople she was wiping away some tears. After the lecture she came up to me, followed by the thugs, on whom she saw my eyes falling. 'Yes, I know', she said, 'my detectives – the best educated detectives in the United States, as they have to come to all my lectures.' She added that they just loved Byzantine history. It was so full of assassinations, it seemed like homework. Later, she told me that the family surname was Johnstone and that they came from Annandale in Scotland; but the Texans had preferred to simplify the name. A few months later I moved myself to a tower-house in Annandale that had been a Johnstone residence and was reputedly haunted by a Mrs Johnstone. Miss Linda Bird came to hear of this, and when she was visiting London the following autumn she wanted to come and see the house. I could not have coped with such an invasion. Her two detectives would have had to accompany her, with Mrs Bruce, the American Ambassadress, as chaperone; and as I was engaged in turning the half-ruined tower into my library, and furniture and books were stacked in the rest of the house, there was not room for them all. Fortunately, Miss Johnson's fiancé decided to join her in Europe and wanted to visit Paris, France.

All this seems far removed from the gambling halls of Las Vegas. Curiously, my next attempt to cross into Nevada was also thwarted by a visit to Texas. The academic term that I spent in Los Angeles in 1971 offered a new opportunity, as I had my week-ends free. I set aside a week-end in March, only to receive an invitation to revisit Austin then, this time as guest of honour at the annual dinner of the Texas Literary Society. It was a strange week-end. I arrived on the Friday afternoon in Austin, and dined with a small group of Texan writers. On the Saturday, a beautiful spring morning, we drove out to the site of the Massacre at Alamo, and in the afternoon were entertained to tea and a discourse by the widow of a distinguished Texan historian, who told us what it was like to travel with a touchy man of letters in Mexico. We then gathered for the dinner, given in the Sheraton Hotel. It was a festive occasion, with alcohol flowing lavishly. By the time that I had to give my address it clearly did not matter what I said. A few simple jokes sufficed. Then the President of the Society handed out prizes, in the form of cheques, for the best books, the best novel, the best book of poems, the best history-book and the best travel-book written by a Texan during the past year. He by then was in such a state of euphoric insouciance that he dropped every single cheque, which I then had to retrieve and hand to the recipient. But, apart from one or two noisy young couples, everyone was so good-humoured and happy that there was no embarrassment.

At last, that April, I was free to go to Las Vegas. Frank Lysinger came with me. We flew from Los Angeles on the Friday afternoon and returned on the Sunday evening. I was fascinated by the splendid vulgarity of the place, with its vast hotels and casinos, and practically every other building either a marriage parlour or a divorce office, all set in a bleak plain, but with grand mountains rising in the distance. We saw it thoroughly. We dined in Caesar's Palace, on Cleopatra's Barge, which is a platform that sways slightly, to give the illusion that one is on water. But I had come to gamble, and I decided to keep to the slot-machines. We started at the airport, where the machines are supposed to be fixed in your favour, to encourage you to go further when you arrive in the town. After one or two tries, which left me even, I waited till we were in one of the great casinos. Next afternoon I settled down in earnest. After a few shots I hit the jackpot; and a gratifying torrent of coins poured out of the machine. A young woman with a basket hurried out to collect them all, and after carefully counting them handed me a handsome wad of dollars. I then tried again with another machine. On my very first shot I hit the jackpot again. This time I thought that the stream of quarters would never stop. The floor of the casino was covered with them. It needed an army of young women to retrieve them; and I had to wait a long time before they were all counted. In the end I received a sum that not only paid for all our expenses in Las Vegas, including our air-fares from Los Angeles, but also left a tidy sum to spare. After that I did not try my luck again.

Next spring I was again in Los Angeles; and Frank and I decided to visit that other centre of vice in Nevada, Reno. We went by car, along a road that skirted the eastern side of the great Sierra. It was a lovely drive; but Reno itself was something of a disappointment. It seemed as vulgar as Las Vegas, and equally full of establishments where marriage or divorce could be quickly obtained, but all on a less grandiose scale. I made for a casino and started on the slot-machines, but I got nowhere with them. So I moved to a roulette table. There, by keeping faithfully to the number 37, I soon collected enough money to pay for all our expenses. So, next day when we drove down through the great mountains and forests back into California, to Sacramento and then on into the wine-country of the Napa Valley, I could feel that our excursion had been worthwhile. I have reason to be grateful to Nevada. But I have never gone gambling again.

 *Orta*

THE LAKE OF ORTA lacks the grandeur of the great Italian lakes, Maggiore, Como and Garda. The Creator designed it on a smaller scale. The hills that surround it are steep but not austere. Vineyards cover many of the slopes. The villages on its shores are simple, not yet overrun by the international tourist world. The town of Orta itself may by now be ruined by visitors, but in the 1960s it was still a quiet resort, a bit crowded in summer but mostly by respectable Italians. In the lake there is an island, the Isola San Giulio, dedicated to an amiable saint, Julius of Novara, who spent his life, under the aegis of the Emperor Theodosius the Great, turning pagan temples into Christian shrines. Here on this island was his favourite shrine, where he lies, mummified and benevolent, to this day. I too have a special affection for the island, as it was the base from which I came to know Lombardy.

When I was in Istanbul in 1937 I made close friends with the Netherlands *chargé d'affaires* in Turkey, and his wife, the Baron and Baroness van Harinxma thoe Slooten. The Dutch are a thrifty race and, where they could do so without great loss of prestige, they liked not to have to appoint fully paid ministers to their legations. The Baron was a Frisian and, like all Frisians, a bit stern and severe, but hospitable and kindly. The Baroness was half-English. Her father was a genial Dutch financier, her mother a lady known in the 1890s as Newmarket Nell, though when I knew her in her old age no one could have been more respectable. So I never knew what the sobriquet signified. I used to love to visit the Netherlands Legation in Pera, where the Harinxmas spent the summer. It was a charming early nineteenth-century building, the work of the Fossati brothers, who were better known for having temporarily uncovered and rather carelessly repaired the mosaics in St Sophia. In 1938 the Baron was appointed Netherlands Ambassador in Brussels. My brother and I spent a night at the Embassy there when we were flying back in his aeroplane from Prague, where my father had been on a fruitless diplomatic mission, the subject of much subsequent criticism, not all of it well-informed.

The Harinxmas escaped from Brussels before the Germans took over Belgium in 1940. They were back there after the War was over; and after my return to live in London in 1947 I used often to go to stay with them. Life in London was grim at the time, as the Labour government believed that unnecessary austerity was good for us all. It was a delight to be able to escape to the more cheerful atmosphere of Belgium. I had another, more reputable, reason for liking to visit Brussels, as the Université Libre there contained the liveliest department of Byzantine studies in Europe. It was headed by an eccentric professor, Henri Grégoire, a man of immense vitality and learning, some of whose ideas trembled on the edge of fantasy. He was always very good to me; and it was wonderfully stimulating to see him and his pupils. Brussels also contained the headquarters of the Société des Bollandistes, a branch of the Jesuits, founded in the early seventeenth century to scrutinize the authenticity of the saints of the Church and to publish scholarly editions of their lives. It was then under the authority of Père Peeters, who became a good friend of mine. He was undoubtedly a holy and pious man, but he took a great delight in showing how bogus were most of the saints of the Church. Once when he was telling me how he planned to demolish many of our favourite saints I asked him if he was going soon to prove that St Peter had never existed. 'I almost think that I could', he replied with relish. He and Professor Grégoire, who was strongly anti-clerical, enjoyed each other's company. I once sat between the two of them at a lecture in Brussels, given by a professor from the Vatican who claimed that the tomb of St Peter himself had been discovered in excavations beneath St Peter's. Père Peeters kept leaning across me with a series of devastating questions that he told Grégoire to ask. I suggested that he might ask them himself. No, he replied, they would come more suitably from a free-thinker.

Those were happy days in Brussels. But in 1954 the time came for the Baron to retire from his embassy there. He went off to live in his grim and chilly castle in Friesland. But first he insisted that he and the Baroness should have a legal separation. Though she had no intention of spending the rest of her days in Friesland she was none the less somewhat hurt. But he pointed out that they could not afford to have their incomes, both fairly considerable, taxed jointly. It was true; so she fell in with his wishes. She had inherited an elegant eighteenth-century villa in the Netherlands, near Arnhem. But she had a weakness for collecting houses. She had already been to Italy and had visited Orta. On the Isola San Giulio she had found a miniature palazzo for sale, and hastily bought it.

I went to spend twelve days with her there in August 1952. It was a charming house, built on the edge of the lake, which in those days was unpolluted. One bathed very happily from the garden steps. We spent a day in Milan, seeing churches and pictures; but most of our time seems to have been spent driving along the shores of Lake Maggiore, to Stresa, to Pallanza and over the Swiss frontier to Locarno, and across to the islands, the Isola dei Pescatori and the Isola Bella, with the Borromeo Palace. At Pallanza we used to be entertained by an eccentric millionaire of

Australian origin called Neil MacEachern, the widower of a high-born German princess, at the Villa Taranto, an imposing building round which he had created an imposing garden. Neither house nor garden showed much taste. The latter, which he bequeathed to the Italian state, was wonderfully maintained and contained a number of rare plants; but it had the air of a municipal park. He was very hospitable; and it is ungrateful of me to record that, after all these years, I remember the food as being pretentious and almost inedible. His house-guests, who were a remarkable mixture of the raffish and the highly respectable, had, I was told, to obey very strict rules of behaviour. But they seem to have returned year after year. So life there cannot have been too uncomfortable.

I much preferred the neighbouring Villa San Remigio, for the Villa Taranto, remarkably for a district where splendid views abounded, was built in a hollow from which one could not even see the lake. The Villa San Remigio had the lake spread out below it. It was a handsome old house with no pretensions to comfort. The garden was lacking in flower-beds but full of old trees and statuary. It had belonged to a Marchese di Casanova and his Irish wife. During the First World War my father, who was then President of the Board of Trade, had gone with my mother to Italy to confer with his Italian counterpart; and the conference had taken place in Pallanza at the Villa San Remigio. So I had known of it since my school-days. I was not disappointed, though it had inevitably suffered from the passage of the years. The Casanovas had died long since and it now belonged to their daughter, Contessa Bonacossa. To maintain it in its proper glory was possible now only for the very rich. She was sadly preparing to sell it. I was glad to have seen it before it went.

I next came to Orta in early September 1955, after having spent an exhausting week of sight-seeing in Bavaria. I was hoping for several days of quiet in the sun. But the Baroness had decided, for financial reasons, to become a Swiss resident and was building a chalet at Bluche, high in the mountains overlooking the upper valley of the Rhône. After two days she insisted on me coming with her there, to see how the chalet was progressing. We drove in brilliant sunshine over the Simplon Pass picnicking on the summit, down into the Rhône valley, pausing to see the pleasant old town of Sierre, then climbed up the mountainside to Bluche, spending two nights there in a simple hotel. The chalet was splendidly placed, with an unbroken view across to the great mountains on the Swiss-Italian border. It was already half-built and was clearly going to be an agreeable residence; but I never saw it again. It remained the Baroness's chief residence for the rest of her long life. Besides the palazzino at Orta and the villa near Arnhem, which I visited on several occasions, she had for a time a mews flat in London and then an apartment in Brussels; and I never thought that the chalet was her favourite house. It was salubrious; it had this wonderful view; it was enjoyed by her daughters and their children, especially in winter, with ski-ing slopes close at hand; for financial reasons she had to live in Switzerland. But living there is never easy, with domestic help hard to obtain and with innumerable regulations imposed by a paternalist government; though the same difficulties were present in the Netherlands as well. She often urged me to visit her there. But, much as I admire the magnificence of Swiss mountain scenery, I have never wanted to stay long in its midst. I prefer the parts of Switzerland that are less sensationally situated, such as Neuchâtel or St Gallen, or even Berne. It was a relief on this occasion to drive back over the Simplon into Italy.

On my last morning in Italy that year, before I took the afternoon aeroplane to London, we drove to the little village of Castelseprio, where in a small church there are some of the finest of all medieval frescoes. They were only discovered in 1944; and since then art-historians have puzzled and quarrelled over them. To judge from what remains of the inscriptions, they were painted by a Greek; and the general opinion seems to be that they date from about the year AD 700. Too little remains of the Constantinopolitan art of the period. The somewhat Classical style is quite unlike anything to be found in Western Europe in those centuries. What the artist was doing painting masterpieces in a building that must always have been a bit ramshackle, in a village that was never of the slightest importance, remains a mystery. But the frescoes themselves are outstanding, even in a country that is rich in great works of art.

My last visit to Orta was in August 1958. Once again I had been in Bavaria. I took a train from Munich, via Innsbruck and the Brenner Pass to Milan, where I spent the night. After spending the following morning in the Brera Gallery I went on by train to Urbania, the station for Pallanza, where the Baroness met me. My recollections of the following days is that the weather was appallingly hot. We had no energy for any excursions. Orta was beginning to lose its charm. Many more tourists invaded the island every day, ruining its quiet. The lake was beginning to show signs of pollution; I no longer wanted to bathe in it. The palazzino kept its charm and my fellow-guests, a tough but civilized German sportsman and another Dutch baroness, were pleasant and easy. But I was quite glad to leave the heat of Lombardy for the coast. Friends of mine had taken a house at Sori, near Genoa. It was far fresher there, though the sea was so full of bathers from all over Europe that I had no great wish to join them. Instead, I spent most days going in to Genoa and wandering round the palaces and galleries of the city.

Genoa seems never to have attracted the glamour that surrounds the other great historic centres of Italy, perhaps because it is still a bustling port and the old town climbs up the hill with little room for gardens. But it is full of splendid buildings and alluring alley-ways; and for anyone with a taste for cemeteries a visit to the Campo Santo at Stagliero, up above the city, is something not to be missed. It is unparallelled in the world. I was there first in the spring of 1923, in my grandfather's yacht. My grandfather had been a sailor. He had run away to sea at the age of twelve and had worked his way up from cabin-boy to be a sea-captain and a master mariner before he was twenty-one, eventually retiring in his forties to become a ship-owner. Somewhat inexplicably, British sailors in the nineteenth century all had a romantic admiration for Napoleon, which my grandfather shared. We had, therefore, after joining the yacht at Monaco, to set sail straight for Corsica, to visit the great man's birthplace at Ajaccio. Alas, when we arrived there, Grandpapa was shocked to see how scruffily the shrine was maintained. He insisted that we should leave the delinquent town at once. The glass was falling; and we all longed to see something more of Corsica. When night fell we ran into the most alarming storm that I have ever encountered. It was a great relief to arrive at Genoa. But we were not allowed to visit many of its sights. The eminent ship-owner the first Lord Inchcape was there with his yacht; and we were summoned to spend the day aboard her. Next morning we had to set sail for Elba, where, happily, greater respect had been shown to the Emperor's memory. I passed through Genoa again with my eldest sister, four years later, on our way to Sicily, but with no time to see anything of the city. Nor did we have any time on our return journey, which we made, bravely for those days, by flying-boat from Palermo, coming down into the Tiber near Ostia on the way. So it was not until 1958, thirty-five years after my first visit, that I was able to appreciate the splendours of Genoa.

On my way home from Genoa that year I stopped first in Geneva. While I was working in Athens I had made friends with a young minister of the Church of Scotland, who was chaplain to the Cameronian Regiment, then stationed in Greece. He had now been appointed minister of the Scots Church in Geneva, a church founded by John Knox himself. I spent a week-end with him there. The high Calvinist banking circles of Geneva form one of the most exclusive societies in the world. Strangers are not welcomed into their midst. But it was the smart thing for them, at least at that time, to attend services at the Scots Church, and to show some hospitality towards its minister. So after the service on the Sunday my host and I were invited to have a drink in one of the most formidable of Genevan households. It was all very stiff and formal. We were received in a handsome and uncomfortable drawing-room, where we made polite conversation. It was interesting rather than enjoyable. From the good Calvinist circles of Geneva I went on to the Calvinist Netherlands, but there I was no longer in a Calvinist atmosphere, as I was staying at the Spanish Embassy.

After a few more years the Baroness became disillusioned with life on the Isola San Giulio and sold her house. I never went there again though I continued to see the Baroness from time to time and kept up a lively correspondence with her till her death. But now that chapter has ended.

The Philippines

In the old days before the First World War only the Great Powers exchanged ambassadors. Lesser countries were represented abroad by legations, headed by ministers, and in return were sent ministers by the Powers. Between the Wars the ambassadors' company was enlarged; but the embassies in London were still outnumbered by the legations, and the legations did not carry the same status in the eyes of smart society. Indeed, to frequent foreign legations was generally considered to be a sign of social failure, unless you were one of the many Britishers who had a favourite small country, preferably in the Balkans, at whose functions you were always to be seen. The legations, whose officials were seldom well paid, were content to be left in peace.

After the last War all this began rapidly to change. With the passing of the old colonial empires new sovereign states kept coming into existence, each requiring diplomatic representation; and none of them were content at being labelled second-class. Legations soon disappeared, to be replaced by embassies. Even the Swiss, who feared that they would have to pay their diplomats higher salaries, agreed grudgingly to follow suit. At the same time the British Government was insisting that we should all live strictly rationed lives of austerity; but the foreign missions were free from such restrictions. If you wanted to have an occasional decent meal, you had to have friends in diplomatic circles. It was all a very happy arrangement. Diplomats coming from faraway countries seemed delighted to be invited into British homes, however meagre the entertainment might be that we offered them; and they seemed to be delighted to welcome us back to their embassies. Then, when rationing ceased in Britain, we could receive them more graciously. When I was living in London, in St John's Wood, in a small house with a large garden, I used every year, from 1954 to 1966, to give a garden-party in July, inviting many more guests than my house could possibly have contained. But fortunately it never rained on my chosen day. I used to make the guests come through the house and be announced as they stepped nervously down a steep iron staircase into the garden. It contained a large apple-tree behind which you could hide if someone appeared whom you had no wish to see. It enabled me to invite estranged married couples without any risk of embarrassment.

Occasionally, however, there were embarrassing incidents. At one of my earlier parties the first guest to arrive was the Liberian

Ambassador, a handsome cultured man who was very black. Next to come were two elderly American ladies from the Deep South who took one look at this distinguished gentleman and fled to a far corner of the garden. Hours seemed to pass before any other guest arrived whom I could send to comfort them.

In 1955 there was sent from the Philippines a new ambassador and his wife, with whom I soon made friends. They were much the best-looking diplomatic couple in London; and they were lively and bright, especially interested in the theatre and the arts, and immensely hospitable. They often came to my house, and I went often to their Embassy. It was due to them that I made my first, and for a long time, my only appearance on the television screen. Someone at the B.B.C. had the bright idea of doing a series on 'tea at the foreign embassies in London'; and the Philippine Embassy was picked to open the programme. The Ambassador and Madame Guerrero were to be shown entertaining friends to tea and telling them all about the Philippines. The guests whom they chose to star in the performance were Margot Fonteyn and myself, with Fleur Cowles arriving a little later. With a battery of cameras around us we walked through the Embassy reception-rooms. Then, after politely sipping tea and asking questions about life in the islands, we were treated to a display of Filipino native dancing, given by some elegant young ladies. I never saw the result. Indeed, I wonder if it was even shown. Certainly the series was not continued. The public were not privileged to see tea at any other embassy.

In the spring of 1957 I was going, as I have told elsewhere, to Borneo, by way of the United States. The Philippine Ambassador insisted that I should stop off in his country. There was, he said, a lively Anglo-Philippine Society in Manila; it would arrange lectures for me there and in other parts of the country. It happened that the British Ambassador at Manila at the time was a friend of mine; he wrote to me to support the invitation from the Society and to offer me hospitality for as long as I wished to stay.

I arrived in Manila, coming from California, on 20 February 1957, having missed out 19 February, through crossing the date line the wrong way. The Ambassador, George Clutton, was a rather frail and lonely bachelor who seemed glad to have an old friend staying with him. Certainly the hospitality was unending. He and his staff gave lunches and dinners for me, as did several leading citizens of Manila and the leading British tycoons living there. I had to pay for it by giving lectures. The day after my arrival I had to talk to the Anglo-Philippine Society, a pleasant civilized group of people. Then I had to cope on the following days with the four universities in Manila. The smallest of them, and the one with the highest standards, was the Jesuit University of Santo Tomas. In both the university of the Philippines and the University of the East the staff was very friendly and seemed competent; but I had no chance of estimating the quality of the students. The largest of the universities, the Far Eastern University, had grand buildings and easy habits. I was told that when you entered your son for a place there you were asked if you wished to pay a little extra to have someone answer his examination-papers for him. My evening there was a gala occasion. I arrived in the late afternoon with the Ambassador, who then had to inspect a guard of honour drawn from the University's O.T.C., youths in a picturesque uniform who looked endearingly like toy soldiers. Then, as darkness fell, we moved to a platform at the end of a huge campus, with a tent draped over it. In the front row were city notables and behind them the University staff; and before us were the students, all ten thousand of them, who had been ordered to attend the function. A sea of little brown faces stretched away into the distance, with flares and loud-speakers at regular intervals. The National Anthem was played. Then a large lady moved to the microphone and sang, loudly but quite tunefully, a patriotic song. Next, the Rector rose to introduce me, at considerable length. Then I spoke. I suppose that barely a hundredth part of the audience understood a word that I said. But everyone listened respectfully. Afterwards there was a party, where I was given an inscribed plaque in memory of the occasion.

I enjoyed several other functions. One evening I went with the Ambassador to a performance of *Macbeth*, given by the boys of the Jesuit school, the Ateneo. I have never seen that difficult play better performed. They spoke their lines admirably, with a faint but attractive accent. The youth who played Macbeth did so with an authority that was very impressive, while the much younger boy who was Lady Macbeth showed a quality of sinister ambition that was rather disquieting. On another evening I attended a St George's Day dinner given by the Anglo-Philippine Society. Just as the Queen in Britain celebrates her official birthday at a more suitable season of the year, so in the Philippines St George is honoured on a different day, the climate in Manila being too sticky and hot for dinner-parties at the end of April. On this occasion I found myself seated next to the wife of the American admiral in command of the Far Eastern fleet. She spent the dinner running down everything British. When towards the end some of the guests got up to dance Sir Roger de Coverley she remarked scornfully that it was like any old Virginian dance. I fear that I was riled into saying: 'But of course, Madam. Don't you realize that the Americans are the British who haven't developed. Think how you use beautiful old words like "gotten", which we have long since abandoned.' She turned her back on me; but her husband, who was sitting opposite me, guffawed and spent the rest of the evening chatting to me.

I interrupted my stay in Manila to fly down to Mindanao, the southernmost of the Philippine islands, inhabited mostly by Moslems who have never taken kindly to the Catholic government in Manila. There was no outward unrest at the time when I was there; but I was warned not to try to travel outside the main town, Zamboanga. I was looked after by the headmaster of the chief school, at which I had to give a talk. He was a lively man, a Dane by origin, obviously well liked by his schoolmaster colleagues, a number of whom he invited to a party to meet me. He told me that he had recently asked the senior girls, all Moslems, at his school each to write him an essay on what they thought about polygamy. With one exception they were in favour of it. Life, they said, was much easier if you had companions to share the burden of a husband with you; and in a polygamous household there would always be someone to baby-sit for you.

On my way back to Manila I paused for two nights at the port of Cebu, where I had to give a talk at a Jesuit seminary. My audience there was the best that I encountered in the islands, though I was a trifle handicapped: as they came to fetch me from my hotel at 7 p.m., I expected to be given something to eat, but all that I received was a glass of Coca-Cola, which did not stimulate my inspiration.

From Cebu I flew across to the neighbouring island of Negros, to a small town called Dumaguete, where there was a small university. I must confess that, while I was struck by the beauty of the island, I remember very little about the University. It was run by Americans, with rather an evangelical atmosphere. I had to give a lecture in the University church that evening, and a talk to the humanities students next morning, before flying back to Manila.

I was met at Manila airport by the Counsellor at the Embassy, Christopher Ewart-Biggs, who many years later was to be assassinated when ambassador to Ireland, and dined that evening at his house. I was due to fly to Borneo the following day; but for some reason the flight was postponed for twenty-four hours, so I spent another day at the Embassy before taking the plane to Labuan.

Two years later I returned to Manila, on my way back from Sarawak. I had been spending three pleasant days in Hong Kong, staying with a writer friend, Dick Ommanney, who was at that time a lecturer at Hong Kong University. I enjoyed meeting members of the University staff and going round that admirable institution. I was also summoned to lunch at Government House. The luncheon was to have been in honour of Mr Willy Brandt, at that time Mayor of Berlin. But a message had arrived that morning from Japan to say that Mr Brandt had overeaten at a banquet there the previous evening and was unable to make the journey to Hong Kong. So the chief guest was Mr Garfield Todd, from what was then still Rhodesia. That afternoon I flew on to Manila, discovering on arrival that I had left all my underclothes behind in Dick

Ommanney's spare bedroom. However, he found them and sent them on to me by the next plane, so all was well.

. George Clutton was still Ambassador there, and I stayed with him. It was not a very good moment to have come, as a British Parliamentary delegation was due to arrive next day. Fortunately, the Embassy did not have to house the members; but the Ambassador was necessarily involved in their entertainment. Before they appeared – it was a Sunday – he and I went out for a picnic into the country, to see some fine baroque churches, returning for a large buffet dinner given by the First Secretary for the delegation.

To free the Embassy of my presence, and to escape from the parties given in honour of the delegation – I was kindly invited to a reception given by the Senate the following evening – I planned to go for the rest of the week to the mountain-resort of Baguio, to the north of the island of Luzon. A kind British tycoon arranged to lend me his cottage there. It involved an early start. I took a train that left Manila at 6.30 a.m., which made a leisurely journey through rice fields into the foothills, reaching some five hours later a small town called Damortis where a car was waiting to take me for an hour's drive up into the mountains to Baguio. I was comfortably housed there, with a couple to look after me, plenty of books to read and a garden full of spring flowers in which to sit. Unluckily, I had escaped from the British Parliamentary delegation only to run into a Universities Educational Conference, which was being held in one of the hotels. Some of the delegates from Manila heard that I was in Baguio, and out of the kindness of their hearts insisted on me dining with the conference on my first evening and listening to interminable speeches. Next day a charming Filipino elder statesman, called Laurel, gave me lunch at the Country Club, together with the Mayor of Baguio. Otherwise I was left blissfully alone, and wished that I could have stayed there longer.

For the return journey I had to leave Baguio at 4.30 a.m. in order to catch the train back to Manila, where I arrived well in time for lunch. I dined that evening with my absentee host of Baguio and could tell him how happy I had been there. I went back to the Embassy to find the Ambassador with the Prime Minister of New Zealand, Walter Nash, and the Japanese Ambassador. Next day the Ambassador gave a lunch for the Parliamentary delegation. I knew two of the members, and was placed pleasantly between them. On the morrow, which was a Sunday, the Ambassador and I went out to lunch at a model hacienda, returning in the afternoon for an early supper before going to the Ateneo school, to see, once again, the boys there act a Shakespeare play. On this occasion the play was *Julius Caesar*. Once again it was well spoken and well acted, though none of the actors were as striking as the Macbeth and the Lady Macbeth of two years before. I wonder if now, after thirty years, plays are still produced there with the same enthusiasm and skill. When the play was over I went straight to the airport, to fly to California.

I was charmed by the Philippines and by the people there. I doubt I would find it all so lovable now, with rebellion smouldering in the southern islands and the whole innocence of the land wrecked by the former régime of President Marcos. Most of my friends there must be dead by now. George Clutton, the ambassador who was so hospitable, died long before he had accomplished his due three score years and ten. There is no one left with whom I can compare memories of those journeys. I like to travel alone; but one pays a price for it in the end.

Queensland

THE BRITISH who visit Australia are seldom indifferent about it. They either love it or are quite unable to take it. My friends all, I am glad to say, belong to the first category. It irritates us to be told by the others that all Australians are brash and graceless, with chips on their shoulders, as though there were no British shoulders similarly burdened. It is pointless to be told that most of them are descended from convicts, as though none of the early settlers had gone there of their own free will. And what is wrong in descent from convicts? Most of us probably have criminal ancestors somewhere along the line. We should remember that most of the convicts that were transported to Botany Bay and other unfriendly spots were guilty of minor crimes, and that, in spite of cruel surroundings, many of them worked hard and made good, and were forbears of whom one might be proud. And anyhow most Australian families of today descend from settlers who arrived later in the last or even in the present century.

I have paid five visits to Australia and was delighted by them all. If I have chosen to select Queensland to be the nominal subject of this chapter, it is not because I have nothing to say about the other States. I have more friends in New South Wales and in Victoria than I have in Queensland, while there is nothing there that can compete with the extraordinary scenery in the centre of the continent, round Alice Springs. Ayer's Rock is unique in the world. But Queensland, with the Barrier Reef and the islands off the coast, and the rain forest close inland, with its lush vegetation and its unparallelled bird life, is visually, I think, the most splendid of the States. Besides, it serves the pattern of this book by beginning with the letter Q.

It was in 1958 that I first went to Australia. I was then working on the history of Sarawak; and a man who had been Chief Secretary there under the Rajahs was living in retirement in Western Australia, and I was eager to see him. So on my way to Sarawak that spring I flew out first to Perth, then on to Adelaide, Melbourne and Sydney, where the British Council had arranged for me to give lectures. On that occasion I did not go to Queensland. But I saw enough of Australia to determine me to return.

The hotel at Perth was a little old-fashioned by European standards. When I came down for breakfast I found one long table at which all the guests were seated, and the head waiter solemnly introduced me by name to them all. It was very matey. I then went out by train to the distant suburb where the retired Sarawak official now lived. He gave me lunch and a mass of useful information, some of which was too indiscreet for me to be able to use. I dined that evening at one of the Colleges attached to the University, and I lunched next day at Government House, before spending the afternoon at the University itself, which is set in a large garden-campus, and flying on overnight to Adelaide. There I stayed at the Adelaide Club, which was very comfortable but seemed to belong to Edwardian days. One of the leading citizens was married to a family connection of mine, and they looked after me, apologizing for not having me to their house, which was undergoing repairs. I escaped on that occasion having to go to the University. Instead, I was taken out to a charity barbecue at one of the great wineries to the north of the city. There, as I was lucky enough to be in the company of the Governor's wife, I was taken up into the house of the family that owned it and was given the best hock that I have ever drunk. My hosts never made enough of it to put it on the market, but kept it for their own private use.

After two nights in Adelaide I flew on to Melbourne, where I stayed at the Melbourne Club, which was, and I believe and hope still is, more splendidly old-fashioned than the Adelaide Club. I spent my first day in Melbourne mostly at its superb Picture Gallery and the second entirely at Melbourne University, where they were kind enough not to make me give a lecture. It was there that I first experienced the vagaries of the Australian climate. During that night the temperature dropped some twenty degrees. After a day of sweltering I found myself shivering. I interrupted my visit to Melbourne to fly for two days to Tasmania, to see an old friend, Lord Talbot de Malahide, the owner of Malahide Castle, near Dublin, with the hereditary title of Admiral of Malahide and the Adjacent Seas. Early in the nineteenth century a cadet of the family, who had been somewhat delinquent, had been shipped out to Tasmania. There he had done well as a sheep farmer and had built himself a house which he called Malahide, after the family seat. His descendants had now died out, and the last of the line left Malahide, Tasmania, to the head of the family in Ireland. Lord Talbot had been out the previous year to look at his new estate; this year he was out again, setting about the task of bringing the house up to modern livable standards. I was fascinated by Tasmanian country life. It seemed to me to be curiously like that in Ireland, except that the inhabitants had rather different accents. The local gentry were farmers whose chief recreation was to go to the horse-races. Many lived in tumbledown houses in the Regency style, built well into the Victorian era. I suppose that no one remembered to tell the Tasmanians that Regency had long since gone out of date in Britain. It was, I admit, un-Irish to see wallabies and parakeets and forests of eucalyptus trees. But otherwise I kept thinking of Ireland.

I returned for two nights to Melbourne, spending the intervening day mostly at the University, then flew to Canberra for the week-end. There I was housed in the Australian National University's guest-house and was well looked after by the historians there. Canberra was still in an unfinished state. The great artificial lake, which now has the effect of uniting the disparate parts of the city, was not yet filled with water and was an unattractive sight. There were pleasant houses in the residential areas; but most of the roads were ominously called 'Circles'; and when you went for a walk you found yourself back in ten minutes at your starting place. But I was impressed by the University. On the Monday morning, before I left for Sydney, I had to hold a seminar of history graduate students and found it rather formidable.

The twelve days that I spent in Sydney were a trifle exhausting. I was overwhelmed by hospitality. I stayed at the Australia Club. But, Sydney being easy-going in comparison with Adelaide or Melbourne, I did not feel so hemmed in by respectability. I was spared having to talk at the University, though I was given a good lunch there. But I was induced to lecture to the sixth forms at two schools, King's School, Parramatta, and Cranbrook School, both of which I thought excellent. Otherwise I was taken to endless parties, given by a great variety of hosts. I was taken to spend days at the seaside, and driven up into the Blue Mountains. I spent a fascinating morning at Sydney Zoo, where I was taken round by a head keeper. We went first into the koala bear enclosure, where I was handed one of those toy-like animals to cuddle. I asked if they were all as tame. All, answered the keeper, except for that one who was sitting on the branch of a small tree. It thereupon climbed down from the tree and walked across and climbed up me. The keeper was greatly impressed and showed me into a number of cages, even allowing me to handle that most delicate and shy of creatures, the duck-billed platypus. Finally we entered the big kangaroo enclosure. Thereupon a huge buck kangaroo came bounding up towards me. 'Take care', cried the keeper as he dragged me away; 'He can become excited.' Two days later I read in a Sydney newspaper that the big kangaroo enclosure was to be closed to all visitors, as a V.I.P. had nearly suffered death or worse at the hands of its largest male.

My only complaint with Sydney on this visit was the weather. On three days there were rain-storms of such violence that I could not go out of doors. It had been arranged for me to fly to see a cattle-station in the Outback. But the airport was flooded that day, and the flight had to be cancelled. I was sorry when the time came for me to go on to Borneo, and very sorry that I had not had the opportunity to visit Queensland.

That opportunity came in 1962, again in February. I flew to Sydney, where friends had arranged for me to be lent a flat at Darling Point. Next morning I left to spend two days in Melbourne and then in Canberra. In both places the University looked after me, and in Canberra I dined one night at Government House, with the then Governor-General, Lord De L'Isle. The dinner itself was rather formal and stiff; but when the guests left I was ushered into a waiting-room and after everyone else had gone I went back to join the De L'Isles for a cosy gossip. On my return to Sydney I went back to the flat at Darling Point, to face as before an endless round of parties. Yehudi Menuhin happened to be in Sydney, with his wife, his daughter and her then husband, the pianist Fou Tsong, and with Yehudi's sister Hephzibah and her husband. Because of Fou Tsong the Chinese community of Sydney decided to give a great dinner for the whole clan. But when the day for the dinner arrived Mrs Menuhin was ill and had to cry off. The Chinese insisted that Yehudi should bring someone in her stead; so I was bidden to stand in for her. It was a sumptuous, rather formal, seemingly interminable but very cordial banquet. The food was interesting but not, I found, kind to the digestion.

After a week in Sydney I flew up, at last, to Queensland, for a week-end in Brisbane. I confess that I was slightly disappointed. Brisbane seemed to be a pleasant city, not as rigidly respectable as Melbourne or Adelaide and not as brash as Sydney, but a bit provincial. Many of the houses were built on stilts, for coolness in the long hot summers. The University there was closed, but friends on the staff looked after me kindly. On the Sunday a charming Indian couple, both University lecturers, took me down to the beaches, to the famed Surfer's Paradise. But one could hardly see the sand for the crowds. On the Monday I had to lecture to the Brisbane Institute of International Affairs, before returning to Sydney. A few days later I left for Fiji.

In 1965 I returned to Australia for a more formidable visit, to lecture for the British Council. I was there for nearly two months, and gave some twenty lectures and held some ten seminars. I went first to Perth, having been told that I should visit Western Australia in its spring. It was good advice. I was taken out one day into the countryside, which I had remembered from my last visit as being featureless scrub. Now it was carpeted with wild flowers, pink and red and blue, in amazing profusion. What all the flowers were I don't know; the names, when I asked, meant little to me. But the spectacle was unforgettable. I went on to Adelaide, and stayed there with my relations by marriage, on a hillside over-looking the city. There too the gardens and the countryside were lush with spring vegetation. From Adelaide I flew into the centre of the continent, to Alice Springs. The desert around Alice was not blossoming like the rose. There were occasional patches of green, and here and there a brackish pool, and Alice itself is in an oasis; but for the most part it was desolation, rather beautiful but strange. There were numbers of tourists in the town, most of them Australian. No one is more splendidly indepedent than the average Australian; but here in the desert on our bus excursions, when the driver stopped and told us that here was something that we must photograph, they all obediently trooped out with their cameras and I, the Pommy, was the only one who did not feel it necessary to obey the order. One had to fly to see Ayer's Rock, that extraordinary boulder the size of a mountain, which turns deep rose-coloured at sunset. The trip involved a not very comfortable night in a tent but was well worth the discomfort.

Next, I spent a fortnight in Canberra, for a series of lectures at the Australian National University. I was housed in a pleasant suite in University House where, to my delight, rosella parakeets used to come to share my breakfast on the balcony. A new Governor-General had just been appointed, Lord Casey, whom I knew. I stood in the crowd to watch him drive to his inauguration; and next day I went to the Caseys' first luncheon party at Government House. The British High Commissioner, Charles Johnston, was also an old friend; and I went several times to his house. It was when dining there that I met the American Ambassador, of whom I have written in an earlier chapter. Canberra, with its lake completed, was looking far more handsome than on my first visit. I enjoyed driving out into the nearby forests. One day a friend took me to lunch at a sheep-station not far off. As we drove back a sheep gave birth to a lamb by the side of the road. She ran away at once; and the lamb decided that our car was its mother. We drove away as fast as we could, but the poor creature came tottering after us till it collapsed. We stopped at the nearest telephone to tell the sheep-station of the mishap; but it was too late.

Sydney, where I spent the next ten days, was as full of social life as ever; and lecturing kept me busy. I escaped one day for a long drive through the Blue Mountains, where the wild flowers were splendid. I stayed at a very pleasant old hotel, since demolished. It was on this visit that I came to know the novelist Patrick White, not a very easy character, but a good friend to me.

From Sydney I flew to Armidale, on the landward side of the Blue Mountains, where there was a small friendly university. It was about to appoint a new Vice-Chancellor; and some of the dons amiably asked me to apply for the post. But somehow I did not see myself spending years of my life trying to be an administrator in a small town on the edge of the Outback, even among such kindly folk. After politely suggesting that they could do better, I flew on to Queensland.

The eight days that I spent that year in Queensland were so fascinating that I consider them to justify my choosing Queensland to head this Australian chapter. I arrived on a Saturday morning, and was taken straight to Government House to stay with the Governor, Sir Henry Abel Smith, and his wife, Lady May, whom I had known before her marriage. They took me at once to the races, for luncheon and the afternoon. I have never been much of a race-goer. Once, forty years earlier, I had attended a race-meeting in Hong Kong. When I was a young don at Cambridge some of my more raffish pupils would sometimes carry me off to Newmarket; and occasionally I would find myself taken to some country point-to-point. But horses tend to give me hay-fever so I cannot be intimate with them. Nor have I indulged much in betting. One of my sisters used to enjoy a flutter on the Grand National; one year I arrived to stay with her on the morning of the race, when she was about to telephone instructions to her bookie. She insisted that I joined in. I asked to see the list of runners and noticed that one was called Red Alligator. I had had a vivid dream the previous night in which a crocodile featured. So I said that I would put my money on Red Alligator. My brother-in-law said that he was a possibility; and all the family decided to follow my lead. My sister lost her head when talking to her bookie and put on twice as much for each of us as we had told her. It was as well. Red Alligator romped home first, and we all did very nicely. Now at Brisbane I had no such heaven-sent inspiration, nor did I know anything of the horses' pedigrees. I had to rely on my eyes, and picked two horses which I thought looked the most elegant. Each came in first. So then I stopped. My hosts were impressed, and I was enabled to leave particularly generous tips at Government House.

That evening we went to a performance of the Brisbane Symphony Orchestra, with Susskind conducting and Tamas Vasary as soloist. Next morning the Governor made me rise early, so that he could drive me round the city, to show me how it was developing under his tactful guidance, before I caught an aeroplane to go northward. It was a small machine, which deposited me at a little airport at Mackay where a smaller machine took me on to Townsville.

I had thought Townsville a somewhat repetitive name for a town, till I discovered that it had been founded by a Mr Town; who could not, I suppose, have called it Townstown. It was then a smallish but growing place, with a college attached to the University of Queensland. The head of the history department there, Ian Moles, looked after me with unceasing hospitality. I was housed in a pleasant small hotel but lunched and dined with the Moleses. On the first morning I was taken round the college, and in the afternoon I was handed over to the leading naturalist of the town, Hugh Lavery. He took me to a piece of wet-land which was a bird-reservation, just north of the town. I had already seen a number of brolgas on the airstrip, grey cranes who seem curiously unafraid of humans, and who have a deep trumpeting call and who are given to perform elegant dances with each other. I saw more of them that afternoon, as well as nearly fifty other species of birds, water-fowl and waders as well as small birds of many types and many colours. Mr Lavery was an admirable showman. Under his guidance I seemed to have time to notice each individual specimen. I wish that I could have remembered half of what I saw. The following day Mr Moles and some friends took me by a little steamer across to Magnetic Island, a few miles off the coast. It was a lovely island, but was beginning to be developed as a resort; but I remember it then as being full of handsome beaches, lush vegetation and colourful birds.

I flew northward next afternoon to Cairns where, thanks to a tycoon in Sydney, I was given an introduction to the manager of the chief local sugar mills. His name, John Smith, was easy to remember; and I remember it with gratitude. He saw that I was housed in a pleasant hotel on the sea-front. He showed me over his mills; and he and his wife gave me dinner. Next morning he saw me onto a boat which took me across to 'Green Island, the nearest to the mainland of the islands of the Great Barrier Reef. The journey in the motor-boat, which was well filled by tourists, took about an hour and a half. Green Island itself is not very large and quite flat, covered with tropical trees. Its tourist attraction is that it has attached to it a glass-walled chamber, built on the floor of the sea, into which you can descend and watch the brilliantly coloured fishes that live round the coral reefs swimming past and occasionally stopping to peer inquisitively at the strange beings cooped in their glass menagerie. I spent several hours there, dazzled by the beauty of them all. The tourists almost all left the island in the late afternoon; but it had been arranged for me to spend the night in a small hotel on the island. While its few guests stayed in the hotel, I suppose to enjoy their cocktails, I wondered alone on rough paths through the island, in quiet except for a curious bubbling noise, like the sound of a melodious turkey-cock, which after a little I identified as coming from the wompoo pigeons, the most colourful of all the pigeon family, of which there were numbers flying around or gossiping in the treetops. Early next morning I meandered again round the island, seeing more exotic birds, and then went again to admire the fishes, before returning to Cairns in the afternoon.

Next day, a Saturday, the Smiths took me for a long drive into the interior, into the Great Dividing Range. It was a magical day, clear and cool in the uplands, in contrast with the steamier heat of the coast. Much of the country was open, and we passed by a number of lakes, mostly, I think, man-made. We had a picnic lunch on the dam of one of them, called Timaroo. But we passed through patches of the tropical rain-forest as we began to descend from the heights, to return to the coast down a great gorge. In one patch, as the sun was beginning to go down, there appeared running along the road ahead of us what looked like an enormous behind on legs. It eventually turned to go into the bush and revealed itself to be a cassowary. The Smiths, for all their years in

Queensland, had never seen one before and were, I think, as excited as I was by the phenomenon. It was the crowning glory of the day.

I left Cairns early next morning, longing to return. But I suspect that it would be a mistake. There were already numbers of tourists there, including a good many hippies and down-and-outs, as an angry old gentleman at the hotel pointed out to me. In that climate one could happily sleep out of doors, unless there was a tropical downpour – rare, I think, at that time of year.

I spent the day that I left Cairns in a series of aeroplanes, one from Cairns to Townsville, one from Townsville to Brisbane, one from Brisbane to Sydney, and finally one from Sydney to Melbourne, in which I found myself seated just behind the imposing figure of Joan Sutherland. I longed to lean over and tell her of the delight that her voice had so often given to me; but I knew that it is never kind to accost the eminent when they are travelling. Many years later I met her on a tour in Egypt and made friends with her then.

I was kept busy all the following week with lectures and seminars at the University of Melbourne and at Monash University. Happily for me I was staying with the Warden of Trinity College, University of Melbourne, Robin Sharwood, who was the kindest of hosts and has remained a good friend ever since that time. I had one day free, in which I was taken to lunch up in the hills, a pleasant escape from Melbourne, which had become very hot, and on to Sherbrook Forest, in the hope of seeing the lyre-birds that live there. The forest warden greeted me with special cordiality as his wife had been born a Runciman, though we could not trace any close kinship. I was lucky with the lyre-birds. First I heard them calling and mimicking, then I saw several, and two of them displayed and danced for me.

After Melbourne I returned to Sydney for a week of social pleasures, marred only by tooth-ache and the need to have the errant tooth extracted. Then I left to cross the Pacific for Los Angeles, and on to Texas, to lecture to Miss Linda Bird Johnson.

My next visit to Australia was in October 1970. I had been in New Zealand for two weeks, giving the Chancellor's Lectures at the University of Auckland. I had been a bit disappointed in New Zealand, perhaps because I did not have time to visit the South Island; and it is from the South Island that nearly all the New Zealanders that I know best have come. The North Island was very beautiful, especially at that time of year, when the many flowering shrubs were blossoming. Auckland itself is superbly situated, almost surrounded by the sea. Perhaps that was to blame for the life there. The Aucklanders seemed to spend all their spare time on the water, healthily enough, but to the neglect of other interests. When I was there, there was neither a theatre nor a concert hall in the city. Dramatic and musical events were left to be organized by a few hard-working amateurs. Outside the University there seemed to be no bookshop, though one could buy popular paperbacks in one or two of the big stores. It seemed strange in a country that has produced a great number of fine scholars, writers and musicians. I did not find the white New Zealanders themselves very hospitable. The British expatriates at the University looked after me lavishly; and I had one or two old friends who had settled in later life in New Zealand. But the only white native house in Auckland to which I was invited was kept by two charming old sisters who asked me twice to tea. However, a former Governor-General, Bernard Fergusson (later Lord Ballantrae) had given me introductions to Maori friends of his, and they were immensely hospitable, though few of them were lively conversationists. I flew down for a long week-end to Wellington, for a lecture and other engagements. I lunched on the Sunday with the British High Commissioner, who told me that he was also Governor of Pitcairn Island where, he said, there was a problem as the women greatly outnumbered the men. Having lived very largely in the Western Islands of Scotland, where the girls all go off to seek a fuller life on the mainland, leaving the boys behind, I suggested that he might well try exporting Pitcairn maidens to the Hebrides, which they would doubtless find wonderfully civilized in comparison with their birthplace. Everyone would benefit from the transaction. But he said that it sounded too much like the White Slave traffic.

It was a relief to cross over to Australia. I had a pleasant week in Sydney, where I was amply entertained; then three days in Canberra and Melbourne, justifying my presence in both of them by a lecture. From Melbourne I flew to Perth for a night, and from Perth to Mauritius, where I stayed for four days. It was beautiful and restful; and a kind British Council officer saw to my comfort. But, brought up on the legend of *Paul et Virginie*, I had expected more dramatic scenery. My next stop was at Nairobi; but that was not a success, as I felt very ill there, apparently because of the height. A Kenyan to whom I had an introduction gallantly took me for a long drive in a ramshackle but perfectly efficient car down into the Rift Valley. I would have enjoyed it greatly had I been in a better state. As it was, I had to pass a day in bed in my hotel before flying back to London.

My last visit to Australia was in 1983, when I went there to attend a Conference of National Trusts. I tagged along behind the delegation from Scotland, but I was actually representing the National Trust for Greece, the British-based branch of the native Greek Elleniki Etaireia, which therefore I also represented. It was an excuse for another journey round the world. I flew first to Los Angeles, then on to stay with American friends who had taken a house in Honolulu, and from Honolulu to Sydney and straight on to Melbourne. After a night there I flew across to Tasmania, to revisit Malahide. My old friend Lord Talbot had died some years earlier, and his sister was living there. The house had been transformed. It was now an elegant and comfortable Regency villa, full of treasures from Malahide Castle – a surprising phenomenon to find in the middle of the Tasmanian countryside. I had three happy days there before returning to Melbourne for a night.

Queensland was not on our National Trust itinerary. But I was determined to go back there. A friend of mine, a professional gardener, whom I had known when he was working on the parks in Canberra, was now employed in trying to introduce gardens into the grim mining centre of Mount Isa in Queensland. I suggested that we might meet on the coast. I would have liked to have gone to Cairns; but it was much more direct for him to come to Townsville. I was glad to see him again. But otherwise the journey was a mistake. Townsville had grown out of recognition. One stayed now at a large impersonal hotel. Magnetic Island was now geared for tourists. We passed a pleasant day there; but it was like being in a spectacular municipal park. I was eager to revisit the bird reservation I had so greatly enjoyed in 1965. But Australia had been through three years of drought. What had been wetlands, full of bird life, was now a bare dusty plain. There were still a few brolgas and I was glad to see them again, though they did not dance for me. I was saddened by it all. My love-affair with Queensland had come to an end.

I flew back to Sydney, where, after staying a night with Patrick White, I joined the National Trusts' conference. We had five days of meetings in Sydney, but with time off, so that I could see many of my friends. We then drove in a bus to Canberra, through the mountains. There we were treated with more meetings, talks and receptions, for two busy days before driving on inland, over the border into Victoria, to a town that had seen better days called Beechworth, where there was a successful attempt to preserve the nineteenth-century atmosphere. Driving through the countryside was interesting but rather melancholy. One saw the cruel results of the three-years' drought, a parched landscape and such cattle as were allowed to survive looking gaunt and sickly. Many of them were feeding by the roadside, where the grass seemed to be less scanty than in the fields. But we enjoyed ourselves at Beechworth, and saw some of the neighbouring country houses and grounds, which must be lovely in kinder weather. Our tour ended with three days in Melbourne, where we had our final discussions and were given our final dinner and reception. Even in Melbourne one was conscious of the drought, with too little water in the parks and the river little more than a trickle. The whole conference had been full of interest. It was impressive to see how the Australians were coping with their heritage, with the many fine nineteenth-century buildings that they possess and with their countryside.

My next stage was Hong Kong. There it was a very different story. Hong Kong had been undergoing one of the wettest winters in its history. We arrived in the evening, in the midst of a formidable thunderstorm. Our Australian pilot cheerfully announced that he was not sure if he could manage to make a landing, but he would try, as the alternative would be to fly to Manila. Happily, he succeeded; but ours was the only plane to land at Hong Kong airport that evening. The rain only stopped for two or three brief intervals during the two days that I spent there. It was a relief to return to pleasant spring weather in Scotland.

It is as well to be reminded from time to time how powerless we are against the forces of nature. If I think nostalgically about Australia and wonder whether I could not have contentedly settled there, I now think too of the drought and the misery that it brings. If I dream sometimes of a little house by the lush Queensland coast, where I could live in quiet, with parrots flying round me, then I remember that typhoons can come and devastate it all. One should be content with one's lot and not seek to be an expatriate.

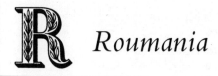

Roumania

OF ALL THE VERSE written by the late Dorothy Parker my favourite piece is entitled 'Comment'. It runs:

> Oh, life is a glorious cycle of song,
> A medley of extemporanea;
> And love is a thing that can never go wrong;
> And I am Marie of Roumania.

It was written, I suppose, in 1926, the year in which Queen Marie had made a much publicized visit to the United States. But I had fallen a distant victim to her glamour many years previously, when I was still a schoolboy. Those years of the First World War were an era of splendid Queens. There was our own great and good Queen Mary. There was Queen Elisabeth of the Belgians, Bavarian by birth but heroically loyal to her adopted country when it was overrun by the Germans. She was also a first-class violinist, and had the further distinction of being the first queen to have her face lifted, in those early days when a lift left one with starry eyes and a permanent smile; tragically so in her case, as a few days later her husband, King Albert, was killed in a climbing accident, and the smile had to be let down for the funeral. There was Queen Elena of Italy, towering over her little husband and owing, we were told, her superb carriage to the fact that in her native Montenegro the princesses had to carry water from the well to the palace in buckets on their heads. There was the tragic young Empress Zita of Austria, desperately eager to make peace for her country, only to see her efforts ignored by the intransigence of the Allies, egged on by the Czech Bureau, which was determined to destroy the Austrian Empire, at the cost of another eighteen months of warfare and the loss of innumerable lives. There was the still more tragic Russian Empress; but she for all her beauty was too obstinately self-righteous and *exaltée* to inspire the sympathy that her cruel fate deserved. Some of the sovereign ladies were, it is true, lacking in glamour, such as the German Kaiserin, rigidly respectable and burdened with a husband and sons who seldom could behave like gentlemen; or Queen Sophia of Greece, maligned by the Allies for continuing a correspondence with her brother, the Kaiser, in the hope of somehow thereby keeping Greece out of the War. In fact she rather disliked him; and it was a sad fate for someone whose idea of bliss had always been to spend a week or two at Eastbourne. None of the neutral queens roused much interest, except for

Queen Ena of Spain, coping bravely with an unsatisfactory husband, and with bull-fights, which she detested.

But none of the galaxy could equal Queen Marie. She acted her role like a first-class Hollywood star and she acted it productively. It was due to her, more than to anyone else, that Roumania emerged from the peace-making at Versailles with her territory doubled in size.

It was natural therefore that I should long to visit Roumania. I acquired other, more professional, reasons as well. Roumania, or rather the Principalities of Wallachia and Moldavia that are the core of the country, remained the only part of the old Byzantine world never to be directly ruled by the Turks, or by the Italian merchant-cities. By a timely submission to the Ottoman Sultan's suzerainty they preserved their autonomy. They were all that was left of Byzantium, as the name Roumania attests. The modern Roumanians like to spell it Romania, to show, they claim, that they are descended from the Romans. But the word is in fact derived from 'Roum', the name given by the Moslem world to Byzantium, the old East Roman Empire. Indeed, most of the later Princes of Wallachia and Moldavia, appointed and usually soon deposed by the Sultan, were Greeks from Constantinople, posthumous heirs of Byzantium. It is in the Principalities that one can see – or could see, until the Ceausescu régime decided to destroy it all – the continuation of Byzantine art. One could see how Byzantine architecture would have developed under patrons free to build churches and palaces. .One could have seen, a little earlier on, the Byzantine love for titles lingering on in the petty courts of the Princes. The Principalities were, as the great Roumanian historian Nicolae Iorga worded it, *Byzance après Byzance*. A visit to Roumania would be for me a great help in my understanding of Byzantium.

It was not, however, till 1934 that I achieved that ambition. After the Byzantine Congress in Sofia that September I went by train and ferry across to Roumania, to stay at the British Legation in Bucharest with a kindly Minister and his wife, Michael and Mary Palairet. Bucharest was at that time eager to think of itself as the Paris of the Balkans. It was not a particularly beautiful city, most of it having been built in the later nineteenth century; but it was full of glittering shops and elegant houses, and here and there churches and monasteries dating from the seventeenth and eighteenth centuries, in a style that was basically Byzantine but with strong Italian influences. The poorer quarters were picturesque and not quite as squalid as in many East European countries. There was a prosperous middle class in the city, which kept mainly to itself; and there was a lively aristocracy, descended for the most part from Greeks who, in the seventeenth and eighteenth centuries, and a few earlier, in the sixteenth, had made a fortune in the Ottoman Empire and had hastened to invest it, before the Sultan confiscated it, in land in the Principalities, safe from direct Turkish rule. They had intermarried with the local landed classes; and a few local families had survived in prominence through intermarriage with the Greeks. Many of the families bore princely titles, when some ancestor had been for a while Prince of Wallachia or Moldavia under the Sultan, or had earned the title from the Sultan through services to the Ottoman government or to the Orthodox Patriarchate. A few generations back all of them had spoken Greek among themselves. Now they all spoke French, only using Roumanian when they had to deal with the lower orders. Their wealth came principally from their vast landed estates, where the peasants had very few rights. But they were not oppressive landlords; and the country was agriculturally rich. Peasant life in the villages was simple and lacking in amenities, but there was always enough to eat.

I enjoyed moving among this bright and not uncultured society, with its rather simple sophistication and its easy-going attitude. Divorce was frequent and obtained without difficulty. It was sometimes hard to remember who was now married to whom. I was, I remember, much impressed to meet a Princess Soutso who, I was told, was aged nineteen and already on her third husband. She had green lacquered toe-nails, such as I had never seen before. Many of them were people of serious worth, such as the architect Prince George Cantacuzene, who was a perfect guide to the older buildings in the city. In the offing was Princess Marthe Bibesco, living in her palace of Mogoşoea, a few miles out from Bucharest. (I have written of her in my chapter on Istanbul.) The great house had been built in the later seventeenth century by Constantine Brancovan, Prince of Wallachia, and it descended by inheritance to Marthe's husband, Prince George Valentine Bibesco, whom she had married when she was sixteen. She had entirely refurbished the old house, adding mosaic walls to the marble ones, buying furniture, mostly gilt, to match the old furniture that had survived, and discreetly introducing modern comforts. The whole effect was ornately splendid, but not garish or vulgar. I went out there several times, usually to have tea with her daughter, Princess Ghika, as Marthe went off to Paris soon after I arrived in Bucharest. But she gave one great banquet before she left. A young peacock had somehow fallen out of a great cedar tree in front of the house and had broken his leg and had to be put out of his misery; he was served up for this dinner. And he was served up in the proper manner, on a golden platter with his head sewn on to his body and the long tail feathers stuck in to trail behind the dish. It was, I thought, macabre; and he tasted like a tough, coarse old turkey.

The highlight of my visit to Bucharest was when I went to tea with Queen Marie. Her sister Beatrice, the youngest of the daughters of Alfred, Duke of Edinburgh, was a friend of mine. She had married the Infante Alfonso of Orleans, a first cousin of King Alfonso of Spain. (I shall tell of them in the last chapter of this book.) I had met her with mutual friends in London; and when she heard that I was going to Roumania she said that I must see her sister. So when I arrived at the Legation in Bucharest there was already an invitation for me to go to take tea at the Palace of Cotroceni, which was now the Queen's residence. Her days of greatness were over. Her husband had died. Her son Carol, who had repudiated his succession to the throne because of his liaison with Mme Lupescu, had come back from exile to snatch it from his young son, King Michael; and his relations with his mother were uncertain. She was, I believe, genuinely fond of him but deplored his way of life. He alternated between showing her deference and even affection, then arbitrarily depriving her of privileges and even cash. But she was still popular and respected in the country.

The British Minister and Mrs Palairet came with me to the tea-party, at which her lady-in-waiting, Mme Lahovary, Marthe Bibesco's sister-in-law, was the only other guest. The palace was redolent with the scent of frangipani and stephanotis; and she herself was dressed in white. She was still beautiful. Her golden hair may have been helped to retain its colour, but her complexion was still wonderfully fresh and her eyes were deep blue. The Minister had told me that if she held out her hand to be kissed, I was not to do so. British gentlemen did not kiss hands, he said. But when she did I could not resist what seemed to me a fitting gesture. I saw him glare disapprovingly at me, but he was kind enough not to reprove me later for my disobedience. She sent me at once to her bedroom, but for no improper reason. Mme Lahovary escorted me to look at the icons that she kept there. Some of them were very fine, but some poor nineteenth-century specimens. Most had been pillaged from Cyprus, with the help of Sir Ronald Storrs when he had been Governor of the island. But what struck me most strongly was her bed, which, together with the cabinets on either side, had been constructed out of a handsome iconostasis. It hardly seemed to be a suitable fate for a piece of holy wood, but perhaps it was all right for a crowned and anointed queen.

On my return to the salon, for china tea and red caviare sandwiches, the Queen talked mostly about her autobiography, which she had just been writing, and the whole question of how frank you can be when telling of the people whom you have known and what you have known about them. She was in favour of frankness, unless it was really hurtful. Her manner was consciously gracious, but she was very friendly and full of humour. I enjoyed it all greatly.

Her autobiography, written in English, came out in three volumes a month or two later and is, I think, the best of all royal memoirs. The first two volumes, dealing with her youth and married life, up to her husband's accession to the throne, are particularly good to read, full of shrewd comments about people and at times very funny. The style can be parodied. It is over-full of laudatory epithets and of old-fashioned slang. Gentlemen friends are usually described as 'good chums'. I sent her a fan-letter. Remembering Mr Disraeli's technique of 'we authors' when writing to Queen Victoria, I wrote of 'we historians'. It went down well. We kept up a correspondence. But, sad to say, her letters to me have perished in a conflagration, with most of the other letters that I had preserved from the pre-War years. When she came to London the following year, I was invited not only to the big reception that she gave but also to a pleasant tea-party for half a dozen intimate friends.

My more serious reason for coming to Bucharest had been to see the eminent historian Professor Iorga. He had refused to attend the Byzantine Congress at Sofia, as he had been indulging in a bitter controversy with Bulgarian historians over the question of the southern Dobrudja, the province by the Black Sea which had been allotted to Roumania in 1918 but which – may Professor Iorga's ghost forgive me for saying so – had long been occupied by ethnic Bulgarians. Incidentally, Queen Marie had built herself a villa with a lovely garden there, on the sea at Balchik, where she was buried. The territory was returned to Bulgaria in 1940 and the villa and garden are now kept up by the Bulgarian state as a literary institute. Though patriotism occasionally blurred his judgment, Iorga was a great historian, with an immense knowledge of his country's archives as well as of all the texts concerning the Byzantine and post-Byzantine world. I have gone laboriously through his works in Roumanian but, fortunately, he wrote mostly in excellent French; and historians owe much to him. His spoken French was curiously accented. When I went to see him he greeted me with words that sounded like: 'Gomme vous êtes jaune'; so that I wondered if I were sickening for jaundice, when in fact he was alluding to my comparative youth. I greatly enjoyed seeing him; and it was he who inspired me to interest myself in a subject about which I wrote a book many years later, the fate of the Christian heirs to Byzantium under Ottoman rule.

Professor Iorga had been a tutor to King Carol and the King was later to persuade him to become his Prime Minister for a time. As such, his liberal attitude offended the Iron Guard, the Fascist group which, backed by Nazi Germany, was to sieze power in Roumania in 1940. Though by then he had nothing to do with politics he was considered to be a potential enemy; later that year members of the Guard kidnapped him and murdered him in a forest outside Bucharest. It is, it seems, a mistake for Byzantine professors to become Prime Ministers. Bogdan Filov, the distinguished professor of medieval art in Bulgaria, was Prime Minister of his country throughout the Second World War. At the end of it, when the Communists took over the government, he met his end in front of a firing squad.

I made one excursion outside Bucharest. The Palairets loved
informality and liked to drive round Bucharest in their own small car. So
they lent me the Legation car for the inside of two days. The Legation
chauffeur, Vassily, accompanied by his comfortable wife, who was a
better linguist than he, set out with me one morning to visit the old
Wallachian capital, Curtea de Arges, with its fine late medieval church,
then on past the handsome seventeenth-century convent of Dintr' un
Lemu, by the town of Monasteremi, to the great monastery of Horez,
also built in the seventeenth century and now occupied by nuns. It was
known to receive guests, and I planned to spend the night there. We
arrived in mid-afternoon, and I was shown into a splendid guest-room.
As I was tidying myself, hoping to go out to see the church before dark, a
flustered nun came into the room, saying that I had regrettably been
shown into the wrong place. She took my small suitcase and hurried me
across a courtyard and up a tower, leaving me in a far more austere
chamber. This was my room, she said, as she went through the door,
locking it behind her. There I remained imprisoned, with nothing to do
except look out of the window onto the neighbouring countryside.
More than an hour passed, and dusk was beginning to fall, when she
returned, wreathed in smiles. It had been another mistake, she said, as she
took me back to the grand guest-room. There an excellent supper was
brought to me, and soon the Abbess arrived, to chat with me in not very
good French. Next morning I was shown the church and the treasury;
and, after making a suitable donation to the convent funds, I left in an
atmosphere of cordiality.

Vassily the chauffeur explained the mystery to me. It seemed that the
convent was not allowed to admit male guests without a lady to
chaperone them. The Legation had thought that by sending Mme
Vassily with me, all would be well. But she was not staying within the
convent. However, as I came with the Legation car, the nuns did not like
to refuse me admittance. But then the local bishop came to pay an
unexpected call, and, as I was there illegally, I had to be hidden until he
left.

A few days later I said goodbye to the Palairets and took an early
morning train to a little station in the north of the country, in Bukovina,
which till 1918 had been a province of the Habsburg Empire. There
I was met by Prince Nicholas Mavrocordato and driven to a country
house at Crasna, the property of his wife, who was one of the Flondors,
the leading family in the province. There the atmosphere was entirely
Austrian. Indeed, the housekeeper was Austrian, while the estate
manager was a Russian prince of German origin, Peter Wittgenstein. I
spent the next few days very happily, being taken to see the chief
monasteries in northern Moldavia, with their churches, nearly all of
which had frescoes on their exterior walls, in a pure Byzantine style,

dating from the late fifteenth and the sixteenth centuries, overhanging eaves protecting them from the weather. They are unique and well deserve a visit. One day the Prince and I drove across the north of Bessarabia, then a province of Roumania and now part of the Soviet state of Moldavia. We had a picnic lunch in the ruined castle of Hotin, built by the Genoese in the fifteenth century, on the banks of the river Dneistr, which was then the frontier between Roumania and the Soviet Union. Russian soldiers on the far bank of the river stared at us through their field-glasses; and I was warned not to try to photograph them, as they were apt to open fire across the river to punish such impertinence. I greatly enjoyed the week that I spent with the hospitable Mavrocordatos. It seemed a happy world, but a world that has vanished for ever.

I returned home from Bukovina through Poland, stopping for a night in Cracow, that most beautiful of cities. I stayed in the palace of the Lubomirskis, being looked after by a son of the house who had been to Cambridge. The reception-rooms were under dust-sheets as the family were still in residence in its country palace; but I was able to have an impression of their dignified splendour. I wish that I had had time to visit the country palace, though life there must have been formidable. Guests were warned not to stray outside the house after dark, as fierce dogs were then let loose to roam in the garden, trained to savage anyone whom they did not know. It was certainly a feudal life. My host told me that his elder brother when he met peasants on the estate always courteously took off his hat to greet them, but thought nothing of horse-whipping them should they offend him. But they did not resent it, I was told, as fathers in all classes treated their sons in the same way, and the estate was regarded as an extended family.

Thirty-five years later, in 1969, I went back to Roumania. It was a different country. At first it had seemed that Roumania might survive the War without too great a social revolution. In 1944 the young King Michael had achieved a coup which had overthrown the rule of the Iron Guard and had brought his country into the Allied camp. He could not keep the Russians from coming into Roumania, but they came as friends and at first treated his government with deference. His mother, Queen Helen, told me some years later that the Russian general, in command of the troops that entered Bucharest, sent almost at once to ask if he might come to see her. He told her that he was anxious to pay his respects to her as, when he first joined the army as a subaltern, the Colonel of his regiment had been her grandmother, Queen Olga of Greece, born a Russian grand-duchess. What a pity, he said, that the Greeks had not known how to treat royalty properly. Queen Helen asked gently if the Russians had done any better in their treatment of their royalty. He was taken aback at first, but then admitted that perhaps the Russian record had not been very good.

King Michael was very popular with his subjects and the Russians let him be for a while; but they soon made it clear that he was to have no control over his government. Then, when he and his mother were in London in 1947, for the wedding of our present Queen, they received a message forbidding them to return to Roumania, where the 'Roumanian Peoples' Republic' was proclaimed. The name was changed in 1965 to the 'Socialist Republic of Roumania', when the Communist Party became constitutionally the only permitted political organization. Meanwhile the pleasant princes and princesses whom I had known, many of whom had suffered under the Iron Guard, had fled the country or had been forced to live in peasants' cottages on their confiscated estates, or else in concentration camps. The dictator, Nicolae Ceausescu, was elected President by the Party in 1967. Things seemed a little brighter then, if only because Roumania had quarrelled with Russia and had made it clear that she would now have no Russian interference in her government. But when I came there in 1969 it was a drab country. Bucharest, the one-time Paris of the Balkans, was a shabby city, with nothing in the shops. Agriculture was being neglected in favour of inappropriate heavy industry; and what had been the best-fed country in Eastern Europe was now short of food. But academic life seemed to be doing well, so long as the professors kept clear of politics.

I was there as the guest of the Roumanian Academy. I was pleased to find that Iorga's house was now an Institute bearing his name. He had been no sympathizer with Communism, but the Roumanians recognized him as their greatest historian. The professors seemed ready to talk, though preferably in the open air, with no one within earshot. Certainly I was very hospitably received. A pleasant and intelligent youngish woman was put in charge of me; and it was soon clear to me that she was not a member of the Party. She escorted me to see the leading members of the Academy and the chief history professors. The professor of medieval art history took me to see the older churches in the city and the suburbs; and, at my request, I went to pay my respects to the Patriarch of Bucharest, a wily old gentleman who had been far-sighted enough in his younger days to keep in with the Left and so was acceptable to the present régime, but who was, I thought, genuinely pious. He saw to it that the state interfered very little in the affairs of the Church, though it was ready, at that time, to pay for the repair and upkeep of the more historic churches and monasteries and for maintaining three seminaries, where many of the ordinands were black young men from Africa. I had to give one lecture, in French, at the Iorga Institute. Apart from a dinner with the British chargé d'affaires, I had the evenings to myself. Bucharest seemed to me then drab but not unfriendly.

The President of the Academy lent me his official car and chauffeur, with a youngish, English-speaking professor to accompany me, so that

I could revisit the painted churches of northern Moldavia and see something of Transylvania. Before we started the professor whispered to me that the chauffeur was a Party agent and probably understood English. I do not think he did, though he certainly knew some French. As we drove northward, not far from the frontier with Russia, we were in splendid sunshine but there were heavy black clouds to the east. I remarked on this to the chauffeur, who thought it a smart political comment and thenceforward regarded me as a friend. We stopped for two nights in Iasi, the ancient capital of Moldavia. There I met the history professors at the University and was shown many of the handsome old buildings in the city. The Patriarch had given me an introduction to the Archbishop of Iasi, whom I was eager to meet as he was said to be the one hierarch who was known to be a member of the Party. But he sent back a message to say that he was too busy to see me. The professors at the University were shocked by such behaviour but said that he was always rude and uncouth and I was missing nothing. I believe that he is now Patriarch. I am sorry for the Church.

From Iasi we drove on to Suceava, the chief town in Bukovina, which was to be our base for seeing the Moldavian churches. When we arrived there, after visiting the monasteries of Neamte and Humor on the way and climbing up to the ruins of Neamte castle, we found that there had been a muddle about our hotel rooms, and as there was a fair of sorts in the town, every hotel was full. So we went out to a neighbouring monastery where we were given adequate rooms and a delicious dinner. I was sorry when we moved next day to the hotel into which we had been booked, as there was a leak in its water supply, and the food in the town restaurants was far less attractive than what we had received in the Monastery of St John. However, the next two days were spent enjoyably if exhaustingly in going round all the main churches and monasteries of the district, in perfect autumn weather. I was pleased to find them in better repair than they had been in 1934. The Abbot of the monastery of Putna told me, quite honestly I think, over rather too many glasses of slivova, the seductive plum brandy of the Balkans, that he found the government always ready to spend money on the upkeep of the monastic buildings and that the professors of archaeology were much more of a nuisance than the state officials. He also said that there was no lack of young men wanting to become monks.

We left Suceava to drive over the Carpathians to Cluj in Transylvania. It was a wonderful journey, through forests splendid in their autumn colouring, outdoing, I thought, even the forests of New England in the fall. At Cluj my professor left me as he and the President of the Academy's car had both to go back to Bucharest. I was put into the charge of a professor of history at Cluj University and a young assistant of his, who during the next two days drove me round several of the old towns of the province. I was especially pleased to see Alba Julia, the historic centre of Transylvania, where in 1919 Queen Marie had organized a magnificent coronation ceremony for her husband, King Ferdinand, and herself as monarchs of Greater Roumania, and where there was a historic library, full of treasures, founded by a member of the great Hungarian family of the Batthany. Unfortunately, the weather had broken, and we drove through lovely country shrouded in mist. My host at Cluj was of partly Magyar origin, and was not happy about the treatment of the Magyars in Transylvania, as he explained to me during a long walk that he made me take with him in pouring rain round a public park. But he was on excellent terms with his fellow professors, who were all very friendly. From Cluj I went back alone by train to Bucharest, befriended on the journey by a Roumanian business-man, who spoke rather bad French and plied me with more slivova than I could manage.

I had three more days in Bucharest. On the first of them I was taken out to Mogoşoea, which was now an institute of sorts. The lady who ran it seemed delighted to learn that I had known it in the days when Princess Bibesco had lived there. I was asked innumerable questions, not all of which I could answer, about how it had been arranged in her time. Incidentally, I found that it aroused great interest, especially among younger Roumanians, when I said that I had known Queen Marie. She had already passed into local legend.

I was sickening for a mild attack of flu by then and wanted to spend the next day in bed but I had to rise to see the Minister for Education that morning and in the evening to dine at the British Embassy. I was to have gone across to Bulgaria on the morrow, but cancelled that journey and returned, rather miserably but without lasting damage, to London.

Two years later the International Byzantine Congress was held in Bucharest. I found then that the atmosphere had deteriorated. Our Roumanian colleagues were all very cordial still, but less at their ease. The young professor who had accompanied me to Bukovina insisted on my lunching with him alone at his flat but took care that no one should see me arrive there. He would be in trouble, he said, if it were known that he was entertaining a foreigner at his home. My hotel room was bugged. I found the apparatus in my bathroom, next to the lavatory seat, as though it was there that I conducted secret conversations. We were well entertained publicly. The President himself gave a large reception for us, at which he arrived, rather scruffily dressed, with a large equally scruffy entourage. It was far more impressive when the Patriarch arrived, fully robed, with a line of robed clergy following him. Some of us were taken up to meet M. Ceausescu, who greeted us in turn with one or two formal remarks. I left the reception early, to go to supper with the Representative of the British Council. As I came out of the People's Palace, where it was held, there was no sign of a taxi. But the chauffeur who had driven me to Bukovina rushed up to me. He was now, he said, chauffeur to one of the Ministers. Where did I want to go? The Minister was not due to leave for another half-hour; so he would drive me to my destination in the Ministerial car. I gratefully accepted the offer.

I tried for some time to keep in contact with my friends in Roumania, communicating with them on postcards or Christmas cards in open envelopes. One or two of them have been allowed out to come to this country. But recently all communication seems to have ceased, and it is only now that I receive an occasional letter. When I remember Roumania as I knew it first, with Queen Marie, with the glitter and glamour of Bucharest in her time, with its churches and monasteries and its rich countryside, it is bitter to think of it lying so long in the clutches of a dictator determined to destroy palaces and churches and even villages in order to create an ugly industrialized land for which it was never suited. The night is ended at last; but the dawn is stormy and uncertain. Let us hope that the people of Roumania will soon enjoy the freedom and the peace that they deserve.

Sarawak

LATE IN 1956 I was unexpectedly asked if I would be willing to write a history of Sarawak. In those days Britain still possessed colonies; and the Colonial Office, perhaps because it saw that the end of the colonial Empire was near, decided that each existing colony should have its history written, as a record of the work of British colonial administrators down the years. Sarawak was on the list for this treatment; but the authorities there felt that it deserved something different. It had, after all, only been a Crown Colony for ten years. From 1841 to 1946 it had been ruled by a dynasty of English-born Rajahs, who, while maintaining their loyalty to the British Crown, had ruled the country by their own methods, deeply resentful of any interference by the British Government. The actual administration in Sarawak was composed of Colonial Office officials; but they were doubtful whether a hack Colonial Office historian would do justice to a government with which the Office had usually been on unfriendly terms.

The Public Relations Officer in Sarawak at the time was a friend of mine called Philip Jones, who was to spend his years of retirement as a much loved clergyman. It was he, it seems, who suggested me for the task of writing the history of the White Rajahs. The Chief Secretary, Hugh Ellis, who had read some of my books, encouraged the idea, and the Governor, Sir Anthony Abell, gave it his approval. When the invitation came, I felt doubtful about it. I never wanted to be commissioned to write a book, and I wondered whether I would be efficient or happy in dealing with modern history. But my mother had just died, and I was eager to get right away for a while; and the chance of travelling to so distant and interesting a part of the world was tempting. Besides, I thought it would be a good discipline to venture into a period of history that was so far out of my experience. And was it so far? From what I knew already about them, the Rajahs were not dissimilar to the Crusader knights of the Middle Ages, while the Ranees showed a kinship to some of the more colourful Empresses of Byzantium.

I still wonder if it was right to come. I enjoyed the experience, or most of it. My intention was to go out to Sarawak for some six weeks in the spring of 1957, to see what papers and records were kept there and what work had been done locally on its history, and to travel a bit round the country; then, after having gone through the numerous papers kept in London and seen as many as I could of the survivors of the Brooke

Rajahs' régime, to return to Sarawak for two months in 1958, to go thoroughly through the local material and complete my travels there: after which I hoped to be ready to write the book. Things did not work out so easily.

This, however, is not the place in which to tell of the difficulties that I had to face when trying to tell the story of the three White Rajahs of Sarawak, the last of whom was still alive when I was writing. The experience taught me never again to try to deal with the history of modern times. But it provided me with the opportunity to see lands that I might never otherwise have visited. On my first journey to Sarawak, early in 1957, I was able to pause at Los Angeles and in the Philippines, as I have told elsewhere in this book. From the Philippines I flew to Borneo, leaving Manila on Ash Wednesday in the evening and arriving on the island of Labuan at 1.40 next morning. Fortunately, Shell Oil ran a comfortable hostel at the airport, where I was able to spend the rest of the night.

I was often to revisit Labuan. It had been the first British colony in Borneo, ceded to Britain by the Sultan of Brunei in 1846. It was very small, but it had the best harbour along the north Borneo coast, also a coal-field, which was in fact not large enough to be of commercial value. Now it also had the best aerodrome in the area; and almost every journey up and down the coast involved a stop in Labuan. My friend Philip Jones met me there and later in the morning we flew across to Brunei. Immediately on arrival I was taken to pay my respects to the Sultan. Brunei was then still a dependency of the British Empire. Indeed, the British had preserved the Sultanate in order to prevent it from falling into the rapacious hands of Rajah Charles of Sarawak, who had managed to annex much of its territory; and their intervention had, unexpectedly, left the Sultan with land that was later found to contain the richest oil-fields in Borneo: thanks to which the present Sultan, the son of my acquaintance, can now claim to be one of the world's multi-millionaires. The Sultan was not greatly pleased to learn that I had come out to write about the Brookes. He told me, rather sternly, not to believe all the accusations that the Brookes had levelled against his ancestors. I tried to appease him by remarking that the Brooke dynasty had come and gone, while his ancient family was still in possession of its throne. That seemed to please him; and when next I was in Brunei I was summoned to see him again. He was not an easy man. The British Resident, with whom I stayed that night, and his successor later on both told tales of careful insults covered by a thin veneer of cordiality. But his people seemed happy enough. The town of Brunei had a certain charm. It was on the edge of an estuary, and many of the houses were built on stilts over the water. The Sultan's increasing wealth was being dem- onstrated in the building of a number of grandiosely ornate public offices and mosques, which added a bizarre effect that was rather endearing. By now, after more than thirty years, the old town is probably engulfed in modern splendour. I doubt if I would wish to see it again.

From Brunei I went to spend a night at Seria, the local headquarters of Shell, and saw over their installations, then flew back to Labuan and on to Kuching, the capital of Sarawak. There I was taken to stay for my first few days in the country with the Governor, in the Astana, the old palace of the White Rajahs.

I had often heard of the charm of Sarawak; but I have to confess that the country round Kuching is not very attractive. One's vision of the tropics as having cloudless blue skies and great forests full of exotic birds and butterflies and brilliant flowers was not confirmed by Sarawak. There the sky was almost always overcast; the rivers were sluggish and muddy; the forests were thick and impenetrable with overgrown scrub, and the bird-life was confined to the tree-tops, out of sight. Occasionally, going along the roads and paths hacked through the undergrowth one might see a turkey-crow, a large unattractive bird, scuttling away. Exotic flowers and butterflies were only to be seen in gardens in the town. Further afield, when one reached the mountainous districts, the air was fresher but the sky seemed usually to be overcast and the rivers just as muddy, while the contours of the hills were blurred by the thick forest growth. Scenically and climatically Sarawak seemed to me to be far less attractive than North Borneo, the present Sabah, which was dominated by the great mountain of Kinabalu, on whose slopes there was pleasant savannah country. The inhabitants of the country, apart from the small number of Europeans, were in three main groups. There were the indigenous peoples, usually lumped together under the name of Dyaks but actually consisting of a number of distinct tribes, of which the most numerous were the so-called Sea Dyaks, who lived on the rivers and seldom penetrated into the sea. These tribes lived for the most part in long-houses, buildings that accommodated the whole local community, under the control of a hereditary headman. Women had a high status, with full rights to own property; but their duties within the community were strictly defined. The religion was a simple animism, with no priests, but sometimes with a local magician, who was dressed as a woman and had to perform women's duties. There was a general belief in an after-life. They had a few slaves, mostly captives taken from neighbouring long-houses; though more recently they had taken to buying unwanted Chinese girls. They would often fight with their neighbours over *Lebensraum* but were not essentially warlike. Indeed, as entry into the after-world involved long ceremonies in which the corpse had to play a part, death and mutilation in battle was not at all desirable. But they nearly all indulged in one unpleasant practice, which was head-hunting. It was a matter of prestige to collect heads. A young man could seldom hope to marry unless he had one or two to his credit, and the wealth of a long-house was estimated by the number of heads hanging in it to dry. As a corpse could not be buried without its head, relatives would pay large sums to have their dear ones' heads returned to them. The choice of victims was arbitrary. A casual traveller's head would do as well as that of an unfriendly neighbour. Heads of women and children were especially esteemed, as that proved that the slayer must have penetrated into the heart of a neighbouring community. The Brooke Rajahs had long struggled to end this national pastime and by the beginning of this century had on the whole succeeded, thanks largely to Christian missionaries. The Brookes did not much care for missionaries, finding them self-important and quarrelsome. In particular, the rivalry between Protestants and Catholics was intense, till the Second Rajah firmly divided the country into areas where each could operate exclusively, rather to the puzzlement of the Dyaks, who found that in some districts the holy men married but would not drink alcohol, while in others the holy men drank alcohol but would not marry. By the 1930s most of the indigenous tribes of Sarawak were Christian, some Anglican, some Catholic, while one of the wildest tribes, the Muruts in the northern hills, were converted by American missionaries to an extreme form of evangelism. All this meant that the habit of head-hunting declined. By 1940 it was considered safe for anyone to wander round the country without running the risk of losing his head. When I was there some of the long-houses still kept a head or two as a sign of past prowess, and would show them to you on request. It was a request that I regretted making.

The Malays regarded themselves as the local aristocrats. Malay principalities had been founded along the coasts of Borneo towards the end of the Middle Ages. The Sultanate of Brunei seems to have been founded, by an ancestor of the present Sultan, early in the fifteenth century. They were firmly established in the coastal areas but had never attempted to penetrate far inland, finding nothing to tempt them to make the effort. They were all Moslems, though not, at least when I was there, at all fanatical. I do not know if Moslem fundamentalism has by now spread there. They were contemptuous of the pagan native tribes; and their contempt was not much lessened when the tribes became Christian. They had been on the whole loyal supporters of the Brooke régime; and it was they who objected most strongly when the Third Rajah sold Sarawak to the British Government in 1947. They saw their independent kingdom being degraded to the status of a colony. And now, as the ultimate outcome of that cession, it has become a distant and somewhat neglected province of Malaysia; the Sarawak Malays, I am told, do not much like being treated as provincial folk by their cousins in mainland Asia. I liked the Malays. They had beautiful manners; they had humour; and they treated you as an equal. It is true that they were touchy and truculent, easy to take offence and unforgiving if they were slighted. Many of them may have been rogues; but I enjoyed their company and had several good friends among them, old men and young. One did not meet their women.

Then there were the Chinese, disliked by both the Malays and the Dyaks, but essential for the country's economy, as they understood about trade and finance, and they worked hard. Chinese merchants had been visiting Borneo for many centuries past. Chinese coins dating from before the Christian era have been found along the coast, while long-houses far inland still possess jars made in China in the time of the Tang dynasty; artefacts dating from the Sung dynasty are not uncommon. The Emperor Kublai Khan is said to have thought of annexing Borneo. There were at that time Chinese trading settlements along the coast; but none seem to have lasted into the sixteenth century, though the maritime trade remained in Chinese hands, and there were Chinese merchants established in Brunei, and in other Malay towns. When James Brooke took over the government of Sarawak, there was a small colony of Chinese in Kuching. He found them helpful and encouraged more of them to settle there; and, as his dominion increased in size, he used them to exploit the mines that came under his rule. They were already operating the gold-mines at Bau, up-river from Kuching. They were at this time organized in *kongsis*, democratically run associations or unions, each of them out for the welfare of its members. The Rajah admired their efficiency, but had to intervene to curb their rivalries. But as time went on the *kongsis* became politically ambitious, in particular the *kongsi* at Bau, the largest of them, which had somehow in the 1840s been brought into touch with the dominant secret society in China itself, the so-called Triad. This in theory preached a mystical union between heaven and earth but in practice was out for political power and was xenophobic and ruthless. There were rumours early in 1857 of a planned Chinese rising. But the government was unprepared when on 18 February several hundred fully armed Chinese burst into Kuching. In the end they were driven back and all of them perished, mostly at the hands of Dyaks loyal to the Rajah, but some at the hands of rival Chinese *kongsis*. But in the course of the rising most of the town of Kuching had been burnt, including the Rajah's residence, with the loss, which he especially regretted, of the fine library that he had amassed. Though a century had passed and the *kongsis* had long since been banned, there was still, when I arrived in Sarawak, some suspicion of the Chinese, particularly among the Malays, and rumours of new secret societies being formed. The Dyaks were less unfriendly, seeing in the Chinese allies against Malay domination. By now the Chinese controlled nearly all the commerce and finance of the country and played a large part in running the machinery of government. The older Chinese tended to keep to themselves, but the younger generations, many of them Christian converts, were almost entirely Europeanized, and it was easy to make friends with them.

I do not know what horrors modern architecture has brought by now to Kuching. In my time it was an unpretentious town, like many others in that part of the world. The public buildings were modest, with a simple neo-Gothic Anglican cathedral, not yet finished, rising somewhat incongruously on a small hill. Residential bungalows sprawled not unpleasantly round the outskirts. The most interesting building was the Astana, the Governor's house, situated across the river and reached only by boat. It had been built for the Second Rajah in the 1860s to replace the Astana burnt down in the Chinese rising, close to the original site. It was an eclectic affair. A Gothic tower rose over the entrance, and on either side there were large wings with high-pitched roofs of wooden shingles. The reception rooms and the bedrooms were all on the first floor, with the kitchen and pantries on the ground floor, next to a row of bathrooms. The house has been many times redecorated since Rajah Charles moved into it in 1870 but has undergone no structural change, though the bathrooms may have been moved upstairs. It is haunted, having been built over an ancient Malay graveyard. When I was working in the library there I used suddenly to feel certain that I was not alone in the room. It was eerie but not actually sinister.

Sarawak was fortunate at that time in its Governor. Sir Anthony Abell had arrived there in 1950 at a difficult moment. His predecessor, landing at Sibu at the end of 1949 to take over the post, had been stabbed to death by a Malay indignant at the British Government having bought the country from the Brookes. The murder shocked even the most fervent Brooke partisans; and the new Governor was received with some sympathy. But his tact and geniality, his obvious fairmindedness and integrity soon won him real affection. The nine years of his rule were probably the happiest period in the history of Sarawak during this century. It was always a delight to go with him round the country and to bask in the sunshine of his popularity. He was a warm and generous host, perhaps helped by being unmarried; for the wives of British Governors have all too often behaved like governesses, didactic, dictatorial and disapproving.

I spent my first four days in Kuching staying in the Astana, going through such records as were kept in its library. I then moved to spend five nights with the Chief Secretary, Hugh Ellis, and for the rest of my visit, when I was in Kuching, I was housed by my old friend Philip Jones. My mornings were usually passed in the Museum library, going through the papers there. It was a curious collection. Very little survived from the First Rajah's reign. He had ruled through personal contacts. Very little had been written down, and what had been written had nearly all been destroyed during the Chinese rising. Were it not for the account published in two volumes written by the Second Rajah while he was a district officer before his accession, there would have been little to tell us what life had been like during those earlier years. For his own reign there were his letter books, with copies of almost every letter that he wrote from 1870 to 1916, an odd collection of Order Books and a number of reports from District Officers, nearly all dealing with trivial matters. Major decisions seem still to have been communicated by word of mouth. There was also a complete set, from 1870 to 1941 of the semi-official *Sarawak Gazette*, usually published fortnightly but sometimes only monthly. For the Third Rajah's reign the material was even more spasmodic, much having been destroyed or lost during the Japanese occupation of Sarawak, from Christmas 1941 to the summer of 1945. But, scrappy though the material was, there was far more in the Museum library than I could fully examine in this first visit to Sarawak, especially as I wanted to see something of the country.

I went for several short excursions. One day the Governor took me with him to visit the country's leper colony, which was pleasantly situated and seemed well run, with the inmates, among whom was an Englishman, remarkably cheerful. But it was sad to see that so much leprosy still existed. It was much less melancholy to visit the local prison. The prisoners were a happy lot. One of them told me how much more agreeable his life was there than in his home-village. Most of them spent their time working on the prison's pepper plantations. For several years after, till he retired, the prison governor used to send me every Christmas a present of peppercorns. I was taken on two occasions to see villages near Kuching that could be visited within a day, my escort being the Malay Assistant Information Officer, from whom I learnt much about Malay life.

My main excursion was to the great caves at Niah, in the north of the colony. The director of the Museum in Kuching, who was also in charge of archaeology and anthropology in Sarawak, was a remarkable man, Tom Harrisson, who in the 1930s had been one of the founders of Mass Observation. He was a trained anthropologist who had come to Sarawak as a paratrooper in the course of the last War and was now the leading authority on its tribes. He was not an easy man, but he had acquired an intelligent and friendly German wife, who could smooth out any roughnesses of his making. He had made it clear that he did not approve of me being invited to write the history of the Rajahs, on the reasonable grounds that I knew nothing about their country. When I arrived in Kuching he was away at Niah, working on an archaeological site at the mouth of one of the caves. With him there was a young zoologist, Lord Medway (now Lord Cranbrook), who was studying the bats that lived in the largest of the caves. He sent me an invitation to visit him at the site, largely, so he admitted to me later, in the hope that I would find the discomfort there too much for me and would be deterred from continuing with my commission.

I set out from Kuching on a Sunday morning with the Police Commissioner and his wife in their motor launch. We spent three nights on the journey along the coast, putting in at a small town at the mouth of a river for dinner every evening. They landed me off the mouth of the Niah river early on the Wednesday. A police speed-boat took me to Niah town, where I was transferred into a boat with an outboard motor, which chugged me up to a landing-place, where Mrs Harrisson was waiting for me. We walked for a mile or so along duck-boards till we reached the hillside and the Harrissons' camp at the mouth of the great cave. I spent the afternoon watching the excavators at work. Up till that time they had not found a single artefact; but I had hardly been there for an hour before they turned up some stones – 'tampan' stones, I think that they were called – which showed signs of human workmanship. Tom Harrisson at once regarded me as a *porte-bonheur*; and thenceforward our relations were of the most cordial.

I spent that night on a camp-bed in the lower cave of Niah. It was damp and eerie; but I slept well enough. Next day I was shown the upper cave, noted for its bats and its birds' nests, from which the Chinese made birds' nest soup. After seeing them I never fancied that dish any more. We had to shelter in another from a portentous thunderstorm. Then, as dusk approached, I was taken to the upper cave to help in counting the bats. I had to stand with my eyes fixed on a small excrescence in the roof by the mouth of the cave and count every bat that passed by. As they came fluttering past in their thousands it was not an easy task. It had a sort of mesmeric effect on one, almost like a mystical exercise to attain enlightenment. But I achieved no enlightenment, merely a feeling of relief when it became too dark to continue the exercise. I forget now how many bats I actually counted. I think that it was close on one thousand.

Next morning, after going some way up the Niah river with Tom Harrisson, I returned to the coast and was taken in a launch to the town of Miri, from which, on the morrow, a Shell aeroplane took me to Labuan and a passenger plane on to Kuching.

I made one other excursion from Kuching during that first visit to Sarawak, going in a small launch, with several stops on the way, to Sibu, a town that had played a large part in the Rajah's history. I spent two days there, mostly in thunderous rain, before flying in a small plane back to Kuching.

It was on my second visit to Sarawak that I made a more serious effort to see the interior of the country. I had been in Australia and flew from Darwin to Labuan, where Philip Jones met me. Two days later, on 19 March 1958, an aeroplane took us across to Sandakan, on the eastern coast of North Borneo. My host there, James Mitchell, was the local head of Harrison & Crosfield, the chief business firm in North Borneo, and was a leading figure in the government of the country. His wife turned out to be an old friend of mine, whom I had known when I had been staying twenty-seven years before with the British High Commissioner in Palestine, and she was governess to his young son. She reminded me that I had told her fortune then and had been puzzled because there was to be a blank period later in her life when she seemed to be dead but she afterwards would later turn to life. She had married soon afterwards and had gone out to live in Borneo, very happily, till the Japanese invasion at the end of 1941. She had then spent nearly four years in misery in a concentration-camp, with nothing to do except to try to keep herself and her young son alive. All that time, she told me, she was sustained by my prophesy that she would come back to life. So I was regarded as a specially welcome guest.

Sandakan itself was an attractively situated town, on a bay with hills around; and the hinterland was far more beautiful than that of Sarawak. We were there for two days, and on each of them the Mitchells drove us up into the mountains. I would have liked to have stayed there longer. But we had to take a boat that would take us round the north coast of Borneo to Jesselton. We sailed mainly by night, spending the inside of a day at Kudat, at the extreme north of the country, where a kindly District Officer drove us up the slopes of Mount Kinabalu. At Jesselton, the capital of North Borneo – and the only capital city to be called after a Jew, unless we count St Petersburg as such; but both cities have had to change their names – we stayed a night at Government House, then flew on to Kuching next morning.

In Kuching I stayed for ten days at the Astana, going across every morning to the Museum to continue work on the papers there. Then, with Easter approaching, the Governor took a small party on his yacht, the *Zamora*, to visit Lundu, the westernmost town in the colony, and Talang Talang Island, on whose beach turtles from all over the South China Sea come to lay their eggs. It should have been an enjoyable weekend; but I spent most of it in bed in my cabin with a fever. However, when we arrived back at Kuching early on the Tuesday, I was sent off at once in an aeroplane to Sibu, to stay with the Resident, Dennis White, who was to take me up the River Rejang right into the interior, to visit long-houses.

My memories of the days that followed are lost in a haze. I was feeling very ill most of the time and did not have the energy to jot down the names of the people and the places that I saw, as I usually managed to do. I remember a very social evening in Sibu, going to a champagne

party given by the leading Chinese citizen. Next day we left in the
Resident's launch to go up the river. In the evening we stopped in a creek
off the river to visit a long-house. I begged to be allowed to stay on the
boat but was told that the villagers were expecting the Resident to bring
a friend to see them. So, with a mounting temperature I landed and
walked over slippery duck-boards to the long-house. Of the evening in
the long-house I now only remember noise and the smells of humanity
and food and the horrible rice beer that they hospitably forced on me,
while two dried heads grinned down from the roof. I hope that I
behaved with adequate courtesy. They were all immensely friendly; and
the headman begged us to stay the night in the house. Space would be
cleared for us and mattresses provided. To my relief Dennis White, who
by now realized that I was far from well, said that we had to go back to
the launch.

I remember very little about the next day. We went further and
further up the river, through scenery that was splendid as we approached
the mountains, and on in a canoe to the rapids of the river near the
settlement of Belaga, then down the river again to spend the night
moored off the riverside-quay at Kapit. But by then I was running a very
high temperature and lay barely conscious on my berth. I was little better
next morning and was very glad to return to Sibu and the Resident's
house. I seemed over the worst next day and was taken down to the coast
to join the Governor's yacht, which had been taking some officials along
the coast.

I do not remember much about the next days. We went up a river to
the town of Semanggang, where the Resident and his wife had to house
me for longer than they had expected, as I was by then quite ill. They
thought that I might be suffering from dengue fever; and I remember a
Chinese nurse coming to take a sample of my blood. The result was then
negative. After three days I was well enough to spend a morning going
up the river to see another long-house, where, mercifully, I was spared
having to drink rice beer. Next day I rejoined the yacht and returned to
Kuching.

After five quiet days living in the Astana I was thought to be well
enough to recommence my journeying, though in a more comfortable
manner. I wanted to see the oil installations in the north of the country, as
they had played a part in the last years of the Rajahs' rule. The head of
Shell in Borneo, who had been visiting Kuching, took me in a company
aeroplane to his headquarters at Seria. But that evening, when staying in
his pleasant house, I was once more stricken by a high fever. Next
morning my host wisely packed me off to the local hospital, which,
being run by the oil companies and not by the Government, was
attractive and highly efficient. I spent a week there. They decided that
my complaint probably was dengue after all but, whatever it was, the

treatment that they gave me was effective. I emerged from the hospital in a rather feeble state; but I had no more trouble with my health during that visit to Sarawak. But I attempted no more travelling about the country. Indeed, I was too busy trying to make up for lost time in my study of the archives. It became clear that I would have to pay another visit to the country.

I came out again in mid-January 1959, after spending two nights in Singapore at that historic hostelry, Raffles Hotel. I wish that I had arrived a little sooner in Kuching, for I just missed a ceremony which I would have loved to witness, when the Governor was made an honorary Girl Guide by Lady Baden-Powell. On this visit I remained in Kuching, apart from a week spent partly in staying with Dennis White, who was now British Resident in Brunei, and partly at the oil headquarters at Seria, without, on this occasion, having to go to the hospital. I enjoyed my time in Brunei, my host being excellent company. I was able to see what papers were kept in the Residency there, and I was received again by the Sultan, who did his best to make the occasion humiliating to the Resident by crudely exaggerating my importance and making him appear as little more than my attendant. I found it somewhat embarrassing, but the Resident was used to such behaviour and amused by it. It was interesting, too, to learn more about the oil installations on the Sarawak–Brunei border.

In Kuching I managed to finish going through the papers in the Museum library and to see a number of the local folk who remembered the days of the Brookes. For most of the time I stayed with Philip Jones but moved to the Astana for the last few days. I did not entirely escape illness but was only out of action for two days. Eventually I left Kuching on 18 February, to travel home by way of Hong Kong, the Philippines and the United States.

I remember Sarawak with affection, not for its scenery or its buildings, but for the kindliness and friendliness of its people. But now it has become part of Malaysia. I am told that many of its people, even among the Malays, would have preferred to be governed from London to being governed from Kuala Lumpur. There are few left who knew the rule of the White Rajahs; but even to the present generation it has acquired the glamour of a distant Golden Age.

Thailand

I WOULD MUCH RATHER call it Siam, the name by which it was known to the West down the centuries. I am aware that its people call themselves Thais and that their language is Thai. But the name 'Siam' carried with it a feeling of gentle mystery, whereas 'Thailand' is a bastard word. But perhaps it suits a country that has now been ruined by excessive tourism and louche expatriates.

When I came back to Cambridge as a young don in 1927 I soon met an undergraduate at Trinity who was a Siamese prince, Chula Chakrabongse, who during the next years became a close friend. His position in the royal family was peculiar. His grandfather, King Chakrabongse, who had brought Siam into the modern world, had remained oriental enough to have had thirty-six wives and seventy-seven children; and of his wives the three ranking highest were half-sisters of his. One of them was raised to be chief Queen; and it was her sons who were designated as being in the line of succession to the throne. Chula's father was the second of these princes. As a youth he had been sent to finish his education in Russia, at the court of Nicholas II, and there he had rashly become engaged to a young Russian lady, whom he married in Singapore on his way home. His parents were furious; but eventually the old Queen became very fond of her, especially when she gave birth to a son who proved to be the Queen's only grandson. On King Chakrabongse's death Chula's uncle, Vajiravudh, succeeded to the throne. Periodically he would become engaged to be married, but then thought better of it. His fiancées were pensioned off but forbidden to marry anyone else. I knew one of them, Princess Lakshami, a lady of great beauty and charm who would have made an excellent Queen; but she was perhaps too high-spirited to suit the King's taste. In the meantime Chula's father, Prince Chakrabongse, was the heir-presump-tive. The succession-law debarred the sons of foreign mothers; but possibly had Prince Chakrabongse survived the King he might have altered the law. As it was, he died five years before the King, and his youngest brother, Prajadhipok, was appointed heir. King Prajadhipok succeeded in 1925, but ten years later he abdicated, after having granted the country a constitution that he resented. The throne then passed to a boy of ten, the son of the late King's senior half-brother. Had Chula been living in Siam and preferably been married to a Siamese princess, he would almost certainly have been appointed Regent, and he would have been a good Regent, if a trifle autocratic. But he had made his home in England and he was soon to marry an English girl. The regency went to another cousin of his, Prince Oscar (called after the King of Sweden) and, after his suicide a few months later, to another cousin, Prince Aditya.

I think that Chula always felt that he had somehow been cheated out of his heritage, but he was far too realistic to regret it. As it was, he had the best of both worlds. He escaped all the tiresome duties and all the intrigues which he would have had to face had he been king or a senior prince living in Siam. In Europe he was accepted as a royal prince. King George V and Queen Mary were both fond of him; and he represented his country at the funeral of George V and the coronations of George VI and of Queen Elizabeth. He had many friends among other royal houses. Though he received no money from the Siamese civil list, he had inherited his father's private fortune, which included large areas of Bangkok, and his grandmother's possessions, which included a vast collection of jewelry. (Alas, I lost the Fabergé cigarette case that he gave me, I think to some nimble pickpocket.) At the same time he was free to lead his own life and indulge his own interests, one of the chief of which was to manage the motor-racing career of his young cousin, Prince Birabongse. In consequence I found myself taken now and then to watch the races, which I found interesting rather than enjoyable.

Chula married his English bride, Lisba Hunter, in the autumn of 1938, and soon after the wedding he took her with him to Bangkok, to spend the winter there. His cousin Birabongse, who had also, a little previously, married an English girl, Ceril Heycock, joined them with his bride and his brother, Abhas; and Chula, hearing that I was planning to escape from Cambridge for a year, and probably for good, urged me to pay them a visit. I had, I thought, been a don for long enough. I enjoyed teaching, seeing each of my pupils singly once a week. I have never much liked lecturing, though I have done it often enough in the course of a long life. I still want the world to end before I go on to the lecture platform. But to have to prepare a lecture is an excellent way of finding out what you really think about a subject. What I definitely disliked were the additional tasks that are now part of a don's life, the examinations and the committees in which one had to do one's share. During my earlier years as a don I had had time to write three books but, as I was sucked further into the system, writing became more difficult. One should never criticize University lecturers for producing so few great works. They have too much other work forced on them. When I was admitted as a Fellow of Trinity in 1927 the historian G. M. Trevelyan was re-admitted as a Fellow at the same ceremony, on becoming Regius Professor of History after having spent several years away from University duties, writing his books. He told me then that I ought to stay for some time in Cambridge, to establish myself as a serious historian, but then, he said, if I wanted to write, I should escape. My grandfather had died in 1937, and I now had enough money to exist without an earned income. So I decided to take his advice. But, before I settled down to my writing, I wanted to go right away for a few months to see distant parts of the world. With war looming on the horizon I might never have another chance.

So the invitation to visit Chula in Thailand was opportune, and I eagerly accepted it. A young man just down from Cambridge, called Eddie Bates, had been promised by his parents a trip round the world before he settled down to a serious career; and they asked me if I would let him set out with me. He too wanted to go to Bangkok, where he had friends; so it suited well, and I was glad to have a companion for the journey out and for journeys later on.

We set out from London on 10 November 1938 to join the P. & O. liner *Chitral* at Marseilles. The company on board was not exciting but pleasant enough. We called in at Malta, where Lord Strickland, then the Grand Old Man of the island, took us on a drive up to the old and lovely city of Mdina – a city where, I am told, every other person whom you see in the streets after dark really is not there. At Aden we were driven round by a young colonial officer who all too clearly hated the place. We called at Cochin, which looked charming, but we had no time to land there; and at Colombo, where we spent a night ashore after driving up to Kandy during the day. Finally we disembarked at Penang early on 1 December. I had seen Penang on my way to and from China thirteen years earlier; and the pleasant impression that I had of it then was now renewed. Business friends of Eddie's father took us to lunch, soon after our arrival, at the top of the peak that dominates the island.

From the funicular on the way down I saw an enormous cobra basking in the sun. It was beautiful, and I was shocked when the car stopped and some boys got out with sticks, to try to kill it. Fortunately it slid safely away. I have never minded snakes. A few months later, when I was walking with friends in Bali, a cobra slithered across my foot. They were all horrified, but I felt no fear. I have worn a young boa-constrictor round my neck, like a feather boa. It was soft and warm and very comfortable. Some twenty years ago a remarkable man called Ionides, who lived in a hut in Kenya, full of books which he read at night, while he spent his days catching poisonous snakes for snake farms, came to London to appear on television. He had read some of my books and wanted to see me. We met at a dinner at the Hamish Hamiltons, to which he brought a basket full of his venomous pets. When the table was cleared after dinner he emptied his basket on to it. As it had a smooth glass top the snakes were unable to move on it. They lay there, helpless and resentful. I wanted to comfort them somehow, but was not allowed to touch.

Eddie Bates decided to stay a day or two longer in Penang. So next morning I crossed alone to the mainland, to Prai, to take the train to Bangkok. It was an agreeable journey. The train was slow and comfortable, with friendly attendants and unexpectedly good food. We meandered through a jungle made remarkable by a number of strange isolated rocky hills. The frontier was crossed, with very little bureaucratic fuss, in the late afternoon and we reached Bangkok next day, just after midday. Chula met me there, dressed in full uniform, with an A.D.C. in attendance, and took me to the Trocadero Hotel, where I was to sleep.

It was a good hotel according to the standards of the time, when there was no air-conditioning and one welcomed a mosquito-net. A car came every morning to fetch me to Chula's own house, Ta Tien. It was officially called a palace, as princes were supposed to live in palaces. But it was actually a rather ugly villa, with large reception-rooms and very few bedrooms. The formal and empty garden stretched down to the river Menam, with the great temple of Wat Arun rising on the opposite bank. The house had been given by Chula's grandmother to his father; but no one had lived in it for many years, and Chula and his wife were having to work hard to make it fully habitable. Princess Chula took me one day down to the cellars, which were full of damaged pieces of furniture and huge handsome dinner-services with half the plates broken. But by the time that I arrived, the sitting-rooms, though rather bare, were perfectly comfortable.

Life in Bangkok was very lively that season. The young king, Ananda Mahidol, who had been at school in Switzerland when he came to the throne, was now at the age of thirteen paying his first visit to his country since his accession, together with his mother, his brother and his sister. He was far too young to appear in society, and the Princess-Mother, a quiet but very intelligent woman, who was unfairly looked down upon by many of the Siamese for not being of royal birth, had no desire to go out to parties. But the King's presence gave the feeling that, in spite of constitutional changes, the old order had not vanished. The two chief figures in the government, the Prime Minister, Field-Marshal Pibul, and the Foreign Minister, a clever lawyer called Pridi, had been leading figures in forcing the constitution on King Prajadhipok; but they were not republicans. They treated the young king and the Regent, Prince Aditya, with proper deference; and there were several princes serving in the Cabinet. There was still some unrest in the country, but Pibul was its target, not the Royal Family. Indeed, shortly before I arrived, Chula had invited Pibul to dinner. He was extremely late in arriving, and when he came he explained that while he was dressing to go out and had one leg in his trousers, a man had burst into his room with a gun, and he was in no position to dodge him. Fortunately, his guards rushed in and overpowered the assassin before he had time to fire his weapon. Later in my visit when I was invited to call on the Prime Minister I was interested to see that before we were allowed to drink the iced soda water, which was the usual refreshment offered on such visits, a taster was brought in, to make sure that the drink was not poisoned.

Chula was eager to show me all the sights of the city. There was hardly a temple or a palace that I did not visit. Many of the temples and the old Royal Palace were remarkably ornate. One's eyes were dazzled by the bright colours and all the gold. But the general effect, though gaudy, somehow was not vulgar. What charmed me most were the *klongs*, canals that traversed the city instead of streets. There were very few roads, and very few cars. Travel through the city was done mainly by boat, and nearly all the market stalls were floating. And, unlike the canals of Venice, the *klongs* were remarkably clean. There were no speed-boats on them, only a few slow motor-boats, and for the most part punts were used.

When I was not seeing sights I was seeing the Royal Family. Chula felt avuncular towards the little King, and he liked the Princess-Mother. She and her children came often to the house at Ta Tien and seemed to be at their ease there. The Regent and his elegant wife were very friendly. I went several times to their house. There were some charming older princes. I remember in particular Prince Naris, a great-uncle of Chula's, who was a capable artist and architect and loved to talk about art. There was another great-uncle, Prince Rangsit, who had a German wife and probably the best private collection of Thai antiquities in the country. Dining with him was something of an ordeal. We were given an ample European – rather Germanic – meal. Then, when it was over, a dinner cooked in Thai style appeared. One did one's best not to disappoint the kind and generous man. When I returned to Bangkok two months later I asked Chula if I could go and pay my respects to Prince Rangsit. No, said Chula; and he told me that the Prince was now in gaol, having been mixed up in a conspiracy against Pibul's regime. He was later released, and even became Regent for a few years after the World War. But I never saw him again.

I went more than once to the British Legation, where there was a genial and hospitable Minister, Sir Josiah Crosby, a bachelor, much loved by the Siamese. He had a peculiar way of talking, bobbing his head up and down and gobbling his words. When Chula acquired a mynah bird it talked in the same way. We called it Josiah. There was also a very pleasant French Minister, M. Lepissier. I lunched with him and his wife one day, where I was seated next to the Royal governess. We all went after lunch to see the royal white elephants, two of them, coloured a rather unattractive pale beige. They each bore a title that was the equivalent of Duke.

The great social event in Bangkok in December was, and maybe still is, the Constitutional Fair. A large open space was covered with tents, one containing a restaurant, another a dance floor, another a theatre where you could see cabaret shows, and another an assembly room. Chula gave two dinner-parties there, one for his house-party and his staff and the other where I met a number of his cousins; and I dined there once with Princess Lakshami, King Vajiravudh's discarded fiancée. A few days after the opening of the Fair there was the opening of the National Assembly, to which I went with the guests staying at the British Legation, and which was followed by a dinner and ball at the Foreign Ministry, where the Prince Regent introduced me to all the members of his cabinet. I had not yet seen the Prime Minister, Pibul; but Chula had already taken me to call on the Foreign Minister, Pridi, and the youngish Minister of Education.

One night at the Fair there was a beauty competition, to choose Miss Thailand for the year. The judges were one of the Cabinet Ministers and Chula, who suggested that I should be added as a third judge. I found it impossible to choose between the charming and elegant young ladies, all very respectably dressed. So I just acquiesced in the others' choice. On another evening there was a ball with prizes for the best costumes. As I was standing there a beautifully attired young woman waved at me as she passed. I asked Chula who she was. He laughed. 'That', he said, 'is the Minister of Education, whom I took you to see the other day. He said he thought of coming dressed as a woman.' He rightly won a prize.

After twelve days of that endlessly sociable life I was exhausted and very glad to leave with Eddie Bates for Cambodia, as I have described earlier in this book. From Indo-China we went to Singapore and saw the New Year in at a party in Raffles Hotel. At midnight a young lady was let down on ropes from the ceiling of the ball-room, laden with confetti to scatter among us all. But the ropes somehow were tangled and she descended head first, screaming, with her skirts falling about her face, leaving her under-knickers all too visible. It was a bad omen for the beginning of 1939. Next day we drove out with his architect to visit the Prince Regent of Johore, who showed us his new house and his zoo and gave us drinks at his Club. We had met the Scottish-born Sultana of Johore in Singapore on New Year's Eve, but were told not to mention it, as the Prince did not care for his step-mother. On 2 January we took a ship for Java, for the city that was then called Batavia.

I spent six weeks in what was then the Dutch East Indies. Eddie and I stayed for three days in Batavia. I had met in Holland the newly appointed Governor-General of the Indies, a grim but friendly Frisian baron, with an American wife, and so was invited to lunch at Government House, some thirty miles inland at Buitenzorg. It was a handsome house, built on the edge of the great botanical garden founded by Sir Stamford Raffles during the Napoleonic Wars when Britain for a time occupied Java. It was still the most magnificent garden in the world; and, thanks to His Excellency, I was able to see the parts that remained his private domain. From Batavia we took the train to Bandoeng, spending the afternoon of our arrival visiting the hill-resort of Lembang and the whole of the next day on a long excursion to the great active crater of Papandajan. This involved, after a considerable car-drive, a long walk along a stony path and a steep climb up the side of the volcano. It was well worth the effort. The views all round were magnificent; and the great crater, with its boiling mud and gusts of steam, looked properly infernal. We returned weary to Bandoeng, to go on the morrow by train to Djokjakarta for two nights and on for one night at Soerakarta. These were the capitals of two small autonomous states in Java, Djokja and Suli, where Sultans ruled on under strict Netherlands suzerainty. From Djokjakarta we drove out to see the eighth-century Buddhist temples at Prambanan and the great ninth-century temple or, rather, stupa at Borobodur. They were interesting and impressive; but one should see them before, not after, visiting Angkor. We also saw the somewhat tawdry public rooms in the Sultan of Djokja's palace.

When I had been at Buitenzorg the Governor-General had spoken well of the Sultan of Suli. He said that he would write to the Dutch Resident at Soerakarta to arrange for me to have an interview with the Sultan. But when I arrived there I had the greatest difficulty in finding the Resident, eventually tracking him down at his house where he was enjoying his noonday siesta. When I asked him if I could see the Sultan he firmly said no. I referred to the Governor-General's letter. He replied that the Governor-General was a new arrival and did not yet realize how the country was governed. Only under very exceptional circumstances were the natives allowed to meet foreigners. I might see the throne-room at the Palace, and that was all.

The episode explained much to me. Java was efficiently adminis-tered, as was everywhere else that I visited in the Dutch East Indies. The towns were clean, the roads well kept, the trains punctual and remarkably comfortable. Everyone looked well fed and well dressed. There were no beggars and none of the ghastly poverty that I was to see a little later in British India. But, except perhaps in Bali, there was no laughter; and one felt that the Europeans were resented. It was a gov-ernment that took great trouble to see that the natives were prosperous, but that allowed them to have no part in it, except as clerks and very junior officials. It took no account of the sad fact that most peoples prefer chaotic independence to an efficient rule by aliens. When I came home I wrote a little memorandum on my impressions; and my father sent a copy to his friend the Netherlands elder statesman, Mr Colijn. He, though considered almost too liberal by most of his compatriots, wrote politely back that he was interested but not worried by my views. The inhabitants of the Netherlands Indies were so well off that they would never want to be rid of their present rulers. He was wrong.

Nevertheless I enjoyed the rest of my Indonesian journey. We sailed from Sourabaya in Java to Macassar, capital of the island of Celebes. Celebes, I am told, is now called Sulawesi, and Macassar, from which in the last century a favourite hair-oil, made from the seeds of a local sapindaceous tree, was exported to Europe, is now Ujung Pandang: so that we ought to call antimacassars anti-ujungpandangs, which is less mellifluous. From Macassar we sailed up the west coast of Celebes to Menado, at the north of the island. I was charmed by Celebes. From both Macassar and Menado we went for long drives into the country, which was mountainous and wild, with very few inhabitants to be seen. A comfortable cargo boat took us from Menado to Ternate, in the north Molucca islands. Ternate had been occupied in the sixteenth century by the Portuguese but was taken over in the early seventeenth century by the Dutch and was for a few years the administrative centre of their Indonesian possessions. But the island was dominated by an active volcano which more than once damaged the town, which was almost entirely destroyed by an eruption in 1763. The present town was then built on the other side of the island. During the morning that we were there we visited the 'Burnt Corner', as the ruins of the old town were called, as well as a handsome old Portuguese fort, now half-ruined, and a fort built by the first Dutch governor in 1607. There we transhipped into a boat that was to go round a number of small ports, collecting copra. We were thus able to see a number of islands that were seldom visited. I remember one in the Sula archipelago where the jungle came down to the shore. We went for a walk in it and became completely lost. We were panic-stricken till suddenly we saw the sea, but not where we expected it to be. In another small island the Dutch Commissioner seemed to be the only white resident. He was a lonely young man who studied history and was thrilled to learn that I was a historian. With tears in his eyes he begged me to stay there till the next steamer arrived. He admitted to me that I would probably have to wait four weeks for it; but his house was full of books, he said, and the island very beautiful. When after some two hours we had to leave, he pressed on me a large old Chinese celadon dish that he had found on the island, so that I would remember him. I certainly did, for it was a heavy thing to carry round with me for the rest of my travels. I wrote to him when I returned home; but I never heard from him or of him again. We eventually returned to Macassar for a night. It had been a fascinating voyage; but there had been one drawback. At every port the ship took on bales of copra, and as the cargo increased so did the smell, till at last the whole ship was filled with that sweet sickly stench. We disembarked without regret.

From Macassar we took a boat to Bali. It was a bad moment for arriving there. During the last previous years numbers of people, Europeans and Americans, men and women, had settled in Bali and had almost all of them become rather too intimate with the natives. The government in Java had at last become aware of these shocking activities; and, barely a week before our arrival, sudden action was taken. Nearly all the male settlers had been taken off to be tried and gaoled in Java, while the women settlers were ordered to leave the country. I had come armed with a letter of introduction to Mr Walter Spies, the now elderly German whose writings had brought Balinese art and, in particular, Balinese dancing to the notice of the Western world. Being interested in all forms of ballet I was eager to talk to him. But when I asked how to find him a stern Dutchman looked at me strangely and advised me to destroy the letter. It was only when we met a French artist who had actually married a Balinese girl and was therefore considered to be respectable, that the awful story was explained to me. The atmosphere was therefore somewhat muted. No Balinese now ventured to talk to a foreigner; though, when it was reported that a tourist ship was arriving, the maidens all hastened to bare their bosoms, knowing that that was what visitors liked, dressing respectably again as soon as the tourists departed. Nevertheless we were able to see Balinese dancing and to hear Balinese music and to witness a great Balinese funeral ceremony; and we drove all over the island, which, however, I did not think as lovely as several other islands that we had visited. I have never been able to feel the enthusiasm for Bali that most later travellers seem to have enjoyed.

After a week there we went back to Java, where Eddie Bates left me, to fly to Hong Kong and then on round the world. I saw him once or twice again when we were both back in England. But then the War came and he joined the Air Force, to be killed eventually on a bombing raid over Germany. I stayed on in Batavia, where I was shown the State archives, and I spent a morning in the gardens at Buitenzorg. Next day I flew from Batavia to Medan in Sumatra, to pass the night there before driving for some four hours up into the mountains for two nights in a hotel on the shores of the great Lake Toba, and a night on my way back over a mountain track at the small resort of Brastagi. The scenery was magnificent, with volcanos smouldering on every side; and the villages of the Batak tribesmen remarkable for houses built on stilts with vast overhanging roofs. On the island of Samosir, in the middle of Lake Toba, there were strange sarcophagi belonging to some older civilization, about which nobody could tell me very much. I was glad to have seen it all; but I was glad, too, to return to Medan to take an aeroplane, early in the morning of 15 February, to fly me to Penang and on to Bangkok.

It was an alarming flight, as many flights in those days were. We ran into a thunderstorm over the Straits of Malacca and were flung about the plane. Then over southern Thailand we flew far too low, I thought, in order that we might admire a herd of wild elephants. However, we arrived safely at Bangkok airport soon after noon, where Chula and his cousins were lined up to greet me and fling garlands round my neck.

It was good to be back in a country that had never been subjected to colonial rule and where the people treated you as an equal. I stayed again at the Trocadero Hotel and again spent the days with Chula and his circle. They kept me busy. I saw the young King again, and the Prince-Regent more than once. It was during this visit that I was taken to meet the Prime Minister. I had an interview with a senior Buddhist ecclesiastic, the Abbot of the leading monastery in Bangkok, who courteously answered all my questions about Buddhist theology, which I wanted to compare with the doctrines of the Dualist heretics in Europe in the Middle Ages, about whom I had been writing a book. I went to a dinner-party at the British Legation. I was taken to see the large and well equipped Chulalongkorn Hospital and the Pasteur Institute with its snake farm. I went all over the University, to which I gave a sum of money to endow a prize for history. I gather that it still goes on but, though I added to the gift a few years later, it is now, owing to inflation, only awarded every other year.

Chula took me one morning to the National Museum, housed in one of the old palaces. It contains some lovely pieces of old Thai and Khmer sculpture. We were still there when it closed for the lunch interval, as Chula was in the middle of discussing some project with the Director. As they were talking in Thai I wandered into a neighbouring gallery. While I stood at one end of the room there came into the other end a lady dressed in clothes which at that time only the poorer classes wore, knickers tight over the legs and an over-tunic, and the hair *en brosse*. I assumed that she was a Museum attendant deliberately dressed in that old-fashioned style. She came so near to me that I could see that her clothes were of the best silk, mushroom-coloured and royal blue. Then, as I was looking at her, she suddenly was no longer there. It was, to say the least, disconcerting. As we left the building, when Chula was out of earshot – I knew that he was terrified of ghosts – I asked the Director if the Museum was haunted. All these old palaces were haunted, he replied. I said rather smugly that I had just seen the ghost. Someone sees a ghost here every day was his answer.

Among the friends that I made during these days was a gentleman called Phya Anirudh, and his enchanting young wife Chalow. Anirudh was one of the richest men in Bangkok, and his wealth was mainly spent on running his own company of Thai ballet dancers. Owing to the recent changes in the monarchy the royal ballet was in abeyance; and he was performing a very useful role in keeping the tradition alive. He hoped, I think, that eventually, when the King returned to live permanently in Thailand, his ballet would be taken over by the crown. We went one evening to a rehearsal of a ballet that he was staging, where he explained to me the meaning of the dancer's every gesture, in far greater detail than I could memorize; but it helped my understanding of it all. A few days later a special performance was laid on for us. The dancing was beautiful and made much of our European ballet seem crude and coarse; but it was a little unearthly, and it moved very slowly.

One day we spent pleasantly going in a launch down the River Menam to the sea, and another very enjoyable day going up the river to the old ruined capital of Ayuthia, to see its decaying temples and palaces, romantically overgrown with trees. Just before reaching the island we ran onto a sandbank and broke a propeller and had to be towed by another boat for the return journey. That involved a stop at the nearby Palace of Bang-Pa-In, on another island, where the young King and his mother were staying. We remained there for dinner and for a splendid fireworks display afterwards. It was 3 a.m. before we arrived back in Bangkok. The Palace of Bang-Pa-In had been built by King Mongkut in the 1860s in the style of the French Second Empire. It was impressive and comfortable – so Chula, who had spent much of his childhood there, testified. Unfortunately, it was burnt to the ground a few months after our visit.

On Sunday, 26 February, Chula, Bira and their wives and Abhas and I took an early morning train for a five hours' journey to Hua Hin, on the western shore of the Gulf of Siam. Hua Hin is now, I am told, a smart resort, full of elegant villas, many of them inhabited by European expatriates. Then it was a fishing village only distinguished by the fact that two successive kings, Vajiravudh and Prajadhipok, had built palaces there, and in consequence a few rich Siamese had followed them. Chula's father had already built a simple wooden house there, on stilts, with a separate guest house, in a pleasant garden close to the sea. There was nothing much to do there except walk in the village and bathe. The only sight-seeing was to the two royal palaces, both of them hideous. I enjoyed three days of rest there. Then on the evening of 1 March I took a train to Penang.

From Penang I sailed to Rangoon, keeping mostly close to the coast and going through the beautiful Mergui archipelago. After two days in Rangoon I went on to Calcutta, to spend some three weeks in India before sailing home from Bombay.

Somewhere in the course of my travels I had caught amoebic dysentery. It may have been in Indo-China, as from that time onward I began to have short bouts of illness. But it was only after I had been home for several weeks that the disease revealed itself in a very virulent form. It was to alter my whole life, as I have written elsewhere. It should have killed any desire that I might have had to revisit those countries. But it failed to do so.

Sixteen years passed before I had an opportunity to go back to Thailand. Among Chula's friends was a young Australian lady whom I had known first as Robin Spencer but who had recently married an able young Irish doctor working in London called Emmet Dalton. She had been appointed to look after publicity for the Thai Embassy in London; and, to help her in her job, the Thai government invited her and her husband to visit Thailand for a few weeks early in 1955. They suggested that I should join them there. A cousin of mine, Sir Charles Lambe, had recently become Admiral of the Far Eastern Fleet, with his headquarters at Singapore and had invited me to visit him there; and I had an invitation to go to Delhi to stay with the French Ambassador there, my old friend Stas Ostrorog. So I decided to go off for two months to the East, to escape the grim British weather. We had hoped that Chula would be there, but he had planned to go that spring to America and put off his visit to Thailand till the autumn. He was slightly annoyed with us for visiting his country in his absence, but he kindly put his house in Bangkok at our disposal and arranged for his agent in Thailand to look after us. The agent was a charming and highly intelligent man called Bisdar Chulasewok. Rarely for a Thai he was six feet in height. I liked being with him as it made me feel less of a Gulliver in Lilliput.

The Daltons went out before me. After a rather tedious flight I arrived in Bangkok in the afternoon of 17 January, to be met by Mrs Dalton and by Bisdar and taken to Chula's house at Ta Tien, which by now had been made quite comfortable.

It is a mistake to revisit after a long interval a place that one has loved. Bangkok had changed. Many of the *klongs*, the canals, that had been such a feature of the city, had been filled in and were now roads; and there were cars and Americans everywhere. Many of the friends that I had known sixteen years earlier were dead. Social life was no longer dominated by the princes with their old-fashioned courtesy but by a new class of millionaire. On the evening of my arrival when, tired from the journey, I had hoped for a quiet evening, I was taken out to dine with one such millionaire, who was half-Chinese and owned a smart Chinese restaurant where we met. I behaved badly. At the best of times I am not very good at many items of Chinese cooking; and I could not face them that evening. Our hostess, next whom I was sitting, kept piling such delicacies onto my plate. When no one was looking I took them in my hands and flung them with all my might underneath the large table, hoping that nobody would be able to trace the ensuing mess to me. My days in Bangkok were not uninteresting. I spent some time at Chulalongkorn University and saw over the new Agricultural University. I saw a Thai boxing match, which was more like a ballet than a contest. Two of the younger princes, whose parents I had known, entertained me, as did the British Ambassador, Berkeley Gage. But this visit to Thailand was made worthwhile by the journeys that we made outside the capital.

Thailand was still officially a democratic kingdom, but in fact at that time it was ruled by the Chief of Police, General Phao, who was a dictator in everything except name. He was a genial man, and I have reason to be grateful to him. I had always wanted to see Chiengmai, in the north of the country; and he took the Daltons and me there in his special train. We set out one evening and spent the next morning winding through lovely country, arriving in the afternoon at Chiengmai, where we were lent a house belonging to a local magnate. I was enchanted by Chiengmai. I have never seen a district where everyone seemed so prosperous and happy. I met there two earnest ladies from the World Health Organization who were worried because they could find no signs of stress illnesses there. There must be something unnatural about the place, they thought. We spent five nights there, going most days out into the country. We saw rice plantations and were taken into a teak forest, where elephants were at work carrying logs. We picnicked by a superb waterfall in the forest and climbed up to an old temple, called Doi Suthop, on the top of a very steep hill. We went out to a charming little town called Lampoon, to be entertained by its ex-prince, who was still the chief landowner in the area. Dr Dalton left us there, to hurry back to London. Mrs Dalton and I stayed on another day, returning by air to Bangkok. It was an alarming journey. When we called at a small airport on the way, the plane was surrounded by a screaming crowd. When we asked the air-hostess what was happening she told us that they were all wanting to get on the plane, and its cargo was already overweight. Most of them did succeed in getting on the plane, crowding the aisle. It was a relief when we landed without mishap at Bangkok airport.

One day we went by car, first to see a newly founded agricultural settlement and then on to the town of Lopburi, about a hundred miles north of Bangkok. The town was enjoying a holiday, to celebrate the opening of a tramway line from the railway station into the town, a two-mile journey, with tramcars bought cheap in Belgium. Everyone was allowed a free ride to the station and back. Unfortunately, we did not have enough time there to enjoy the privilege. On another day Bisdar took me to the town of Petchaburi, near the coast on the way to Hua Hin. King Mongkut had built another palace there, in the same Second Empire style as his palace at Bang-Pa-In. It had a fine situation but no charm. The Director of Monuments then took us to some nearby caves, where there were traces of early human occupation. They were more attractive than the palace.

I left Bangkok on 7 February, to fly to Penang. There I joined the Lambes to sail slowly down the coast of Malaya to Singapore, where I stayed for a happy fortnight in Admiralty House. From there I flew to Delhi, to spend ten days under the aegis of the French Embassy, and so back to London.

Chula is now dead, and so is his wife and his cousin Birabongse, and my good friend Bisdar. Bangkok, I am told, has become a noisy bustling city. Even Chengmai may now be full of stress illnesses, being too near to frontiers beyond which civil war is raging. But I am glad to have been there; and I shall always remember the country and its people with affection.

U Ur of the Chaldees

HAVING BEEN brought up to read the Bible and having always found romance in the names of far-off places, I was enchanted as a child by the cities mentioned in Holy Writ. Babylon was my favourite, 'the glory of kingdoms, the beauty of the Chaldees' excellency', to quote Isaiah. How could one not be excited by a city that aroused the grand minatory curses of the Hebrew prophets? But I had a special liking for Ur of the Chaldees, the place where the whole Biblical story seemed to begin, with Abraham going out into the unknown to be father of the Chosen People. When first I began to learn German, a language that I was soon to take against, as I have told elsewhere, I was delighted to discover the German prefix 'ur', meaning 'original' or 'basic'; and with the inaccurate ingenuity of the precocious I decided that the Germans must have been thinking of the ancient city. My governess firmly disillusioned me. But I would still like to imagine that Martin Luther, that great Biblical scholar and founder of modern German prose-writing, had invented the prefix in the interest of theology.

My liking for Ur was well justified in the 1930s, when Sir Leonard Woolley's excavations brought to light the splendid works of art from the royal tombs there. It was a little disappointing to realize that these treasures came from Ur of the Sumerians. The word 'Sumerian' lacks the resonance of the word 'Chaldee'. Under the Chaldaeans Ur, though still a holy city, was no longer a royal capital. Its art lost its splendour. But Ur retained its glamour for me; and, though the treasures were taken away to be housed in museums and the site was left empty, I still wished some day to make a pilgrimage there.

My first attempt to do so was when I visited Iraq in the spring of 1938, on my roundabout way to Syria. I had come out by train from London. That year you could stay on the same compartment from Calais to the Syrian-Iraqi frontier, the carriages being taken in a ferry across the Bosphorus. As the train passed through the Tyrol and stopped at Innsbruck, the station was empty except for a few men in uniform. The wagon-lit attendant explained to me that Hitler's troops had entered Austria that morning. Everything had been so well organized that the train was only ten minutes late leaving Innsbruck. At Tel Kotchak on the Iraqi frontier we had to leave the train and take a bus to Mosul. It was pouring with rain, and the mud on the unpaved road made progress slow.

Next morning the rain had stopped; and we had time to see something of Mosul and to cross the River Tigris to the site of the great Assyrian capital, Nineveh, before taking a bus on to Kirkuk. I liked Mosul. It contained no monuments of any note, but it had escaped any deliberate modernization. It was, as it had been in the Middle Ages, a bustling commercial town with a cosmopolitan population, Iraqis, Syrians and Turks, Jews, Armenians, Jacobite and Nestorian Christians. From time to time there were moments of inter-racial or inter-religious tension, but on the whole they all lived contentedly together. Some of the old walls remained, and some old churches and synagogues, the former mostly converted into mosques. The handsome Turkish bridge across the Tigris was never completed. One crosses to Nineveh by an ugly iron construction.

When I studied history as a child I was always fiercely partisan. Prominent among my dislikes were the ancient Assyrians who, I thought, compared very badly with their Babylonian neighbours. The Babylonians were civilized. They were skilled in mathematics and astronomy; they founded law-codes; and they built hanging gardens, though how the gardens were made to hang remains a mystery. The Assyrians had none of those accomplishments. They were crude and wanton militarists. They seemed to have no intellectual pursuits; and their art was heavy and unattractive. I always sympathized with the prophet Jonah when he was angry because the Almighty refused to destroy Nineveh. So it is with sorrow that I have to admit that the site of Nineveh is far more attractive than that of Babylon. Nineveh rises up from the banks of the swift-flowing Tigris, in fields that are covered with wild flowers in spring. I do not know what recent excavations may have taken place on the site. In the 1930s there were few signs of archaeological work. One could see where Frederick Layard had dug nearly a century earlier. On the mound below which the great king Sennacherib lay buried there was a Turcoman village, and on its summit a mosque believed to contain the body of the Prophet Jonah. There were lesser mounds all round, awaiting excavation. It was vast and impressive, but dead.

A bus took us that afternoon to Kirkuk, where we caught a night train to Baghdad. I spent six days in Baghdad, staying with the brother of a Cambridge friend of mine, who was First Secretary at the British Embassy. He was a vague, absent-minded man, of little use as a civil servant, but so well-liked that nobody minded. It is, after all, useful for an Embassy to contain a member whom everyone loves. He was certainly the kindest of hosts. Modern Baghdad, as I had been many times warned, bore no resemblance to the great city of the medieval Caliphs. Though now, after centuries of neglect, it was trying to adapt itself to be the capital of a modern state, the result was undistinguished. A few old buildings survived, but none of any importance, with the exception of the great Shia mosque at Khadimain, in the northern suburbs, with its golden domes, its elegant minarets and its tiled gateways. But no infidel is allowed within its precincts. The great River Tigris provided some character to the city, and the residential quarters on its western bank were pleasant enough.

A busy social life left little time for sight-seeing. I asked about Ur; but it was too far away. I was taken to Ctesiphon, to see the great arch built by King Chosroes and the surviving wing of his palace, impressive ruins, but looking lonely and inapposite in a flat featureless plain, with just a few warehouses for company. I went on a picnic to Babylon. I knew not to expect to see any ruins of significance, except for the Ishtar gate, with its bas-relief carving, but without the tiles that once had covered it all. What was impressive about Babylon was the sheer size of the site. Within an area some ten miles long and ten miles broad there were mounds and ditches, traces of ceremonial avenues, the foundations of bridges over the old course of the river Euphrates. But all is desolation. The Hebrew prophets have triumphed. 'O Lord, thou hast spoken against this place . . . that none shall remain in it, neither man nor beast, but that it shall be desolate for ever.'

I was next in Baghdad in the autumn of 1944. I was on leave from Istanbul, and was on my way back from Teheran, where my brother was then Air Attaché at the British Embassy. In those days the British Council was eager to find anyone able and willing to lecture in far-off places. So by offering to give a lecture or two one was allowed the facilities for travel that were needed in the War years. I had spent my summer vacation in Egypt and Palestine. On 14 September I flew from Lydda to Damascus, and next day from Damascus to Teheran. It was a lovely flight over the mountains on the western border of Iran. But the mountains are high, and the aeroplane was un-pressurized. I had been rather ill in Palestine, and, at the best of times, high altitudes do not suit me. I arrived at Teheran feeling far from well. Teheran itself stands nearly four thousand feet above sea-level, and my brother's house, the former Roumanian Embassy residence, was in a suburb that was higher still. In consequence, till I became acclimatized, I did not enjoy the lively social life of Teheran. My brother, who did enjoy it, was disappointed in me. One evening soon after my arrival he took me to a grand dance held in a smart hotel up in the mountains, where he planned to have a happy evening with his favourite Persian girl-friend. But after a little I was in a state of collapse, in terror that I was going to faint. I begged him to take me home. He was most unwilling to have his pleasure interrupted and seemed ready to leave me to my doom. But fortunately the husband of his girl-friend, who, like me but for a different reason, was not finding the party very enjoyable, offered to drive me home himself; and so I escaped. A few days later I had recovered and, indeed, spent a happy Sunday with my brother walking higher up in the mountains.

Teheran was not an attractive city. There were wonderful works of art to be seen in its museums, but all the buildings, even the palaces, lacked charm. Its inhabitants at that time were friendly. When I lectured at the British Institute the house was full, though I wondered how many of the audience understood a word of English. There was a historic Armenian colony, some of whose leaders I met. In the bazaars I found that most of the merchants were Azerbaijani. When my brother talked to them in his very adequate Persian, he won little response; but they were delighted when I tried to talk to them in Turkish.

While Teheran was unattractive, the old capital, Isfahan, was among the most enchanting cities that I have ever seen. I had to give a lecture there too; and that justified my brother, who as Air Attaché had his own aeroplane, to take me there in it. The flight-route was over a lofty mountain-range; and, to punish me for complaining about heights, he tried to frighten me by winding through narrow gorges and skimming over mountain passes. But I believed him to be a competent pilot, so curbed my fear.

The splendours of Isfahan have often been described. There is no need for me to add another description. I hope that they survive intact. I was only there for forty-eight hours, and wish that it had been for longer. My brother was in a kindlier mood for the return flight. Indeed, he made a long detour to the south, to fly me low over the ruins of Persepolis.

I had one more night in Teheran before flying to Baghdad. On this occasion I was there for just over a week, staying with my old friend Stewart Perowne, who was Oriental Counsellor at the British Embassy. He was sociable and hospitable. I was taken to meet the chief Iraqi and British officials. I had an audience with the Prince Regent, whom I had met three years previously in Jerusalem. I made friends with a number of Iraqi intellectuals, and I found several friends among the British archaeologists working in Iraq. But my plea to be allowed to visit Ur of the Chaldees was again refused. It was too far away, they said. But, in recompense, I was taken to see Samarra, some ninety miles to the north of Baghdad, the city which for forty years in the ninth century, under the Caliph Mutasim, replaced Baghdad as the capital of the Caliphate. The ruins stretch over a vast area. In the centre is a small modern town, clustering round a handsome Shia mosque. Round it for miles one can see the traces of a well-planned city. The one edifice still standing erect is the minaret of the Great Friday Mosque, built in the form of a ziggurat. Of the old palaces only a few walls are standing.

Nearly twelve years passed before I next came to Iraq. I was invited to spend ten weeks in Baghdad early in 1956, to give a series of lectures at its College of Arts and Sciences, which was soon to be raised to the status of a University. The Representative of the British Council in Iraq, Jock Jardine, who was responsible for my invitation, was an old friend of mine, and, I think, one of the best officers that the British Council ever employed. He hid his considerable administrative ability under an easy-going manner; and, though he was no linguist, he always made a great number of friends in the countries in which he worked. Later on, when he was in Pakistan, he brought me out to be a professor for a term at the University of Peshawar. His last post was to be in Turkey, and when he retired he had hoped to settle there in a house on the Aegean coast. But there were bureaucratic difficulties with the Turks; eventually he made his home in Corfu. But the house that he acquired there was notoriously accursed. He died of a heart-attack before he had fully moved into it; and his two successors as its proprietors both died within a few months of taking possession.

All that was in the future. In 1956 Jock had a charming house, old and in places a bit decrepit but perfectly comfortable as regards essentials. I stayed there while I was in Baghdad. Next door there was the British Institute of Archaeology, inhabited, when they were not digging at Nimrud, by Professor Max Mallowan and his wife, Agatha Christie. They became close friends of mine. Life in Baghdad seemed very pleasant at that time. Perspicacious observers would remark that there was dissatisfaction mounting in the country against its government. But I saw no sign of it; and the revolution two years later, in which the young king and all the royal family were shot and the chief elder statesman, Nuri es-Said hounded to his death, came as a shock to me. I knew that Nuri had his enemies and that many Arabs disliked him for being a Kurd; and I knew that the former Prince-Regent, Abdulillah, the young King's uncle, though amiable to meet, had never managed to be popular and was thought to have been over-oppressive to dissidents. But I thought that the King was popular and that he was starting his reign amid general good-will. He was certainly a very likeable young man. I was twice summoned to see him and found him a trifle shy at first but eager to talk about education and greatly interested in history. He seemed to be rather diffident and rather lonely. He hinted to me that he had too many older relatives and advisers who kept telling him what to do and were unwilling to allow him to have views of his own. He would, I think, have become a good king. He certainly did not deserve the fate that was in store for him.

My duties at the College were not arduous. I gave two lectures a week, on Mondays and Wednesdays, and was supposed to be available to see staff or students on Tuesdays, should any of them wish to talk to me. It was usually the same ones who came week after week; and they wanted to talk, not to listen. My subject was the relationship of the

Caliphate with the Christian world in the Middle Ages. In those days, before the rebirth of Islamic fanaticism, I never met with any hostility, even from Shia students. This was, perhaps, because I preached tolerance and understanding, and was known to consider the Crusades to have been a Bad Thing. I spoke in English, which most of the students understood; but at the end of each lecture my Iraqi assistant would give a summary in Arabic. My own Arabic was far too poor for me to be able to check how good his summaries were; but Arabic-speaking friends who listened to him reported that it was all quite adequate.

I had the second half of the week free; and the authorities encouraged me to travel round the country. My first excursion was only for the inside of a day, to see the holy city of Kerbela or, rather, as much of it as an infidel was allowed to see, then on to the great ruins of the palace of Ukhaydir, a building whose history is unknown but which seems to have been built for an Abbasid prince in the eighth century. Then, after a week-end spent over the frontier in Kuwait, I achieved my old ambition and went to see Ur of the Chaldees.

I went there in style. I had a young Iraqi friend whom I had known ten years previously, when he was a student at Robert College on the Bosphorus, and who now was a successful business-man in Baghdad, well connected with the government of the day. He arranged for a special coach, with sleeping-berths and a small kitchen, to be attached to the train from Baghdad to Basra. We left Baghdad at 8 o'clock on a Friday evening. The train meandered slowly next day between the Euphrates and the desert, and reached the small station of Ur at about 10 o'clock next evening. There our coach was detached and moved into a siding. Next morning we drove some two miles to see the vast ruins of Ur.

The remains of great cities that have been thoroughly and efficiently excavated and have had their treasures removed are somewhat sad to see. Ur was impressive from the vast extent of the site and from the signs of its town-planning, with its great outer walls and its greater inner walls enclosing the temple area, with a huge mound that had been the ziggurat in the centre of it all, and suburbs stretching away outside the walls; though the Euphrates, which must have provided the chief means of access to the city, had long since changed its course, to flow well to the east of the ruins. But everything had been dead for centuries. It was hard to imagine the rich bustling city from which Abraham and his family had fled.

After some three hours of wandering round Ur we drove to Eriddu, the city of Ea, the god of water, set in a waterless plain, then back to Tel el-Ubaid, to see what remains of the oldest monumental construction yet discovered. After a late lunch in our railway coach, we drove in the afternoon to the pleasant little town of Nasriyah, on the Euphrates, glad to see a living community. That evening our coach was hitched onto a train that took us a stage back to Baghdad, to the town of Samawah. We spent the next day at Warka, the Erech of the Bible, the city of Nimrod, the mighty hunter. There was a German archaeological team working there, who kindly showed us round the excavations and invited us to a sumptuous lunch that they were giving for the German Ambassador and some of his staff, who had come to visit the site. That night our coach was fixed onto the end of a goods train, which chugged slowly northward during the night and deposited us at Baghdad at 9 o'clock next morning.

The expedition had enabled me to see in comfort sites that had long haunted my imagination. But I must confess that in fact I find greater interest and enjoyment in later periods of history. Such tastes were to be well gratified during the next two weeks. Soon after my week-end at Ur, the College broke up for a fortnight's holiday, and I was free to travel further afield, though the British Council saw to it that I justified my journeys by giving an occasional lecture. The following week-end I went with the second-in-command of the Council, Cyril Eland, to lecture at Basra. Basra itself lacked charm; but I greatly enjoyed a morning that we spent in the old town of Zubayr, the port from which Sinbad the Sailor set out on his voyages to the Further East. There was nothing spectacular to be seen there, and the harbour was empty now, except for a few dhows. But if one could penetrate through the rather grim, windowless house-fronts, one would see elegant courtyards, with flowers and now and then a fountain. We were taken to lunch in one of these, which was filled with roses.

Still more I enjoyed a day that we spent in the marshes of the Euphrates, going in a punt through twisting waterways to a village full of houses made of reeds. They were strange buildings, rather Gothic in their feeling. Though in fact they were small, if one saw them without any human being nearby to give a scale of proportion one could almost think that one was looking at a medieval Western church. The people were gentle and shy, but friendly, especially as our guide had come originally from the village. These Marsh Arabs have been vividly described in a book by Wilfred Thesiger, published in 1964, after he had lived among them for some time. Whether their way of life still exists or whether it has been undermined by modern trends or destroyed by the bitter war against Iran, I do not now know. But I am very glad to have seen it.

I followed my visit to Basra with one to Mosul, travelling overnight by train. Mosul had not, I thought, lost its charm, with its various communities living in tolerable amity with each other, in an atmosphere inherited from Ottoman days, not yet badly spoilt by modernity. The British Council officer with whom I stayed was a friendly man called Archibald Ross Thomas, who liked to spend his time painting street scenes or tending his garden, in which he grew loofahs. He gave me one, which I use to this day, though it is now a bit bedraggled by age. Whether he was an efficient administrator I would not like to say; but he and his wife were greatly liked by all the communities, which is something that efficient officials do not always achieve. After spending the morning calling upon the local governor and other notables, I went in the afternoon to see a village inhabited by the Yezidis, followers of that strictly Dualist sect, called by their neighbours 'Devil-worshippers', because they regard the Devil, whom they treat with respect but in fact do not worship, to be as powerful as God. There are few of them left now; and in this village they seemed to be gentle self-effacing folk, taught by centuries of cruel persecution not to draw attention to themselves.

Next morning a car came from the Iraq Petroleum Company to take me to its headquarters at Kirkuk; and I spent the next four nights in their guest-house at Arrapha, just outside the town. I had reason to be grateful to the Company in the past, as its representatives in Syria had twice lent me a car, free of charge, to enable me to visit castles and battle sites connected with the Crusades, only asking in return to be thanked in the preface of a forthcoming book. I was even forgiven for seriously damaging one of the cars when I insisted on being driven up a mountain track in the Anti-Lebanon. So I could not be churlish when I was required to give a lecture to their staff at Kirkuk and then at their subsidiary station at Ain Zaleh. I was taken round to see every local aspect of the oil world; and I hope that I showed the same polite interest as did my lecture-audiences, to whom my subject, Moslem influences on European civilization, must have seemed similarly remote. What I most enjoyed was to be taken one evening to see the Eternal Fires, the pit in the ground from which flames have shot up ever since the beginning of history. Pedants tell us that it was the burning fiery furnace mentioned in the Book of Daniel. The hospitality of the Company was exhaustingly lavish; but I was given a slight holiday one day, when a Kurdish employee of the Company drove me up into the mountains near the Iranian frontier to lunch with local officials in his native town of Suleimaniye. I have always felt a liking for the Kurds, a fierce, proud race that have seldom been well treated down the centuries.

I drove back early one morning from Ain Zaleh to Mosul, and was taken almost at once by the Ross Thomases to have a picnic lunch on the banks of the River Zab and then to visit a Syrian Uniate monastery, before returning to the town to give a lecture. Next day we started out in pouring rain on a longer excursion. We lunched at Erbil (Arbela, near which Alexander the Great routed the forces of the Great King of Persia, and so altered the history of mankind). It is the oldest town in the world to be still inhabited and to have retained its ancient name. Now it is perched on a high mound underneath which lie, each below the other, the previous towns of Erbil. From there we drove on through the rain into the mountains, to spend the night at the small town of Salehuddin, where, surprisingly, there was a pleasant small hotel. Next morning we went on, in fine weather, past the town of Shaqlawa, into the valley of Haria, to see the last remnant in Iraq of the old Assyrian Church. This is a branch of the great Nestorian Church which in the early Middle Ages spread from Syria to China and which might well have become the dominant religion in the Levant had the Mongols, who gave it their support, not been defeated by the Mamelukes at the crucial battle of Ain Jalud in Palestine in 1260. Thenceforward the fortunes of the Church rapidly declined. In Mesopotamia it came to be called, for no good reason, the Assyrian Church. Early in the nineteenth century a section of the Church seceded to come under the jurisdiction of Rome and to enjoy the political protection of France. It is now known as the Chaldaean Church. But the Assyrian Church lasted on, being treated by the Ottoman government as an autonomous *millet*, or nation; and this status saved it from overgreat persecution by its Moslem neighbours. During the First World War the Assyrian levies formed a valuable adjunct to the British forces. But this was resented by the Iraqis; and when Iraq became independent under King Faisal there was in 1933 a deliberate persecution, followed by a massacre, of the Assyrians living in Iraq. The survivors sought refuge in other countries, who were not very willing to receive them, while the Iraqis put difficulties in the way of their going. Eventually the Patriarch and his chief followers made their way to America; and it is now in Chicago that you will find the main seat of the Assyrian Church. But a few stayed on in the Kurdish hills; and it was this remnant, under its Metropolitan, whom we now visited.

His Grace the Metropolitan received us graciously. His post, though ecclesiastical, was hereditary; but as he had to be celibate each Metropolitan was succeeded by his nephew, his younger brother's eldest son. I enquired from an English-speaking deacon what happened if the Metropolitan had no brother or if his brother had no son. I was told firmly that God had always seen to it that the successsion was uninterrupted. Our host certainly had a nephew, a pleasant-looking youth who spoke adequate English, learnt at the school in Mosul. He was accompanied by his father, who, we were told, was in charge of the finances of the community but who was too much in awe of his brother to utter a word. The Metropolitan informed me that his nephew was going that autumn to spend a year at an Anglican theological college in Nottinghamshire. Would I, he asked, look after the boy when he passed through London? I agreed; and, indeed, a few months later I was informed that he was due to arrive there. I met him at the airport and took him to my house. He was too tired and bewildered to want to go sight-seeing, but was ready to chatter, his one interest seeming to be the cost of things in England. He even asked me what rent I paid for my house and began to enquire about my income but then realized that perhaps that was an unsuitable question. I gave him dinner and housed him for the night, and saw him onto his train for Nottingham. I received a polite postcard from him a few days later and then heard nothing more. I suppose that now he is in a charge of his community, if he has managed to survive the turmoil of the last few years. I am sure that he will be managing its finances carefully; and I hope that he learnt enough theology and ethics to see to its spiritual needs.

On leaving the Assyrians we drove up through the magnificent Rowanduz Gorge to have a picnic in the still wilder Berserini Gorge, with snow-capped mountains towering over us, before journeying back to Mosul. I spent the next day with Max Mallowan and Agatha Christie, seeing all over Max's excavations at Nimrud. Indeed, one of the happiest outcomes of this visit to Iraq was my friendship with them both. Thenceforward, so long as Agatha lived, I visited them yearly, usually over Easter, at her house on the banks of the River Dart. I made one more excursion from Mosul the following morning, to lunch at the picturesque old town of Aqra, in the hills to the north, before catching a night train back to Baghdad.

I had three more weeks there, lecturing and going to an exhausting number of parties. The College was much concerned at the time in drawing up the statutes and regulations for the University that it was about to become. I was invited to some of the discussions; but my advice was unheeded when I begged the committee to abandon its insistence that no one could be appointed to a professorship unless he already held a doctorate. In vain I pointed out that the majority of professors at Oxford and Cambridge at that time had never become doctors. In vain I told them that the degree of Ph.D. had been invented in the 1920s by those two great Universities in the hope of luring rich American research students to their colleges, and Americans would not come unless there was a title to be obtained. In vain I said that in my young days at Cambridge we called the Ph.D. the 'badge of shame'. The committee was unmoved. It was devoted to the Germanic notion that nobody was worthy of academic advancement unless he was a Herr Doktor.

I left Baghdad in mid-April that year, and I have never been back to Iraq. I was invited to the opening of the University of Baghdad next year, but was committed to be lecturing elsewhere. I was less pleased to be invited in July 1961, to celebrate an anniversary of the murder of the royal family. But I am glad to have seen so much of it in happier days and to have visited Ur of the Chaldees.

V Vancouver Island

In 1967 Canada celebrated the centenary of the British North America Act, which raised the country to be a self-governing Dominion; and, as part of the celebrations, the Canada Council, the Dominion's equivalent to the British Council, was empowered to invite three scholars over from Britain to give lectures at universities all over the Dominion. I was fortunate enough to be one of the three.

I had twice been to Canada before this occasion. When first I crossed the Atlantic, in 1952, I went on from the United States across the border to Toronto, travelling in a comfortable night-train from Chicago. It probably no longer exists. I stayed close on a fortnight in Toronto, giving five lectures there. I have always had a great respect for the University of Toronto, with a special affection for the Pontifical Institute of Medieval Studies, not least because it seems to have the best cuisine in North America. My most formidable task was to address the University Women's Club. My subject was the rôle of women in modern Turkey; and, looking at those grim faces seated before me, I lost my head and declared that in spite of the part that women now played in public life no Turk thought that there was any point in paying attention to them unless they were attractive. I repented at once of my discourtesy. But I need not have worried. After the lecture a hatchet-visaged lady came up to me and said: 'How sweet of you to imply that we were all attractive.' The experience taught me to avoid such institutions. When a few years later I was honoured by an invitation to be guest-speaker at the annual dinner of the Association of British Headmistresses, I panicked and somehow found that I had an engagement abroad that week.

From Toronto I went by train through snowy forests – it was already December – to Ottowa for a week-end, and then on to Montreal, where I had no lecturing duties, though I was given a luncheon at McGill University Faculty Club to meet the Principal.

I was back in Toronto in 1957, on my way to Los Angeles and then across the Pacific to the Philippines and Borneo. I had hoped to arrive there on a Saturday evening. But the British Airways plane that was to take me there was ailing. After we had sat in it for a while we were unloaded and told to go back into London for the night. But the plane into which we were transferred next morning, after calling at Manchester and Prestwick, gave up at Shannon. We were told to spend the night there, but soon after midnight a TWA plane arrived which was willing to take some of us to New York. There I had to wait several hours for a plane to Toronto, where I arrived late on the Monday afternoon. I spent four pleasant days there, with only one lecture to give, before going on to Chicago and so to Los Angeles.

I was particularly delighted with the invitation to visit Canada in 1967, as I was told that I would be sent across to the Pacific coast, to Vancouver and to Vancouver Island and the city of Victoria, with the famed Empress Hotel. The tour began rather badly. My first assignment was to lecture in Montreal, at McGill University. The day before I was due to leave London I received a cable telling me that neither McGill University nor the Canada Council had realized that they had fixed my lecture to take place on a public holiday, Canada Thanksgiving Day. They now planned for me to give it the following day, and all my subsequent programme would have to be re-arranged. However I did not postpone my departure, hoping to spend the spare day visiting the great centenary exhibition, 'Expo' '67', that was being held on an island in the St Lawrence river. My hosts had already arranged for me to have one day there, the day after my arrival. It was not a very happy visit as it poured with rain all the time. However, I hopefully thought that I would go back on my own on the morrow, the public holiday. However, that day was even wetter, so I gave up the idea. In the meantime a pleasant young man from the Canada Council had brought me my revised programme. But it clearly had been revised in a hurry; and, going through it I found that I had on occasion been committed to giving a lecture and catching an aeroplane at the same hour of the day. But it was all sorted out.

After giving my lecture at McGill I left at dawn next morning for Toronto, not, sadly for me, to the University of Toronto but to a new establishment called York University. This consisted of a grim series of high-rise buildings in a large clearing in a forest some miles outside the city. I was given a guest-room in one of these edifices. It was an austere room. The electric lights were so placed that I could neither read in bed nor at the small writing-table. For one's clothes there was just one large cupboard with twenty-four immovable hangers in it, no shelves nor any drawers. When I looked into the bathroom there was no toilet paper there. When I remarked on this I was taken to see the Head Porter to ask for his help. His answer was: 'If you think I'm going to drive five miles to the nearest shop just for toilet paper, you had better think again.' In the end the kindly Warden of the building, by name Mr Polka, gave me a roll from his store. The food was unlovely even by North American university standards. The students seemed nearly all to have come from the United States as refugees determined not to be drafted to Vietnam. I found only two students whom it was a pleasure to teach. One was a Red Indian, still in his twenties but already with a wife and six children, a frail young man who looked as though he had not had a proper meal for years. The other was an ambitious Armenian. I met him some years later in California, when he was studying for a doctorate at Berkeley.

I ought not to be ungracious about York University. Its academic staff were all extremely friendly and anxious to be helpful. My chief cicerone among them even invited himself some years later to visit me in Scotland. So I hope that my distaste for the place went unnoticed. All the same it was with great relief that I left it after two nights for the University of Toronto, to stay with friends there. On the following day I was driven out into the forests to see their cottage there and to call on the Canadian elder statesman, Vincent Massey, in his country house.

I wish that I had asked to be sent across to British Columbia by train. I would have loved the journey through the Rockies. As it was, I travelled by air on a clear autumn afternoon; but it was already dark before we crossed the mountains to Vancouver. There I was met by a young man whom I had known when he was studying in London, by name Bryan Gooch, a gifted musicologist who was now a lecturer in English literature at the University of Victoria, but whose parents lived in Vancouver. He took me to spend the night very happily at their house. Next morning I had to give a lecture at the University of British Columbia, a large, competently run and, I thought, rather impersonal institution; but I saw very little of it. Then in the afternoon I went with Bryan by the ferry through a wooded archipelago to Vancouver Island and the town of Victoria, where, as I had specially requested, I stayed at the Empress Hotel.

I found Victoria charming. As the capital of the province of British Columbia it had some handsome if undistinguished public buildings; but it seemed mostly to be filled with pleasant houses occupied by retired gentlefolk, a sort of Canadian Cheltenham, though without the architectural elegance of that old town. The Empress Hotel came right up to my expectations. There one was back in the late Victorian age. It was spacious and dignified, with large bedrooms filled with heavy furniture. Apart from the provision of bathrooms nothing had been done to modernize it. In one of the ample reception rooms the ladies of Victoria would come in every afternoon to drink tea while a light orchestra played suitable melodious music. I was able to join them the following day. The Canadian Pacific Company, to whom the hotel belonged, had, I was told, planned to make vast alterations to bring it up to date, and more profitable. But there had been such an outcry that their schemes had to be dropped. Whether it still exists in its pristine glory I do not know. But I am very glad to have seen it.

The 1960s were notoriously a period of student unrest in the universities of North America. I was lucky enough never to come across it, though at the end of the decade I was in California, to lecture for the University of California first at Los Angeles and two days later at

Berkeley; and it was suggested that I should spend the intervening day lecturing at the University's campus at Santa Barbara. I refused, not wishing to give the same lecture three days running. I was wiser than I knew. I would have arrived there just as the students were in full riot, burning down the University library. The students at the University of Victoria were less violent. But I was warned that they had recently invaded the Senior Common Room and left a garrison there and were still in a rebellious mood. But when I heard that their chief grievance was the authorities' determination to dismiss a popular lecturer on the grounds of personal immorality and that the students, to whom his private life was of no concern, were shocked and angered by such illiberalism, my sympathies were with the students. I certainly found them all well-behaved and friendly. I had some time to spare next morning before I gave my official lecture; so Bryan Gooch asked me to talk informally to his English class on the writing of history. It was a pleasant experience. The students were attentive, laughed at the right moments and asked intelligent questions. As we walked away a large young man came puffing up from behind and solemnly shook my hand and thanked me for my talk on behalf of all the class. He was, I was told, the leader of the student rebellion. The audience at my official lecture was large and attentive; and next morning I gave another informal talk, this time to a history class.

I would have liked to have stayed longer in Victoria at the splendid Empress Hotel and to have seen more of Vancouver Island. A kind professor took me for a drive through the forests that second afternoon; but there was no time left for us to go very far. That evening I had to fly back to Vancouver itself, to spend the night at an inn near the airport, and to start out early next morning for the University of Notre Dame, Nelson, British Columbia.

When I had asked in Vancouver for information about Notre Dame University nobody could tell me anything except for the obvious fact that it must have been founded by the Catholic Church. At last I found someone who knew of it as being placed so far into the mountains that it was in close reach of permanent snow fields. It was thus popular with students who were enthusiasts for winter sports. Indeed, the lady ski-ing champion of the time, Miss Nancy Green, was studying there at the moment. I met her there in due course and found her attractive, unassuming and bright. She dutifully came to all my lectures.

I travelled there in a small aeroplane that wound its way alarmingly through narrow valleys and after two hours deposited me on a small landing-strip at a town called Castlegar. There I was met by the Professor of History and was driven some twenty miles to Nelson, where I was housed in a rather bleak motel about a mile from the University.

The Canada Council had asked me to provide four subjects on which I would be prepared to lecture; and they had circulated the subjects to the various universities which I was to visit. I had also been told not to give more than three lectures at any one of them. When I arrived at Nelson I found that I had been scheduled to give six lectures during my forty-eight hours' visit, three of them on subjects which were not on my list and on which I was not qualified to talk with any authority. I had to make a protest. In the end I arranged to lecture on all of my four chosen subjects, two on the day of my arrival, with a radio interview thrown in as an extra, and two on the following day. The history staff at this Catholic university consisted of a professor who was a retired clock-maker and a Quaker, the Theosophist daughter of a former British ambassador whom I had known when he was *en poste* in Bulgaria and in Greece, and a young Mennonite, who was the brightest and most interesting of the three. In the course of my visit I was summoned by the Reverend Father who was President of the University and asked if I had any idea of how the history staff taught the history of the Reformation. I told him that after talking with them all I was sure that each of them would be careful to say nothing that might cause offence. I hope that I was right.

My two days at Notre Dame were exhausting. When I was not lecturing I was being hospitably entertained without intermission. So few people came there from the outside world that I suppose it had to make the most of my visit. My lectures were crowded with students from all departments. How much they understood I cannot tell, but they listened attentively. The weather did not permit me to visit the snow-slopes; but I doubt if I would have had the time to go out to them.

On my last evening there it began to snow, and during the night the snow turned to rain. In the morning we learnt that the airstrip at Castlegar was flooded and there would be no flights to or from it that day. I was invited to stay on in Nelson till the weather improved; but I was anxious to return to Vancouver, as the Gooches, with whom I was to stay, had arranged a party for me that evening. We found out by telephoning that the next nearest airport, at Pendicton, about a hundred miles away, was functioning normally. Fortunately for me, a couple had come down all the way from the North-West Territories in order to hear me lecture; and they kindly offered to make a detour on their return journey in order to take me to Pendicton. We started out through mist and cloud, but as we went westward the weather improved, and the last part of the journey was very beautiful. When eventually they deposited me at Pendicton, at 5.30 p.m., I found that I would have to wait till 9.50 for a plane to Vancouver. I was able to telephone to the Gooches to tell them of my delay. Eventually I reached their house some time after 11 p.m., just as their last guests were leaving.

The next day was a Sunday; I was grateful for a day of rest. It poured with rain all morning, but cleared enough in the afternoon for Bryan Gooch to take me to see the newly founded Simon Fraser University, built on a mountain-top some miles to the east of Vancouver. In fine weather the view over the sea to the islands must be superb. But when we were there even the tops of the buildings were hidden in mist; and that, I gathered, was far from being unusual. It seemed to me a strange site on which to build a university. I would not have cared to work there.

From Vancouver I flew on the Monday to Calgary, and from Calgary two days later to Saskatoon. In both places the Universities were lively and efficient; and I found their professors hospitable and kind. But they both seemed to me to be charmless cities. From Calgary one had a distant view of the Rockies as a consolation. Saskatoon was surrounded by prairie, and there the winter snows had begun to fall. It was a relief to return to Toronto, where I spent two nights at the house of a friend before flying the next Sunday evening to London, Ontario. I liked London and the University of Western Ontario, where I found old friends and made new friends. I spent three nights there, then flew via Toronto to New York, and from New York to Dublin, where I had to attend a conference of the Pen Club on History as Literature. I came back to Scotland very tired.

I have revisited Toronto since then; and I would like some day to revisit British Columbia. But I fear that I shall never now see it again.

West Indies

To ME it has always seemed more natural to travel to the East than to the West. It is from the East that all the fundamental elements of our civilization came, and it is to the East that anyone with an interest in the past must turn. The West should have remained, as it was long ago, a vast area of mystery, bounded by an impenetrable ocean, beyond which there was, perhaps, the rim of the world, the great cliff that led to nothingness, or perhaps the Happy Isles, where the ghosts of past heroes survived. The realms beyond the sunset had, maybe, their allure; but they were alarming and better avoided. 'Comrade, look not to the West. 'Twill have your heart out of your breast', said the poet Houseman. I feel that I know what he meant.

Christopher Columbus spoilt it all. It would be pleasant to believe that St Brendan managed to cross the ocean in his coracle. The Norsemen certainly managed it, reaching a coastline that they called Vinland, a curious name for an area that was to become Puritan New England; and though there are vineyards further inland, the wine that they produce is not the best of North American products. But the Norsemen were not there for long. Climatic and political changes forced them to abandon the hope of settling there. The lands beyond the ocean returned once more to the realm of mythology.

With Columbus it was different. Byzantine superstition was not all of it ill-based. In Constantinople in the later Middle Ages many folk, even some of the wisest philosophers, believed that the world would last for seven thousand years and that it had been created in 5508 BC. If you do your sums correctly, that brings us to the dreadful date of 1492. Unlike the Norse pioneers, Columbus started a fashion. Soon all the nations of Western Europe were seeking to found colonies in this vast newly discovered continent. Had I been living at the end of the fifteenth century I would, I think, have felt the same disquiet that in my own time I felt when men from earth stepped upon the moon. Mystery, which is the true basis of religion, has been eroded once more by man's arrogant technology. Too many apples have been eaten from the Tree of Knowledge.

It would, however, be foolish not to take advantage of the achievements of mankind. The Americas are there. One should go to see them. It was not till 1952 that I plucked up courage to visit the United States; but I had already seen some of the less formidable areas of the New World. Early in 1935, when I was teaching in Cambridge, I was suddenly rendered immobile by an attack of lumbago. After two days my back recovered; but by then my sciatic nerve had become inflamed. For the next four weeks I was in appalling and unceasing agony. For some fifteen years to come I was liable to suffer such attacks, though now four decades have passed since the last of them. But I learnt better how to cope with them. This first attack has remained the most painful in my memory; and no form of treatment seemed able to ease the pain. I moved to my parents' house in London; and at last, in early March, I was able to walk a bit, with the help of a stick, to ease the pain of putting the stricken leg to the ground. I felt by then that if only I could get away and lie somewhere in the sun for a few weeks, I might recover. But where in early March, in those days before aeroplanes could take you anywhere, could one find somewhere easy to reach where sunshine would be sure? The answer seemed to be the West Indies.

At that time Messrs Fyffe, the banana merchants, used to take a few passengers on the ships that they used to send to the West Indies to collect the fruit. Early in March I set out in one of them from Avonmouth. She took some eighty passengers in simple but perfectly adequate comfort. The next two days were miserable as we made our way through storms across the Bay of Biscay and the Portuguese coast; and the misery was prolonged, as we had to make a detour, unnecessarily as it turned out, to help a ship in distress. I spent the time in my bunk, not seasick, but not daring to get up and be hurled about when I was not in good control of my limbs. But then we reached the district of the south-easterly trade-winds and sailed smoothly, in sunshine, across the ocean to Barbados. I could start my treatment of lying in the sun. My fellow-passengers were not exciting. I spent most of my time with a pleasant and lively widow and her married daughter, both of whom seemed to wish to mother me, which they did with amiable tact. I remember very little about the other travellers.

We spent the inside of a day in Barbados, with enough time to drive round the island. It seemed to me to be a placid place, with one or two good buildings in the capital, Bridgetown. Freya Stark, who later spent some months there, as wife of the acting-Governor of the island, claimed that it was called Bridgetown because the only occupation of its inhabitants was to play bridge. The scenery in the countryside was agreeably tropical and there were some handsome houses and gardens, but I have no wish to revisit it.

Trinidad, which was our next port of call, I found much more interesting. Scenically it was much more exciting, though the great asphalt lake in the centre of the island was not beautiful. There were flowering trees and a rich bird-life. One felt traces of the Spanish past of the island; and the coloured population, African and Indian, seemed to have their own ways of life, which I would have liked to explore.

From Port of Spain in Trinidad we sailed by night along the northern coast of Venezuela to La Guaira, the port of its capital, Caracas. La Guaira was not on our programme; but it seemed that the ship called in there to have something done to her engines and it was thought that the work could be quickly and cheaply managed there. Consequently we had some time to spend there; and it was arranged that we should all go up to Caracas for the night. We none of us had visas for Venezuela, but the authorities were easy-going and amiable and admitted us all. Venezuela at that time had not begun to benefit from its rich oil resources. It had been ruled for the last forty years or so by a dictator called Gomez, whom nobody liked but nobody had the energy to displace. The road from the port to Caracas climbed over a high mountain-pass. It seemed to be well-engineered but ill-maintained. Every few miles one saw by the roadside a hugely enlarged photograph of the remains of a car that had fallen over the precipice. But the driver of our bus was competent; and I was delighted by the sight of a scarlet macaw that flew across the road in front of us. Caracas at that time was a shabby and dusty city, very different, I gather, from the large and pretentious city of today. In the hotel where we were housed nothing worked very well, but the members of the staff were friendly. There seemed to be little to see in the town apart from some baroque churches built by the Spaniards. We had arrived in Caracas in the afternoon, and we were told that we would probably have to spend the next day there. So I began to try to make plans for a drive down into the jungle; but then we learnt in the evening that we would be embarking next morning.

That has been my only visit to the South American continent. We had been scheduled to call in at Cartagena, on the Colombian coast, a historic city that I would have liked to visit. But to make up for lost time we sailed straight to Colon and the Panama Canal, through which we sailed to Panama City. I suppose that by now the banks of the Canal are covered with buildings, with warehouses and barracks and modern technological installations. In those days we passed through lovely lakes with unspoilt wooded islands. It was all far more beautiful than the scenery round the banks of the other great Canal of Suez. Yet somehow, as so often when one compares the achievements of the Old World with those of the New, it is the former's that carry the splendid romance of history. At Suez one is conscious of all the efforts that have been made for more than three thousand years to make a passage that should open the way from the Mediterranean to the Red Sea and the Orient. In comparison the Panama Canal is just a magnificent parvenu.

Neither Panama nor Colon, nor Puerto Limon in Costa Rica, where next we called in, left much impression on me; though I would like some day to see more of Costa Rica, a country which seemed to me then and, I am told, still is, beautiful, friendly and competently governed. But our visit there was very brief. We soon went on to Jamaica, where we all disembarked.

Jamaica was not yet the tourist paradise that it has since become; but it was well on the way there. The hotel in Kingston, the capital, to which I went on arrival, had all the amenities that a tourist could desire, and lacked a soul. It was situated in the town; and, though walking was still rather painful for me, even with a stick, I was able to wander through the colourful streets and the bazaars. On the following day I went with my two lady-friends from the ship to visit the old capital, Spanish Town, with its handsome eighteenth-century public buildings. But after I had been for two nights in the hotel a message came from the Governor of the island summoning me to stay at Government House. My father, then in the British Cabinet, seems to have mentioned to his colleague at the Colonial Office that I had gone to Jamaica; and the latter had thought that I should be properly entertained. I felt grateful for such kindness, but in fact would have been happy to have been left at my hotel. Government House was a fine building, with a lovely garden; but it was a good many miles outside Kingston; and a governor's guests cannot expect to have cars put at their disposal. It was tiresome to have to summon a taxi to come all the way out there if one wanted to do a little shopping. But the Governor himself was an admirable man, able, well liked and very amusing; and his staff were helpful about my plans for visiting other parts of the island. I enjoyed the three days that I spent in Government House. I passed most of my time sitting in the garden, educating myself about Jamaica from books that I found in the house's excellent library.

The Governor, properly anxious to push his colony's amenities, told me that for my sciatica I ought to patronize some mud baths, up in the hills. But a lady resident, who overhead him making the suggestion to me, begged me not to listen to him. The baths, she said, were horribly dirty, as was the inn at which one would have to stay. There was nothing attractive about the site, and I would probably emerge having caught some nasty infection. So I did not follow His Excellency's advice. Instead, I took a taxi and was driven over the mountains to Montego Bay.

The drive was through beautiful country, and Montego Bay was still a quiet resort. I stayed at a comfortable and friendly hotel and spent most of the time on the beach. Ordinarily I can think of nothing more boring than a holiday given over to nothing but bathing and sun-bathing. But at that time it was what I wanted and needed. The bathing was delicious. The water was almost too warm near the shore, but you could go out into deeper and cooler water in perfect safety, as a reef stretched across the bay, which kept the sharks from entering it. I always wore something when lying in the sun, as I sunburn quickly and very painfully. This régime was wonderfully effective. After a few days I was more or less free of pain and could throw aside my stick.

I found several friends in Montego Bay, some who were settled there and some who were visitors like myself. Among the latter I was delighted to run into an elderly couple whose three sons I had known well at Cambridge and whose house I had often visited in London. It was a remarkable house. My friend, Sir Ernest Debenham, had bought up all the remaining William de Morgan tiles that he could find and used them to cover the outside walls, while for the interior he patronized mosaicists. Portraits of his many children done in mosaics greeted you from the walls as you went upstairs. The house still stands, surrounded by a large garden, in Addison Road, and is rightly scheduled as being of artistic importance. In his younger days Sir Ernest had founded the great store Debenham & Freebody. He told me on one of the drives that I went with him and Lady Debenham from Montego Bay that when he started on his career every important shop seemed to have two names – Dickins & Jones, Marshall & Snelgrove, and so on. So when he came to choose a name for his establishment he felt that he must invent a partner. So a non-existent Mr Freebody had come into existence, the surname having been chosen because it was his mother's. By the time that I came to know him he had sold the store and was losing money on experimental farming in Dorset. It was a great delight to go out with them for gentle excursions into the Jamaican hills.

After having greatly benefitted from my stay at Montego Bay I went in a taxi to a newly opened hotel on a hill overlooking the north coast of the island. The scenery was lovely, and there was always a small car at hand with a friendly black driver who would take you down to a secluded bay for your bathing. The hotel itself was a trifle brash, and I did not feel drawn to any of my fellow guests. On the second night that I was there two over-friendly gentlemen came up and suggested that I might enjoy a game of poker with them. I have always been lucky at cards; so I agreed, with richly rewarding results. I have often wondered whether they deliberately let me win in order to encourage me to join them again next evening, when they would fleece me. I shall never know, as I left early next morning for another hotel along the coast, at a pretty small town called Ochos Rios. From there I took a rather primitive train that twisted in and out of the mountains and eventually brought me back to Kingston. I spent two more days at Government House before driving up again to the north coast, to take a banana boat back to Avonmouth.

It was a quiet voyage. The boat only took two or three passengers, and I only had one fellow-traveller. He was a quiet man who wanted to be left alone. So we only conversed at meal-times. That suited me. I spent the days sitting reading in the small saloon. It was grim on deck. The boat, being laden with bananas, made her way northward to reach cold weather as soon as possible for the sake of the fruit in those early days of refrigeration. I was glad when we reached Avonmouth. A few days later I returned regenerated and refreshed to my duties at Cambridge.

Fifteen years later I returned to the West Indies, on my way to Mexico. A brother-in-law of mine, who had died a few years previously, had a cousin in the Colonial Service, called Ray Arthur, married to another cousin; and I had stayed with them at the end of the last War, when he was Colonial Secretary in Cyprus. I was especially fond of his mother-in-law, Lady Spring-Rice, whose husband had been British Ambassador in Washington during the First World War and was the author of the poem 'I vow to thee, my country'. Ray Arthur was now Governor of the Bahamas; and I was invited to spend ten days at Government House in Nassau.

I enjoyed my visit. The Arthurs were kindly hosts; and Lady Spring-Rice was a fellow-guest. It was interesting to see how the colonial government was trying to prepare the islanders for independence. The Governor was particularly anxious about the future of education in the islands. He took me round the chief schools in Nassau, which I thought well-run, considering how ill-endowed they were. I left a sum to provide a small annual prize for history at the Government High School. I do not know if it still exists. No one has told me anything about it since Independence; and I suppose with inflation it is worth very little nowadays. But I cannot say that I found the Bahamas very attractive. Low flat islands covered with palm-trees bending in the wind soon lose their charm. For those who like sailing or surfing or just lying in the sun they may be very agreeable. But the Europeans who had come to visit or to settle there, lured by such attractions, were not themselves very attractive. They did not much care for the Arthurs, who never invited them to bridge-parties or dinner-dances or other glamorous entertainments that they felt to be their due. Instead, at the quiet lunches and dinners given at Government House one met men and women who were doing useful work in the colony, many of them coloured people.

The chief event during my visit was the arrival of the great singer Elisabeth Schwarzkopf to stay at Government House and give a concert in Nassau. There was considerable fuss over her coming, as her agent seemed to have muddled her timetable, and the United States officials tried to detain her accompanist for having something wrong with his visa. Telephone-calls to Washington were needed to sort things out. She arrived a day late, quite ready to give a concert that evening. The concert-hall was packed; but the only white faces to be seen were those of the party from Government House. The other Europeans in the Bahamas were uninterested in this opportunity to hear one of the finest singers of our time. There was a lively party at Government House afterwards filled with enthusiastic members of the audience.

She stayed on for several days. On the Tuesday we flew across to bathe and picnic on Harbour Island. I took some photographs of her bathing, which were jolly rather than beautiful. I subsequently sent her copies but received no acknowledgement. I ought not to have sent them. I left Nassau the following afternoon to spend three days in millionaire circles at Palm Beach, Florida, where it poured with rain for most of my visit.

My last visit to the West Indies was in 1963. I had spent all January that year in bed with a mild but depressing form of hepatitis, a complaint that had attacked me in 1943 and 1953. I was nervous when 1973 came, lest the decennial visitation should recur. But all has been well since then. I had to go to America that March, to spend a month as a visiting professor at the University of Chicago and for other engagements before I went there; and I wanted to have a warm and restful respite before my duties began. A friend of mine had recently been appointed Spanish Consul-General in Puerto Rico; and he suggested that I should visit him there.

The easiest way to reach Puerto Rico from London was to fly to Jamaica for a night and then fly on next morning to San Juan, the island's capital. It was a very interesting visit. San Juan itself had become a rather brash American city. But in the countryside there were houses and whole villages whose inhabitants resented American domination. They were still very consciously Spanish; and to them the Spanish Consul-General was their Viceroy. In such places my host was treated with the deepest respect. It was fascinating to drive round the island, usually through splendid scenery, to some handsome old house where we would receive a vice-regal reception. Unfortunately, I was out of practice in Spanish, which anyhow I speak without elegance as I am always confusing it with Italian, a language that I similarly have never learnt to speak properly, though I read both of them with ease and understand most of what is said to me. Unfortunately, too, after my illness I was forbidden alcohol, which on such occasions gives confidence to one's efforts. But my various hosts necessarily knew English; and once I had done them the courtesy of trying to address them in Spanish they were ready to switch over to English. Altogether my nine days in Puerto Rico were very enjoyable and fitted me to face the ordeal of a term in Chicago.

Xanadu

THERE IS much to be said for enjoying ill-health when one is young. One learns how to cope with it and not to take it too seriously; and it usually means that one will have a healthy old age. As a child I literally enjoyed it, as it was only when I was ill that I was allowed a fire in my bedroom, which otherwise was quite unheated and usually icy, as my mother believed in the virtues of fresh air, and our windows were kept open even when the snow came swirling in. Even at school, though the sanatorium was seldom attractive, at least one had something of a holiday there; and if you were ill enough you might even be sent home. In my first year at Eton I was lucky enough to grow seven inches in height. Thenceforward I was too frail and anaemic to have to work hard, and I was excused from playing rough games. There was tuberculosis in the family; and my parents told me many years later that they feared that I might be stricken by it. So I spent much of my school-days happily at home. I doubt if my education suffered badly, as I was always an eager reader, especially of history-books, but was also ready to keep up with the Classical languages. Maybe my knowledge of the sciences was impaired; but they were not very well taught at Eton, much as we liked the hours that we passed under the aegis of John Christie, later the founder of Glyndebourne, whose scientific knowledge never seemed much deeper than our own. There were certainly gaps in my mathematical education. I was away from school when my contemporaries were taught about logarithms, and I had subsequently to pretend that I knew what they meant. I gather that they are now considered out of date; so perhaps that does not matter. But I acquired a wide knowledge of history; and when at the earliest opportunity I became a history specialist I rather looked down on my teachers as being ill-informed. Many years later, when tidying up my father's papers, I came across my brother's and my school-reports, which we had never been allowed to see at the time; though if they were bad we were informed of their contents quickly enough. In one of them a history master, whom I liked but arrogantly thought not very learned, had written: 'I wish this boy were kinder to me.'

During the last Christmas holidays of my Eton years I had a very bad attack of influenza: thanks to which, instead of returning at the proper time to school, I was sent off to Switzerland for a fortnight's ski-ing with my eldest sister. I quite enjoyed it, but not enough ever to face life in a winter-sports hotel again. I suppose that it was good for me. During the following three years, when I was an undergraduate at Cambridge, I suffered from nothing worse than an occasional feverish cold. But in my fourth year at Cambridge, when I had begun to do research for a dissertation that I hoped might win me a Fellowship at Trinity, I had another bad attack of flu, which developed into pleurisy. I moved to London and spent some three or four weeks in bed there, then was sent to Brighton, a town which I have always found enjoyable, for a week; after which my mother took me, with one of my younger sisters, to the south of France, to Costebelle, near Hyères, a quiet resort which was thought to be suitable for two young innocents. She deposited us and there we remained for nearly a month, quite happily, though all the time we were the only people in the hotel under the age of fifty. It was then that I made friends with the great American writer Edith Wharton, who had a handsome house built among the ruins of a castle behind Hyères. I was well enough to return to Cambridge for the summer term, but not very satisfactorily, as I was ill on and off, and continued to be ill during the following summer vacation. I managed to finish the first draft of my dissertation; but it was not very good.

By the end of the summer my parents decided that it would be good for me to be sent off on a long sea-voyage. They loved the sea and had faith in its curative powers. They also thought, so they told me later, that as I was a very shy youth it would be good for me to have to spend several months on my own. I was not very keen about the scheme, till I realized that it could give me an opportunity that might never recur. I agreed, therefore, on condition that I might go to China.

So on Saturday, 10 October 1925, I set sail from Liverpool in a liner called *Patroclus*. She belonged to the Blue Funnel Line, whose proprietors were friends of my family; and, indeed, my brother had recently spent a year in their Liverpool office to learn about shipping. So I could count upon kindly treatment. I felt lonely and apprehensive; and when, on that first night, my rubber hot-water bottle leaked and soaked my berth I was sure that the journey was doomed. However, after four grey windy days which I spent for the most part reading unsociably in my cabin, we passed through the Straits of Gibraltar and the sun came out; I began to make friends with my fellow-passengers. There was no one else of my generation. Most of them were middle-aged ladies, wives of business-men working in the Far East. Some of them had their husbands with them, and some of them had children. All of them were friendly and pleasant, but few of them were of much interest and all of them were shocked when I refused to play deck-games. There was a charming wife of a naval captain, whose brother I knew in England, with her well-behaved little boys. There was a bright and amusing couple on their way to Peking, where the husband was Acting Head of the China Customs Service, which at that time was run by the British. I got on happily with them, so much so that they kindly invited me to stay with them when I should come to Peking. There was a glamorous Dutch lady, aged about forty, with the strange Christian name of Femme, going out to Shanghai to join her husband, for whom she did not seem to have much affection. I found her entertaining but rather fey. She wore a large, rather ugly ring with a cat's-eye stone set in it, which, she said, had been bequeathed to her by a friend who had lived in Java. She told me that since she had acquired it she had been suffering from nightmares and nervous crises, and that, shortly before she left Holland, a woman whom she had never seen before had come up to her in a restaurant and begged her to throw the ring away. It was cursed and evil, she said. I persuaded Femme to let me wear the ring for a night. I passed a very unpleasant night, waking at intervals with the sensation that someone was trying to throttle me. The sensation may well have been self-induced as I believed the ring to be sinister. But when I returned it to her and told her about my experiences she said that she had often had exactly the same feeling. Two nights later she was found by a sailor sleep-walking on deck and apparently about to throw herself overboard. Next morning she gave me the ring, and I flung it into the sea.

We called in at very few ports on our way east. We arrived at Malta at a very early hour, but had time enough to drive round the town. It was nearly as early when we arrived at Port Said. There we only had three hours, a visit I have described in the chapter on Egypt. We spent the rest of that day going through the Suez Canal, but paused only briefly at Suez. After Suez our next port of call was Penang, off the Malayan coast. It was while we were crossing the Indian Ocean that there took place the inevitable fancy-dress ball. There were to be side-shows, to raise money for charity; and, as I used in those days to tell fortunes, I rashly promised to do so that evening – £1 for a reading of the client's hands and another £1 if they wished the cards to be read for them too. I was not in a good fortune-telling mood that evening but was managing all right, as most of my victims gave themselves away by the questions that they asked, and with one or two I established a sort of telepathic connection. Then a woman came who was one of the few who wanted cards as well. As I laid out her cards I suddenly felt inspired. Without stopping to think what I was saying I told her that she would be a widow soon. Her friends rightly rebuked me for giving her a fright. Then, to my horror, when we reached Singapore she received a message to say that her husband was seriously ill. She left at once to go up-country to the station where he worked. Whether he survived or not I do not know. It was a salutary lesson for me. Thereafter I kept control over what I said.

We spent the inside of a day at Penang, which I liked, and again at Singapore. There the agent of the shipping line invited me to lunch. The Bishop of Singapore was present at it; and I asked him about a problem that had always puzzled me: at what season of the year do birds nest on the Equator? He could not tell me; he had never thought about it. We managed to skirt round the edge of a typhoon on our way from Singapore to Hong Kong, where I think we arrived on 11 November.

For November and December 1925 I have to be dependent on my memory. I had brought with me an engagement diary which I filled up with brief notes at the end of every day, but it was a diary made for the use of the Cambridge University world and ran therefore for the period of the academic and not the calendar year. There was no space for entries in it after mid-October, apart from a page or two which I had filled before the end of the month. I was not greatly worried as I wrote every week to my mother and was sure that she would keep the letters: so that I would have, should I need it later on, a record of all my doings. But at that time letters to England from China travelled by train across Siberia and Russia and many of them never reached their destination. I was surprised when I came home to find that my parents had no knowledge of some of the incidents that I had reported to them; and when after my mother's death I went through the letters from abroad that I had sent her, three or four that she should have received from China were missing. At the New Year, 1926, I acquired a new diary, which I conscientiously filled up. At the same time the mails to England became much more reliable. One letter that I wrote in January was missing. Otherwise my remaining weeks in China were well documented; but, as regards November and December 1925 I cannot supply accurate dates and I have forgotten many names.

We were, I think, for two days at Hong Kong, one of which I spent out at Repulse Bay with the Naval Captain's family and the other in the town. We went on to arrive in Shanghai on 16 November, where I stayed with the local head of that great China firm, Butterfield & Swire. There my host gave me good if rather depressing advice about how to plan my tour of China. It was a period when the country was filled with rival war-lords, all fighting against each other. I had hoped to go up the great Yangtze Kiang river. But that, I was told, was out of the question. One could too easily find oneself in a war-zone. However, my main objective was Peking. Ever since as a schoolboy I had read the *Travels of Marco Polo* I had longed to see Xanadu. That was considered to be feasible. I was advised to rejoin the *Patroclus*, which was due to sail in a few days' time up to the Yellow Sea, to Taku, the port for Tientsin; and from Tientsin it would be easy to go on to Peking. That suited me, as the British Consul-General at Tientsin was a first cousin of my mother's, and I knew that she had written to him to warn him that I might suddenly turn up there. So, after spending one lovely autumn day going by train to see Hangchow, a city of great beauty, I re-embarked on the *Patroclus* on 21 November and two days later arrived off Taku.

The Yellow Sea is so shallow that larger ships had to anchor out of sight of the low shore. Launches came out to meet us passengers and to take us to Taku at the mouth of the Pei-ho and then up the winding river to Tientsin. We were warned that there was fighting going on round Taku, but that we ought to get through all right. The journey that afternoon was a very unreal experience for me. Owing, perhaps, to our sudden arrival in the wintry weather of northern China I had acquired a feverish cold and had a temperature of 103°. As we went up the river under a grey grim sky there was gunfire to be heard all around, and a few shots seemed to be directed against our launch. However, Tientsin itself, which we reached in the early evening, was out of the danger-zone. When we landed I at once telephoned to the British Consulate, to announce my arrival. The news came as a surprise to Cousin Bill Ker, for he had never received the letter that my mother had sent him. But our families had always kept in touch, so he knew who I was; and he and Cousin Lucy, his Canadian wife, made me very welcome at the Consulate.

I spent the next three or four days in bed, and when I emerged I was considered by the doctor to be unfit for further travel. Indeed, I had a relapse a few days later. The delay was disastrous. By the time that I was pronounced to be ready to travel it was no longer possible to reach Peking. The whole area was the scene of fighting between the troops of the Manchurian Warlord, Chang Tso Lin, and the Christian general, Fung Hu Hsen, whose army was said to march to the tune of 'Onward, Christian soldiers', sung in Chinese. Chang Tso Lin still held Peking and Tientsin, but the Christian general's army had closed round Tientsin and we were being besieged. So I had to be prepared to stay on indefinitely in Tientsin.

It was not the most interesting of cities. It had a certain character as one of the great Treaty ports of China, where, in those days, the Great Powers each had their own Quarter, or Concession, self-governing under its Consul-General. Staying at the Consulate was thus like staying at a minor colonial Government House. The Kers were extraordinarily good to me. Cousin Bill was a quiet little man. Cousin Lucy was far larger, very exuberant and a trifle bossy, but immensely kind. They had been in China for nearly thirty years. In 1900 they had been among the British besieged in the Legation Quarter at Peking during the Boxer Rebellion and had lost two children in the course of it. But they bore no resentment against the Chinese in general, by whom Cousin Bill was well liked. They even kept a grudging admiration for the monstrous old Empress-Dowager, whom they had met on several occasions. They were hospitable. One met most of the British residents in Tientsin at their house, and many Americans too, as the United States was then officially too anti-imperialist to have a Quarter of its own, and its

Consul-General thus lacked the prestige of his British, French and Japanese colleagues. Among the Americans who came several times to the house when I was there was Owen Lattimore, who was later to achieve fame, first as an explorer and then as a China expert, and was hounded out by the American authorities for warning them against putting much trust in Chiang Kai Shek. He was about to make his first expedition in a camel caravan across Mongolia and the Gobi Desert and was, like me, waiting to be able to travel to Peking. Many decades later I met him when he was Professor of Chinese at Leeds University. He vaguely remembered the Kers, but he did not remember me at all. He had suggested that I might like to join him on the journey. It was a tempting idea, but hardly practicable while my health was insecure.

To me the most interesting episode in my stay in Peking was the opportunity that I had of meeting the ex-Emperor of China. Henry Pu Yi, as he liked to call himself, after having been dethroned at the age of six, had been allowed to stay on in Peking, in the Forbidden City, until he was sixteen, when he was ejected by the Chinese Republican government. His guardians moved him to Tientsin, where they found him a house in the Japanese Concession, where he lived with his Household and his formidable tutor, Mr Johnston. Mr Johnston seems to have been away from China in the autumn of 1925, though he was certainly back in early February next year, when I met him. One day in November – I cannot, alas, give the actual date – his understudy, of whose name I have no record but who was, I think, an Australian, came to call on the British Consul-General on some matter and met me there. He at once asked me if I played the piano. A little, I answered. He then told me that the Emperor had just started to learn the instrument and what he liked most was to play duets. All that he could manage so far was very simple music, like nursery rhymes, with both hands playing the same tune; and he wanted someone to go thump-thump in the base. Would I come and supply the need?

I went twice to the Imperial residence. It was a large villa, full of rather showy occidental furniture, with an upright piano in the drawing-room. The Emperor was a frail etiolated youth, not at all good-looking but with an air of race, suitable for the last head of an old dynasty. After our musical sessions, which sadly revealed that he would never be a pianist, we settled down to chat over cups of jasmine tea. His English was adequate, and he was interested in history, liking to question me about Court rituals in the past. His general background knowledge was full of gaps; and I doubt if I ever convinced him that the Byzantine Emperors and the Ottoman Sultans were not the same people. He was better informed on English history, and he told me that he was devoted to the Tudors. He called himself Henry because of his admiration for King Henry VIII. His chief wife, of whom he was clearly not fond, he called Mary, after Bloody Mary, but his chief concubine was Elizabeth. I never was privileged to meet the Imperial ladies, so I cannot tell how appropriate the names may have been. But certainly he bore little resemblance to Bluff King Hal.

After those two sessions I never saw him again. Early the following February, soon before my departure from China, Mr Johnston arranged for me to go and take my leave of him. But when the day came the Emperor was ill and the visit cancelled. I followed his subsequent career with interest and with sadness. I think that he always accepted with uncomplaining endurance whatever role he was told to play, whether it was that of puppet Emperor of Manchuria under the Japanese or of market-gardener under the Chinese Communists. The recent film that was made of his life, though splendidly decorative, gave him, I thought, too positive a character. It omitted, too, I suppose out of ignorance, the final episode that rounded off his life. In 1966 Queen Elisabeth of the Belgians, who was known to the world as the Red Queen, from her passion for visiting Communist countries, was invited to China by Mao. When she arrived in Peking with her daughter, Queen Marie José of Italy, Mao provided the two Queens with the ex-Emperor to be their guide to show them round the Forbidden City, which had been his childhood home. Queen Marie José came to see me soon after her return to Europe. She was writing her *History of the House of Savoy* at the time and thought that perhaps I could give her hints on historiography. I told her that I wished I could have known that she was going to see him, as I would have liked to send him my respects and to have asked about his piano-playing. She reported that he had been an excellent guide, proud to tell them about the Palace treasures and to talk of his old life, but wistful and sad. He died a few months later. It is good to know that before his death he could move for a few days among ladies of his old exalted class.

As December advanced the Christian General's army tightened their siege of Tientsin. Coal and even food began to run a little short. The General had already occupied Peking; and just before Christmas Chang Tso Lin's garrison in Tientsin surrendered. I went out to the outskirts of the Chinese city to see the Christian troops march in. To my disappointment no hymns were sung. They shuffled along in silence in the bitter cold. Just after I returned to the Consulate a large car drew up outside the gate and a bemedalled general emerged, to inform the British Consul-General, as the senior Consul, solemnly and courteously, that his Commander was now master of the city. Within a few days the railway to Peking was re-opened. Unfortunately I fell ill with flu on 27 December. It was only on 4 January that I was able to take the train to Xanadu.

The four weeks that I spent in Peking were among the most enjoyable in my life. My hosts, Mr and Mrs Edwardes of the Custom

Service, were unfailingly kind, as was everyone else that I met there; except, perhaps, Lady Macleay, the wife of the British Minister. When I remarked to her about the kindness that I found everywhere, she replied: 'You need not think that it is due to your beaux yeux. It is just that we like new tea in the tea-pot.' However even she liked new tea enough to invite me round on several occasions to the Legation. The Edwardes's house was in the Legation Quarter, which was a collection of Chinese-style residences, adapted to European standards of comfort. As Mr Edwardes was Acting-Head of Customs he could have moved into the rather larger house of the Head of Customs, a post which was vacant at the moment but to which he eventually succeeded. But that house was reputed to be badly, even unpleasantly, haunted; so he preferred to stay where he was.

Peking was still unspoilt. The great walls that surrounded the various rectangular quarters of the city were still all extant, massive and mustard-coloured, pierced by occasional gates over which were built pagodas with turquoise and green tiled roofs. The buildings were almost all of one storey, the better houses with gardens round them. The only high-rise structure was a hotel, which, if I remember rightly, had five storeys. The weather in January was icily cold but clear. The sky was almost always cloudless, pale lemon-coloured rather than blue. The earth outside the city was bare and yellow, with very few evergreen trees to break the monotony. The canals round the city were frozen stiff and provided a splendid means of transport. These were barges with long metal rollers under them, which were propelled by barge-poles with a metal tip. Adept young Chinese took charge of this type of ice-punting and could soon reach enormous speeds. It was exhilarating but alarming, as every mile or so there would be a crossing at right-angles with another canal, and collisions with fatal consequences were not infrequent.

There were a number of agreeable Europeans staying in the Legation Quarter, whom I used to see; and I met a number of highly interesting European journalists. I remember in particular Mr Donald of the *Manchester Guardian*, at whose house I used to find eminent Chinese. My favourite among those was Mrs C. T. Wong, whose husband was the well-respected Chinese delegate to the League of Nations and head of the Foreign Office and so indispensable that, no matter who might be ruling in Peking, he never lost his post. Mah Jongg was much played in Peking society circles; and Mrs Wong took the trouble to teach me the finer points of the game. Such expertise as I acquired was unfortunately wasted, as once I had left Peking I never played it again. She was an elegant and lively lady, very ready to talk about the Chinese way of life. She was, she told me, Mr Wong's second wife, but as his first wife disliked parties and was terrified of going abroad it was she who accompanied him everywhere. There was nothing derogatory in being a second wife, she said. It was, she thought, like marrying a younger son in England. You were not the chief lady in the family, but you enjoyed a perfectly respectable position.

Much of my sight-seeing was done in the company of Lady Delia Peel, who was staying at the British Legation. She was the eldest sister of the Lord Spencer of the time and had herself a position at the British Court. She was an excellent fellow-sightseer, eager, well-informed, full of humour and almost too energetic. It was with her that I went all through the Forbidden City and out to the Winter Palace and the huge Summer Palace, which looked rather desolate in winter-time. It was, however, a Chinese silk-merchant with whom I visited most of the temples. He was a dear old man from whom I had bought a few pieces of silk but who seemed to have taken a fancy to me. On our first expedition he took me to see first the Lama Temple and then the Temple of Confucius. The latter was a large high rectangular hall with frescoes round the walls, not, I thought, of very good quality. A rickety wooden staircase led up to an equally rickety wooden gallery from which more frescoes were to be seen. It all looked so unsafe that when my kind friend asked me if I wanted to climb up to inspect them I said no. He seemed to be inordinately pleased. It was only much later that I learnt that those frescoes on the upper level were all of them pornographic, and the respectable Chinese were shocked by the eagerness that most Europeans showed in wanting to see them. My unwillingness to see them proved to him that I was well brought up and clean-minded. After that he was eager to take me round to see more temples than I could manage. We remained good friends. Every Christmas he used to send me for many years to come, until, I suppose, he died, a lacquered tin containing jasmine tea.

My longest outing was to the mountains to the west of the city. One week-end Mr Donald organized an expedition for a few of us to go out to the old Imperial Hunting-park. We drove out on the Saturday morning over the flat yellow plain till suddenly the foothills appeared and behind them higher mountains, with the fantastic shapes that one sees in Chinese paintings. This was where in older days the Emperors had gone to hunt deer and to shoot game-birds. Even in the bleakness of winter, with most of the trees without leaves, it was all very beautiful. We spent the night camping in a monastery called the Ladder to the Cloud Mountains. I was eager to go on next morning to see the Great Wall. That was forbidden. The Wall was in bandit country, and the government did not want the embarrassment of having visitors robbed or held to ransom. But Mr Donald, who knew the countryside well, drove us over rough tracts to a hill from which one could see in the clear winter air, some twenty miles away, a long section of the Wall, climbing up and down the mountainsides. It was immensely impressive.

I would have gladly stayed on in Peking, but I could not decently impose myself upon my kind hosts any longer; and I had already committed myself to go to Japan. So at the end of January I took the train back to Tientsin for a few days with Cousin Bill and Cousin Lucy before embarking on a boat to cross the Yellow Sea.

There are many places in China that I would dearly love to see, but I have no wish to see what Mao and his successors have done to the city which we are now told to call Beijing. Beijing is not Xanadu.

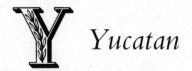

Yucatan

Late in 1961 I met in London a newly arrived Mexican Ambassador, for whom I took at once a great liking. He was highly intelligent and well-informed, and he had enormous charm. He came to lunch with me several times, and I used now and then to dine at his Embassy. Our friendship did not last for long. After about a year in London he was summoned back to Mexico to be its Foreign Minister. But he did not forget me. A few months later I received an invitation to visit his country as the guest of the government. They would be glad if I would be willing to give a lecture at the University of Mexico. Otherwise I should go round the country seeing its major monuments. The invitation arrived at a suitable moment. The Representative of the British Council in Mexico at the time (who, under the pseudonym of John Lincoln, was to write the best book that I know abut modern Mexico) was an old friend of mine, having been my second-in-command when I was trying to run the British Council in Greece. He at once agreed to house me while I was in Mexico City and to drive me himself round the towns of Central Mexico. When I went further afield, to Yucatan, everything would be arranged by the Government.

So, after visiting the Bahamas and Palm Beach, Florida, I arrived in Mexico City on Saturday, 6 February 1960, to be met by the British Council Representative, Maurice Cardiff, and by the Chef de Protocol of the Foreign Ministry, and taken to stay with Maurice and his wife at their pleasant house on the edge of the town. I had many apologies from my friend, the Foreign Minister, who unfortunately had had to go on a tour abroad.

My days with the Cardiffs were very enjoyable, though at first I found the height above sea-level of Mexico City a little hard to take; and when on the day after my arrival they took me for a picnic to a mountain-top some several thousand feet higher still, I barely had the energy to walk. The city itself is now, I am told, the largest in the world. It already sprawled in all directions, but there were fine buildings in the centre of the town, and some handsome suburbs. I admired the palace of the Emperor Maximilian and the Empress Charlotte, in spite of its melancholy atmosphere; and I loved the suburb of Xocomitlo, where you travel by boat down canals past flower-stalls. There are splendid objects in the Museum. But I find it impossible to like Aztec art. There is a harsh unfriendly cruelty about it. I would not like to possess any Aztec artifact. The Aztec temples are cold and hostile, well suited for human sacrifices. Even the scenery round Mexico City, which is of extraordinary beauty, especially when you travel over the mountains westward, is somehow hostile. You felt that human beings are unwelcome intruders, not wanted by the gods, who must therefore be appeased by blood.

Society in Mexico City seemed to have a similar element of unease. I was delighted to meet again an artist whom I had known years before on the fringes of Bloomsbury, Leonora Carrington – not to be confused with Lytton Strachey's Dora Carrington, but a far better artist, who had been for many years the lady-friend of Max Ernst. She was now living in Mexico with a husband who was a psychiatrist. She was charming and eccentric. 'Leonora always goes mad in April', her husband said to me. 'At other times you will find her fairly normal.' She took me to a party where I saw two very handsome and very sinister young men, who had been involved a few years before in a ritual murder, but, each belonging to an eminent family, they had escaped prosecution but had been advised to retire for a while to California. The party was held to welcome them back. Sorcery was rife. Mrs Cardiff took me to the herb-market, where, she said, one could buy love-potions. I hoped to purchase some as I thought that one could have a happy time fixing up love-affairs between one's friends. Unfortunately, the witch that sold them was away ill. All that I was offered were the dried corpses of humming-birds, said to be highly effective in attracting lovers if you kept one dangling in your bosom. I did not like the idea.

After a few days Maurice Cardiff drove me over the mountains to the towns of Guanajuato and then Guadalajara, stopping to see some Aztec sites on the way. After two nights in Guadalajara we took a small aeroplane to go down to the Pacific coast at Puerto Vallarta. It was a charming unpretentious resort, which in warm weather must have been delightful. Unfortunately, while we were there an icy north wind was blowing, and the hotel was designed to cope with heat-waves. I have seldom been so miserably cold. It was a relief after two nights to fly back to Guadalajara and thence to drive to Morelia on our way back to Mexico City. Those towns, especially Morelia, were full of handsome buildings dating from Spanish colonial days. The Spanish baroque, ornamented by Indian craftsmen, was, I thought, very beautiful. To the Mexicans, however, anything that dated from Spanish imperialistic days was not to be admired. I had to curb my enthusiasm.

I hoped to find Maya architecture much more to my liking than Aztec; and after a few more days in Mexico City I set out to see the temples in Yucatan. First I was to visit the temple of Palenque, in the jungle near the Guatemalan frontier, which was said to be the most fascinating of all Maya buildings. To go there I flew in awful weather to a town called Villahermosa, the 'Beautiful town', from where a small aeroplane would take me on to Palenque. When we arrived at Villahermosa, which did not live up to its name, the north wind was blowing hard, with blinding rain. There was no question of the little plane being able to fly on into the jungle. I must confess that when I saw the plane I was not sorry. It seemed to be tied together with string and the pilot looked not a day older than sixteen. I thought of flying straight on to Merida, the capital of Yucatan; but the airport was soon closed down; and anyhow I was not expected at Merida till the following evening. So I had to remain in Villahermosa. The headmaster of the local school and the lady directress of culture in the town had been told to look after me and to see me on to the plane for Palenque. But now they were saddled with me for nearly two days. It was not easy for them, especially as my Spanish was very weak, and they anyhow talked to each other in a local dialect. They valiantly did their best. I was shown round the town and taken to call on the Governor, who gave me lunch, and they found me a room in the local inn. But then there arrived on a bicycle, dripping in the rain, a huge young lady from Finland, who was bicycling from Chicago to Buenos Aires. She was called Helen. I never discovered her surname. She was a splendid girl, who at once took charge of the situation. She spoke Spanish and English, and was very amusing when telling us of her experiences. Her cycling costume was practical rather than elegant, but she had a blue cotton dress to wear in the evenings. Thanks to her we had a hilarious afternoon and evening, spent largely at the local cinema. Next morning the weather was slightly better, and we went to see the Archaeological Park (which was not very interesting). At noon, the rain being over, she set off on her bicycle to Yucatan; and I begged my hosts not to bother themselves with me any more. In the late afternoon an aeroplane appeared, rather late, which took me on to Merida.

I was met there by the secretary of the Governor and the secretary of the Mayor, and a reportor from the local newspaper. They took me to a hotel and gave me dinner there. But there was an international Gas Convention taking place in the town; and next day the delegates took over all the available taxis to go sight-seeing. My hosts, with many apologies, left me to myself all day. I was quite happy wandering round Merida, and I made friends with a pleasant Mexican, now resident in Chicago, who had come back to visit Merida where he had been born. He was willing to act as my guide. Next morning a car appeared which drove me to the Maya temple at Chichén Itzá, which I thought very impressive, far more interesting architecturally than the Aztec temples, though a trifle sinister. One could well believe that it was the scene of human sacrifices. I spent a pleasant day there.

Next day the same car drove me, over the rather featureless countryside, to the temple of Uxmal. I spent the afternoon in the ruins, and, after a night in the local hotel, returned there in the early morning. I found it even more impressive and, somehow, more sympathetic than Chichén Itzá, though it too had a sinister feel about it. In the evening, as I was having drinks in the hotel with some very conventional Americans, I looked out of the window and saw a bicycle arrive. I rushed out and told Helen to put on her blue cotton dress and come and dine with me. She found some lodging-house in which to spend the night and then appeared in the hotel. My American acquaintances were puzzled by her at first, but soon fell for her charm. I gave her my address in London and begged her to send me a postcard when she reached Buenos Aires. But I never heard from her.

I was back in Merida to give an interview to the local press, and took an afternoon aeroplane back to Mexico City. I am very glad to have been to Yucatan and to have seen examples of Mayan art, but on the whole I do not care for Pre-Columbian art.

In the aeroplane I rashly ate some fly-blown sandwiches. I had barely arrived back at the Cardiff's house before I was stricken by what is archly called Montezuma's Revenge. I have seldom felt so ill. For four days I was wholly incapacitated. Unfortunately, I had promised to lecture on one of them. I could not possibly go out to the University. But the Cardiffs had a large drawing-room, and as the University was in vacation my audience was restricted to the staff of the history faculty and a few professors of other subjects. So the lecture was given there. I tottered from my bed and was just able to give a slightly curtailed address before having to hurry away again. One or two professors, who did not know of my situation, thought it rude of me not to stay to answer questions. But I had done my best.

I recovered in due course. The Cardiffs were kind and considerate, though I must have been a nuisance. After emerging from my bed and spending two days of gentle convalescence, I was well enough to leave Mexico and to fly on to a less restful life in Dallas.

 *Zion*

THIS BOOK began with an account of a visit to the Holy Mountain. It is proper that I should close the alphabet by telling of my visits to the Holy City. To our ancestors in the Middle Ages the pilgrimage to Jerusalem was the noblest of all journeys that could be made on this earth. In our over-worldly wisdom we may now no longer believe that to worship God in the holy places of our ancient faith will bring us remission from our sins. We may no longer identify the earthly Jerusalem with the Golden City of Paradise. We may no longer hope to arrive when life is over to the Halls of Zion, all jubilant with song, which St Bernard of Cluny promised us eight hundred years ago. We may see strife and bitterness where the Prince of Peace should reign. Yet, in spite of all the anguish and hatred, there is some transcendental aura surrounding a city that is holy to the three great religions of the world. Here are shrines where down the centuries millions of men and women have prayed for peace, for faith and hope and charity. Surely something must remain.

Even in my rather pagan youth my liking for history made me long to make the Jerusalem Journey. It was not till 1931 that my opportunity came. I had had a friend at Cambridge in our undergraduate days whose confidant I had been when he was struggling to be allowed to marry the girl that he loved. All that was happily settled by now; and I was accepted almost as one of the family. In 1931 his father was British High Commissioner in Palestine, under the League of Nations Mandate. When he heard that I wanted to spend my Easter vacation travelling round those parts I received an invitation to spend as long as I liked at Government House in Jerusalem.

I have told elsewhere of my journey by train across Anatolia and Syria to Baalbek, and thence by road to Damascus. I continued by road from Damascus, through Galilee, stopping at Tiberias for a night and Nazareth for lunch, to Haifa. After a night in an inn on Mount Carmel, I took a train from Haifa, which journeyed slowly down the Palestinian coast and then, when it reached Jaffa, turned to climb still more slowly up the hills to Jerusalem, where an A.D.C. met me and drove me to Government House. It was situated some way out of the city, high up, with splendid views. It was tactful not to remark that the hill on which it stood was traditionally called the 'Hill of Evil Counsel'. It was a handsome new building, but cold. The wind howled outside and all the chimneys smoked, except for one in a little boudoir reserved for distinguished guests. There was no proper garden as yet, and the surroundings were desolate. In those days jackals barked round the house at night, and twice I heard a hyena. But the house had a happy atmosphere. My hosts, Sir John and Lady Chancellor, were unfailingly kind. They had with them a very young son, with his nursery governess, whom later I was to meet in Borneo. The other guests in the house when I arrived were the then Lord and Lady Lytton, with their beautiful daughter Davina. When they left after two days their place was taken by Lord Athlone, Queen Mary's brother, and his wife, Princess Alice, Queen Victoria's youngest (and eventually last surviving) granddaughter, and their daughter, Lady May.

Their coming was very fortunate for me. An extra A.D.C. had been brought in to accompany them wherever they went. But Lord Athlone liked to visit military camps and installations and municipal improvements, while Princess Alice was an indefatigable sight-seer who was determined to see every possible place of historic or religious interest. So, while he went off in one car with the A.D.C. I went off in another with the Princess, earning my keep by acting as an informal A.D.C. As everything was opened up to be shown to so distinguished a visitor, I too saw everything, in the utmost comfort and ease. I was lucky enough also to find in Jerusalem an old friend from Cambridge days, Stewart Perowne, who was working in the administration of the city, of which his knowledge was unrivalled. He was a perfect guide.

My sight-seeing was thus well catered for. Stewart took me round the streets of the old city. He showed me the great Roman drains which only that year were being replaced by a modern installation. We went to the village of Abu Gosh, to see the Byzantine pavement and frescoes in the crypt of a chapel there, and on to wander through Bethlehem. The afternoon after my arrival I went with the Lyttons – the Athlones had not yet appeared – to the Russian Convent on the Mount of Olives, to take tea with the Abbess, a dignified lady of Imperial Russian birth. After tea we listened to the nuns singing their chants most beautifully. Among them was a sister who might have been Chaliapin *en travestie*, a magnificent figure with a resonant bass voice. With the Athlones I was shown round the Church of the Holy Sepulchre by the *locum tenens* of the Orthodox Patriarchate – the last Patriarch had recently died and his successor had not yet been elected – who then took us to see the icons and the plate in the Patriarchal Treasury. Another morning we went to the Armenian Patriarchate, to see its superb collection of medieval manuscripts. For the Dome of the Rock and the mosque Al-Aqsa our guide was the Grand Mufti, a sinister red-bearded Arab who was rather over-affable. He entertained us to tea and a few days later invited us to his balcony to see the Moslem Nebi Musa procession. Some years later, when war broke out, he was sent into exile for his anti-British intrigues.

We went to Hebron. We went to Jericho, to be shown round his excavations by Professor Garstang, and then to a lunch in an orchard, given by a former Minister of Education of the Ottoman Empire. There Princess Alice was offered the supreme delicacy of a sheep's eye. She hastily said that a religious taboo forbade her to eat it. The Governor of Jerusalem had to swallow the dainty morsel in her stead. We went twice down to the Dead Sea. Once we crossed to the Moab shore, to bathe in delicious hot springs; and once we bathed in the middle of the sea, in which it is impossible to sink.

The Athlones interrupted their stay in Jerusalem to go on an expedition to Petra. There was no room for me in the wagon-lit put at their disposal, so I spent the three days at a Royal Air Force camp near Amman in Transjordan. The officers were kind. One of them without complaining spent a day driving round Moab, to see the Christian villages there and, in particular, Madaba, with its sixth-century floor mosaic map of the world, which was being given preservative treatment by a learned archaeologist, Dr Goussus. On the third day I rejoined the Athlones at Amman, before driving back to Jerusalem, picnicking in a pine forest on the way.

The climax of my visit to the Holy Land that year was provided by the Easter ceremonies of the Eastern Churches. On Holy Thursday, 9 April, we went early to the courtyard of the Church of the Holy Sepulchre to witness the Washing of the Feet, when the Acting-Patriarch in his robes knelt before a row of beggars and saw to their ablutions. The ceremony, though a yearly occurrence, could, one felt, have done with a rehearsal beforehand. It was a bit hugger-mugger, yet with a tense feeling of piety in the air. A similar service, conducted in the afternoon by the Armenian Patriarch in the Chapel of St James, was a far more dignified affair. On the Good Friday morning I went to a service in the Monastery of the Holy Cross, and in the afternoon, after spending two hours looking at the manuscripts in the Armenian Patriarchal library, I went to the Burial Service in the Cathedral next to the Patriarchate. The spoken Armenian language is, I think, unattractively guttural and harsh, but the Armenians have by far the best singing voices in the Levant. The music in the cathedral was superb. But the liturgy had its longueurs. The *Kyrie Eleison* was repeated, if I counted correctly, thirty-three times.

The great ceremony on Holy Saturday was the Miracle of the Holy Fire, of which I shall speak later. For the midnight service I went to the Holy Sepulchre, then on in the early hours of Easter Sunday to the Russian cathedral, till 2.30 in the morning. But previously, in the late afternoon of Saturday, I attended what was, I think, the most moving of all the ceremonies. The Ethiopian Church only possesses a chapel on the roof of the Holy Sepulchre. There the Archbishop, splendidly robed and

attended by his clergy, went in procession round and round the dome, to
the sound of drums and rattles, swaying from side to side, searching for
the body of Christ, and pausing from time to time to lament that it was
not to be found. I watched it for several hours but had to leave before
midnight, when the news came that Christ had risen and there was no
need to continue the search. I asked why the Ethiopians were restricted to
tents on the roof, and was told the following story.

In the old days the Ethiopians had occupied one of the chapels in the
rotunda round the Holy Sepulchre itself. One morning in 1913 they
arrived to find their chapel occupied by the Copts. The Coptic Church is
in full communion with the Ethiopian, but has always regarded it as
somehow subservient. To save riots between the sects the allotment of
chapels had been fixed by the Turkish authorities. So the Ethiopians
went to the Turkish governor of Jerusalem to demand the return of the
chapel. He told them to produce their title-deeds, endorsed by the
Sultan. But, to their horror, they found that the title-deeds had
disappeared. They had to retreat to the roof. In the course of 1914, after
the outbreak of the World War, a Coptic priest appeared in St
Petersburg and offered to sell a document to the Tsar. It turned out to be
the Ethiopian title-deeds. The Tsar bought it, intending to return it to
Ethiopia, no doubt in return for political concessions. But, what with the
War and increasing political troubles, he never did anything about it.
When the Revolution came, one of the grand-dukes, who was close to
the Tsar, before fleeing the country, prudently looked through the
drawers of the Imperial desk to see if there were anything worth
rescuing. He came across the Ethiopian title-deeds and took them with
him into exile. When he reached Paris he wrote to the Empress Zaoditu
(Judith) of Ethiopia – who had recently replaced her nephew the
Emperor Jesus when, inappropriately, he was converted to Islam – to
offer her the deeds. She promised him a sum down and a pension for life
if he would personally deliver the document to her. Eagerly he went to
Marseilles to take a boat to Djibouti, on his way to Addis Ababa. But he
had a night to spare there and unwisely visited a brothel. He emerged to
find that the document, which he always kept with him, had been
removed from his pocket. His dream of a comfortable future was
shattered. Some years later a British orientalist looked in at a brothel in
Brussels. The Madame, chatting with him afterwards, asked him his
profession; and when he told her she asked him if he could identify a
piece of paper that one of her girls had left behind with her. Excitedly he
saw that it was the Ethiopian title-deeds, and asked if he could buy it.
But, seeing his excitement, she named a price that he could not possibly
afford. On his return to London he made contact with the Ethiopian
Embassy; but, unfortunately, he had forgotten to note the address of the
brothel. For a year or more Ethiopian diplomats were ordered to visit all

the brothels in Brussels, but in vain. The document has not been seen again. So, sadly, the Ethiopians are still confined to the roof of the Sepulchre.

The Miracle of the Holy Fire is the most sensational of the Easter ceremonies. It dates from early Christian times. On the morning of Holy Saturday the Orthodox Patriarch, accompanied now by the Armenian Patriarch and the Archbishop of the Syrian Jacobite Church, goes holding a candle into the Tomb in the centre of the rotunda of the Church of the Holy Sepulchre. There he and his colleagues wait with the entrance sealed – and they have been frisked before they enter to make sure that none is concealing matches or a lighter – and sooner or later fire descends from heaven. They knock on the door, which is then unsealed, and they emerge, candles ablaze; and all the congregation, each member with a candle in his hand, hurries to have it lit by the sacred flame. We in the Governor's party were standing in the main gallery, from which we had an excellent view of the ceremony, and of the congregation. Among the many guests who used to come to lunch or dinner at Government House was the colonel in command of the Warwickshires, the regiment that was garrisoning the Holy City. We all took a great dislike to Colonel Montgomery, as he used to lecture us on the luxurious lives that we led – he cannot have had any idea of how icy were the rooms in Government House – and how idle and spoilt we all were. He had been particularly censorious at dinner the previous Thursday, not even sparing Princess Alice from his strictures. Now, as we were standing in the gallery waiting for the ceremony to end, holding our lit candles, Princess Alice nudged me and pointed downwards. There, just beneath us, was the Colonel with his staff. 'See if you can get him with your wax', she said to me. So I tilted my candle and a drop fell off right onto his head. He looked up angrily, but we were piously gazing heavenward. 'Your turn now', I said to the Princess. Her aim was excellent; she hit the bald spot on the centre of his head. Stewart Perowne, who was on my other side, had a shot, but he missed, as our victim moved. It was as well that we soon left the church. Several years later, when I met Princess Alice for the first time after the War, she said to me: 'Do you remember what fun we had dropping wax on Field-Marshal Montgomery?' Till that moment I had not realized that the unloved Colonel was the same as the great Field-Marshal. However, when she came to write her charming book of memoirs, the Princess referred to her sin in dropping boiling wax by mistake on the Field-Marshal's head. I told her that it was a far worse sin to tell a lie about the incident. She replied that there were times when tact demanded a modification of the truth. 'But', she said, 'when he and I are both dead, I give you leave to tell the whole story.'

I left Jerusalem two days later, travelling by car up to Beirut with an Air Force officer who was engaged to the High Commissioner's daughter and was at the moment British Air Force liaison officer with the French authorities in Lebanon. From Beirut I drove next day to Rayak, in the Bekaa valley, where I was able to take a train for Istanbul. It was a slightly tedious journey as we were held up by floods in Cilicia, so that I arrived in Istanbul too late to catch the Orient Express which would have brought me back to England in time for the beginning of the Cambridge term. I was in slight disgrace for being a day late.

Ten years passed before I was next in Jerusalem. In early April 1941 I was on my way from Bulgaria to take up a job under the British Embassy at Cairo, and paused for three nights in Jerusalem, staying at Government House. Apart from one day spent at Jericho and by the Dead Sea, I remained in the city, meeting a few old friends. I had brought all my possessions from Bulgaria with me, and as I was told to go on by air to Cairo I obtained permission to leave them stored in Government House which gave me an excuse, once I was settled in Cairo, to go up to Jerusalem to collect them and return by train to Cairo. That enabled me to spend three pleasant days there in May, and gave me the chance to make friends with Owen Tweedie, the British Director of Publicity. The result of that friendship was that when in July I fell rather seriously ill, and, my main task in Egypt having been accomplished, it was decided that I ought to be moved to a kinder climate, Owen Tweedie asked for me to join his staff in Jerusalem.

The months that followed were the most agreeable in my war-time career. Though there was already tension between Arabs and Jews in Palestine, for the time being there was something of a *détente*, chiefly owing to the temporary restriction of Jewish immigrants. It was possible to invite professors at the Hebrew University to meet Arab intellectuals. Indeed, most of my friends at the University were there because they were interested in Arabic studies, and they were alarmed at the prospect of a Jewish state that might cut them off from their Arab connections. At the same time it was a great asset to have an excellent Hebrew orchestra established in Jerusalem. My work was varied and interesting. Sometimes I was called upon to act as a film censor, not an easy task in view of the religious and moral sensibilities of the local population and the need for political discretion. The cinema proprietors used to try to sway one's judgment by offering one glasses of local whisky, a particularly nasty drink which prejudiced one against them. Occasionally I would go out in the evening to show mildly propaganda films to Arab villagers. I used to love the drive back in the warm summer evenings to Jerusalem, with gazelles leaping across the road. Now and then, usually on a Sunday when the regular staff was absent, I used to have to write the news bulletin for the Palestine radio, which was not always easy. It was my task to produce the bulletin when news had just come through of the Japanese attack on Pearl Harbour; and it was difficult to draft anything encouraging when one had little to report except for Japanese victories in the Far East. I was required to give a certain number of lectures, the most alarming being when I had to talk to Australian convalescent soldiers on the history of the Holy Land, a subject in which they were wholly uninterested. I learnt then that with a microphone one could shout down unruly elements at the back of the hall. What I most enjoyed was going to see the heads of the various religious communities and attending their services. It was a very ecumenical life. Soon after I arrived in Jerusalem Owen Tweedie was moved to Egypt; but his successor, Christopher Holme, was a good friend and a kindly colleague.

I lodged at first with another colleague until I found myself an old Arab house, just outside Herod's Gate, with vaulted rooms built round a courtyard and a garden full of cyclamen, where I was looked after by a large Armenian lady, gruff and moustached, but very amiable and an excellent cook. I found many old friends in Jerusalem, and many others passed through. One day I went with Stewart Perowne to Bethlehem. There a little Arab boy attached himself to us. He showed us first a shed full of human bones, coming, it seems, from an old cemetery which had been dug up when new drains were being provided for the town. He told us with glee that he informed tourists that these were the bones of the Holy Innocents, though anyone could see that they came from adults, as he pointed out, holding a thigh-bone against his own little leg. He then took us past a photographer's shop, in the window of which there was an enlarged portrait of a blonde little girl. 'That', he said, 'is Saint Helen. She can cure the sick.' We made enquiries when we returned to Jerusalem. There was an orphanage at Bethany run by three Scots who had become Orthodox and were called Brother Lazarus, Sister Martha and Sister Mary. Two or three months previously a little girl had appeared at the Orphanage announcing that she had been told to go there by God. They discovered that she was the daughter of a Christian Arab living near Acre and that she had the gift of healing. Her father had tried to make money out of it; but she thought that to be wrong and had set out alone and had somehow made her way on foot to Bethany, to this institution of which she could never have heard. She refused to return home; and, after some negotiation through the Orthodox bishop of Acre, the Orphanage was allowed to keep her. She seemed a perfectly normal child, till, a few days later, she suddenly said that she had to go for a walk. When they tried to dissuade her she became hysterical, so they let her go, Sister Mary following at a discreet distance. She went straight to a village where she had certainly never been before and to a cottage where indeed a man was lying desperately ill. Sister Mary saw her go to the sickbed and lay hands on the man, who at once seemed to revive. She came out calm and happy and was delighted to have Sister Mary guide her back to the Orphanage. There had been several similar instances, the little girl always knowing exactly where to go. She soon acquired the reputation of being a saint, at least among the villages, as our little boy in Bethlehem, who was incidentally a Moslem, testified. Indeed, she did not discriminate between Christians and Moslems. The Orphanage was having some difficulty with its landlord, a rapacious Jerusalem merchant; and one day the little girl said to Sister Martha that when next the Sister went to see the landlord she was coming too. When they arrived at the landlord's house she sent Sister Martha out of the room. A little later the landlord emerged with tears in his eyes and, instead of increasing the rent, offered to reduce it. I met the saint myself. The children of the Orphanage used at Christmas time to go round singing carols, and I invited them to my house. There among them was this fair-haired, fair-skinned girl, who must, I think, have had Crusader blood, but who otherwise was as normal as her companions. I do not know what happened to her in later years. When I was back in Jerusalem three years later I was not able to go to Bethany; and I gathered that as she grew older her powers faded. I believe that as soon as she was old enough she retired into a convent. But I am glad to have known a saint.

Though I was far from home and though the War-news was seldom encouraging at that time, I was happy in Jerusalem and innocently thought that I would like to stay there for ever. I was not pleased when the order came that I was to move to Turkey, where, as I have described elsewhere, I was to lead a very different life.

When I returned to Jerusalem on a visit three years later I realized that I had done well to move to Turkey. The atmosphere had changed. There was bitterness now between the races. There were the beginnings of terrorism. The Stern Gang was setting an example that certain Arab elements were only too ready to copy. I myself was in a low state. I came from Egypt, where I had vainly hoped to be able to arrange to go home on leave. I had just arrived in Jerusalem when I received the news that my eldest sister, with whom I had always been exceptionally close, had been killed in the course of her service as an aviatrix. My health was bad at the time, and I spent much of my visit in bed. But I saw a great many friends, some living there and some passing through; and the Old City was still as beautiful as ever. To many travellers the Holy Sepulchre is a sad disappointment. They are put off by the tensions and rivalries between the Christian sects and by the garishness of the present building. But I found it consoling to go there when I was depressed and to kneel in the Tomb itself. There I always felt the almost physical presence of Faith, Faith compounded, it is true, of hatred as much as of love, of bellicosity as much as of peace, Faith in a God who is jealous and fierce, maybe, but omnipotent and unknowable, and there to remind us of the smallness and the transience of our lives and our emotions. I found that somehow it freed me from the cage of my sorrows. So I am grateful for Jerusalem.

I was once again in Jerusalem, coming over from Jordan for the inside of a day in 1952. It then had the sadness of a divided city, and I had no wish to linger there. Instead, I shall bravely hope that what the saints of old have told us is true and that when my travels are ended I shall reach the New Jerusalem, Zion, city of our God.

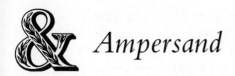

Ampersand

My travels have taken me to places of which I have made no mention in this book. Some of them did not fit into the alphabetical pattern that I had chosen. Some are omitted because my visits to them, though pleasant enough, were without any memorable episodes. Then there are countries to which I have been only briefly, and I cannot write about them with any profundity.

Of this last category the most important is, I suppose, India. I have been there three times. I have a splendid memory of the mountain mass of Kanchenjunga towering snow-capped over me as I gazed at it across the valley from Darjeeling. I am full of admiration for the great buildings of the Moghul Emperors. I was charmed by Goa, with its churches that blend Portugal with the Orient. But, for all its beauty, I do not find India sympathetic. The grim poverty in the cities and even in the villages is all too visible. And I cannot like the Hindu attitude that combines an aggressively self-righteous holiness with a tolerance of the caste system. Nor can I believe in any Indian guru. But so many of my friends are devoted to India that I am impelled to think that I must be wrong. So I had better say no more about it. I found Pakistan, where once I spent a term as a professor at Peshawar University, a little more agreeable; but I have a certain understanding of Islam, at least until it lapses into fundamentalism — but Christian fundamentalism is almost as unpleasant, though mercifully it is less bloodthirsty. My days in Pakistan were interesting enough; but I have no great wish to return there.

There are, however, many places in the world where I have spent happy days; and I feel that it would be ungrateful not to say so. There are many districts in Greece which I have not mentioned in the book, but which I love to revisit, such as Epirus in the north and such of the islands that have not yet been sacrificed to tourism. There is Serbia, with its lovely medieval churches and its great forests. I have said nothing about Southern Italy and Sicily. It is sad that the island's coasts now seem to be an almost ceaseless chain of hotels; but the bleak haunted interior still keeps its beauty. I have paid many pleasant visits to Belgium, Holland and Denmark, and to Portugal. I have always enjoyed Morocco, though when I was last there, with my sister, in 1987, we hit upon the one wet week in an unusually dry spring. The Moroccans were delighted with the rain. We were not. Further afield, I would gladly return to Jordan, of which I have happy memories, and one that was rather embarrassing, when in 1944 I was taken over to Amman to lunch with the old Emir, later King, Abdullah. Knowing him to have been educated in Istanbul and to love to talk in Turkish, I did my best to oblige, to be told by him that if I could only speak that vulgar modern Turkish I had better revert to some language that I could speak decently. Indeed, his Ottoman Turkish was so full of elegant Arabic and Persian words and phrases that I could barely understand him.

There is one country that I greatly regret not having been able to fit into the alphabet. That is Spain. I first was there a few months before the outbreak of the Civil War, and the atmosphere was already strained. Madrid was an uncomfortable, unhappy place. I then went south, to stay with an eccentric English baronet and his family at Torremolinos, near Malaga, then a small village with two or three other equally eccentric English residents. My host's main occupation was to help his Spanish friends organize Communist meetings in the Malaga bull-ring, rather to the disapproval of his sister-in-law's husband, the historian H. A. L. Fisher. It was all quite good-humoured, but there was uneasiness about. I did not greatly enjoy it. My next Spanish visit was in 1950. I had been in Portugal and had gone north from there into Galicia, to the splendid city of Santiago de Compostela, with its great cathedral and its dark alleyways, in one of which I stayed, in a student hostel. I took a train from Santiago to Madrid, where I was looked after by a very gifted young Spanish pianist, Gonzalo Soriano, who died a few years later, when he was barely thirty. I was there for the Easter processions, before going south to Seville and Jerez. From Jerez I was taken by car to Sanlucar de Barrameda, the town at the mouth of the Guadalquivir from which Columbus sailed to America. There I stayed with a couple who were to become my closest Spanish friends.

The Infante Alfonso of Orleans was the son and the grandson of Spanish Infantas, each of whom had married a prince of the French Orleans dynasty; and their husbands had become naturalized Spaniards. Neither King Alfonso XII nor King Alfonso XIII had brothers; so, during the latter's reign, Alfonso of Orleans was his only adult male relative living in Spain, and was therefore given the title of Infante. The King relied on him for political advice, which then he seldom took. Indeed, though the Infante was strictly loyal in everything that he said about his cousin, he clearly thought him feckless and unreliable. The Infante was also the first Spaniard to obtain a pilot's licence and was the founder of the Spanish Air Force. When in 1931 the King gave up the throne, the Infante accompanied him into exile, and then took a job in Ford's works in Detroit, under the name of Mr Orleans. So able was he that within a year Mr Ford offered him the job of being his chief representative in Europe, which, however he refused. When the Civil War broke out, the Infante joined up with Franco, who promised him that he would restore a constitutional monarchy. But he became disillusioned with Franco's aims and methods and went into retirement, but remained in Spain. The Infanta was a granddaughter of Queen Victoria and the youngest sister of Queen Marie of Roumania. But while Queen Marie always struck me as being a beautiful actress playing the part of a Queen, the Infanta was by birth a beautiful princess. Some found her a little alarming, but she was always charming to me and very amusing company. When first I visited them they lived in a garish palace, built in the 1840s, vast, difficult to run and impossible to heat in winter. During that first visit I was housed in a huge salon, where my bed was placed between two grand pianos. A few years later they built themselves a smaller and far more comfortable house in their Botanicó, a park surrounded by a wall some three miles out of Sanlucar. I had met them in London in the 1930s, when the Infanta was living in England, where her sons were at school, and the Infante would visit her from America whenever he could manage it. But it was now that I really came to know them. Henceforward I went to stay with them roughly every other year. One's fellow-guests were remarkably mixed, royal relatives, old and young friends from France, Germany and Italy as well as from Spain. I remember Professor Messerschmitt, the aeroplane-designer, coming there, a dear, gentle old man, quite unsuitable to be the creator of such deadly machines. I remember a Mlle Maricq, the first French-woman to fly an aeroplane, who, when she arrived at Sanlucar, had just crossed the sands of the Sahara on skis behind a camel. English was the dominant language; but one had to be ready to switch into French, German or Spanish – and I was never fluent in the two latter tongues.

The Spanish believe in sex-equality when it comes to titles. A man who marries a lady of title takes its masculine form. So I planned to find a Spanish duchess in her own right. If I married her I would become a Duke, and were she to pre-decease me, I would be a Dowager Duke, a title that I greatly fancied. So I asked the Infanta to find me an elderly duchess. She did produce one, married but with an aged husband who would not – and did not – last for long. But the Duchess herself, though she had a resonant title, seemed to me unsuitable. She was old but she looked as though she were made of leather, tough enough to outlive any number of husbands. So I did not pursue the scheme. My ambition remains unfulfilled.

The Infante was a great letter-writer. So long as he lived I used to receive every two months or so a long letter dealing not only with personal news but also with world affairs, about which he had an extraordinarily detached and objective view, due, he claimed, to his being a prince, born into a class that was basically international. I kept all the letters; and after his death I wondered what I should do with them, as they were, I thought, of too great interest to be destroyed. Eventually I was told that as they were written by a Spanish prince they should go to the Royal Archives in Madrid, where I have now deposited them. The Infanta, on the other hand, hardly ever put pen to paper. But in the late spring of 1965 I received a letter from her in which she said quite simply that she was going to die in the coming winter and that if I wished to see her again I must come to Sanlucar during the summer. It was a summons that I could not disobey. She was very frail but still bright and ready for a good gossip. But when I left, I knew that I would never go to Sanlucar again. In fact she lingered on over the winter. It was in July 1966 that the Infante telegraphed to me to tell me of her death.

He lived on for another nine years, sad and lonely. I still received letters from him, and I saw him once more, when he was visiting London.

These Spanish pages fit awkwardly onto the structure of my Alphabet. But they contain a tribute to friends which I would have hated to omit. So I am grateful for the symbol AMPERSAND.